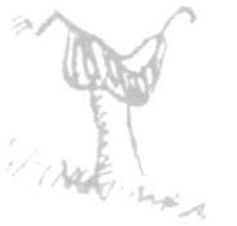

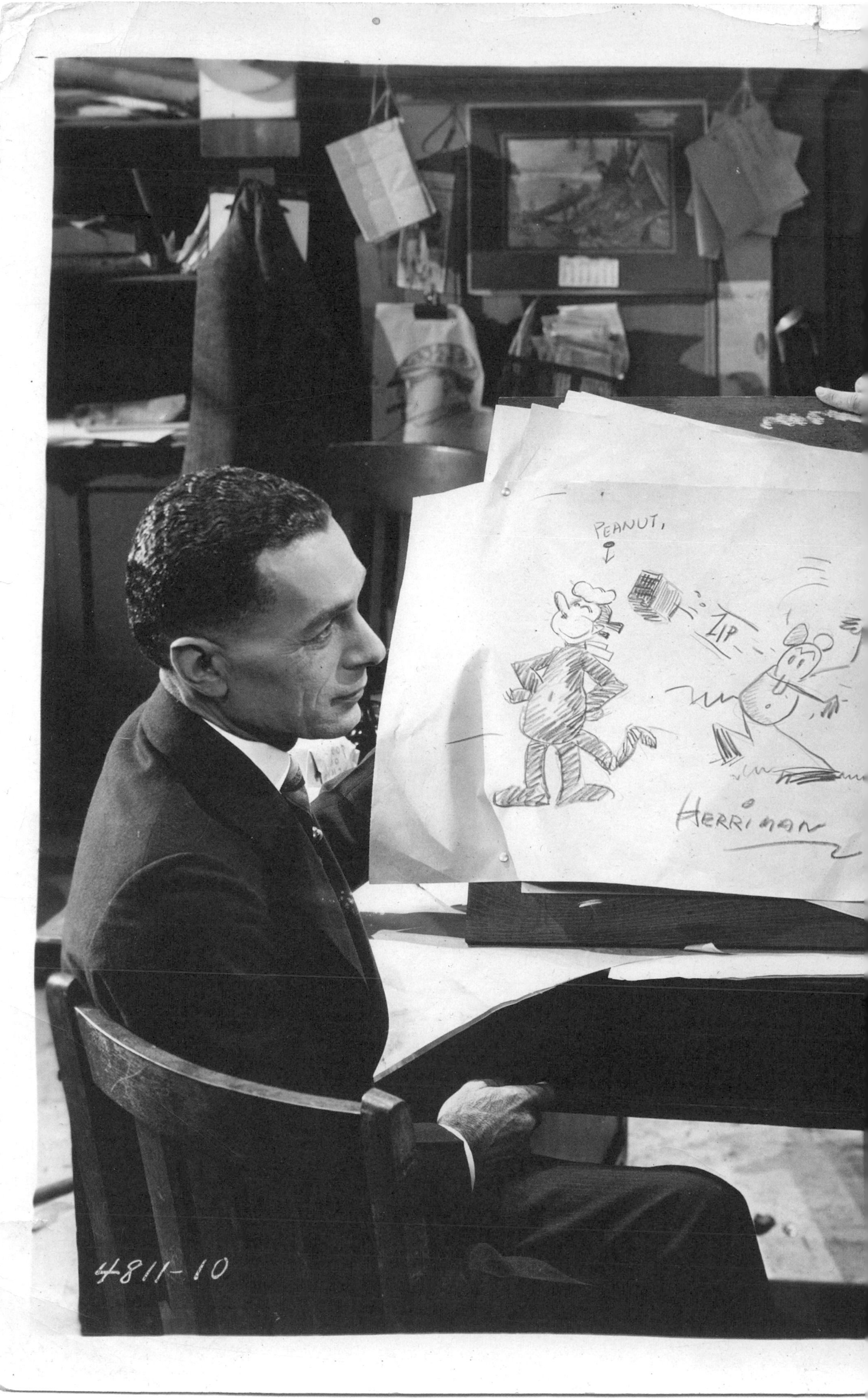
PEANUT,
ZIP
HERRIMAN
4811-10

OSWALD'S RABBIT PUNCH
"WHAT'S YOUR IDEA IN BRINGING THAT UP?"
I'm THERE TOO- JEAN"
TO-NIGHT OSWALD AND JEAN HERSHOLT MAYVILLE OPERA HOUSE
LEN — HIGGINS

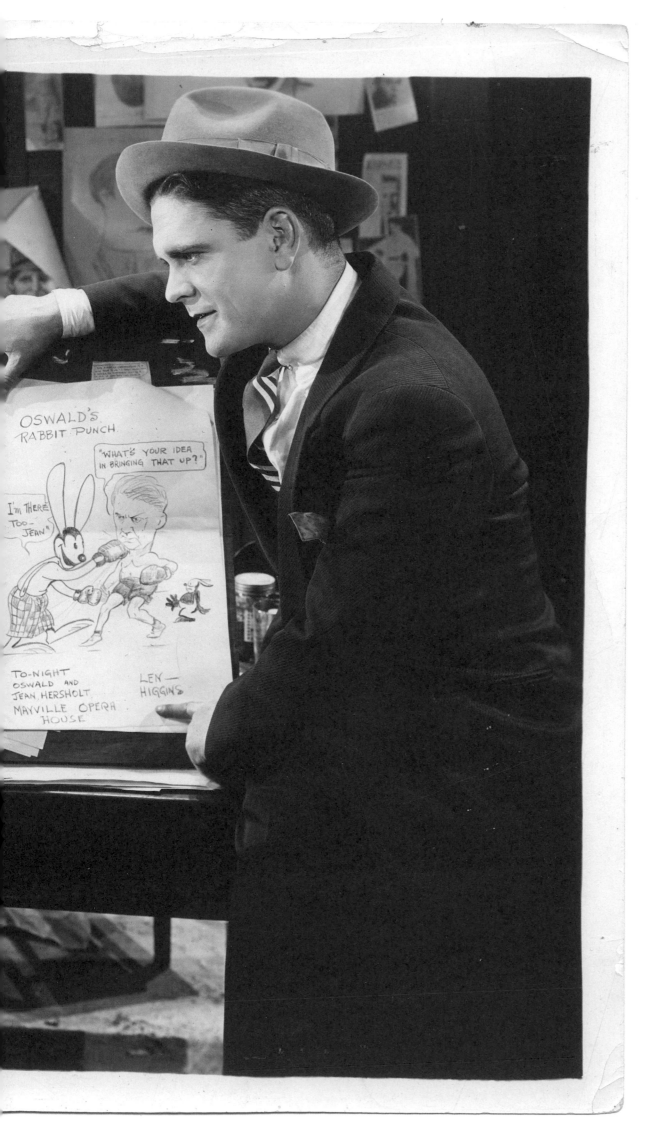

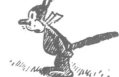

Previous pages: George Herriman and an unidentified companion, c. 1935, in a publicity still of uncertain purpose, though the drawing on the right, presumably also the unidentified fellow's handiwork (? — the drawing seems to be signed "Len Higgins") shows a drawing of Oswald the Rabbit boxing a caricature of what is presumed to be actor "Jean Hersholt." Possibly this was a publicity still for the later *Krazy Kat* animated cartoons produced by Charles Mintz for the Columbia Studios in the early 1930s — though these were so imitative of *Mickey Mouse* that they resembled Herriman's work in name only.

Above: the cardboard packaging for an abbreviated child's version of early *Krazy Kat* cartoon from the nineteen-teens, issued in the 1930s when toy projectors became an affordable luxury for tots and the Mouse-like Kat cartoons were being shown in the local cinemas; below: the lithographed pressed-tin top for the "Krazy Kat Chasing Ignatz Mouse" tin toy produced in 1932 by an unidentified company and copyrighted "F. H. Herriman." A *Felix the Cat* scooter tin toy was also produced, but, ironically, when the Felix character fell out of public favor, the remaining stock was resold as a *Krazy Kat* toy to capitalize on the popularity of the *Mickey Mouse* version of the (by this time) commercially diluted character. All items collection C. Ware; thanks to Charles I. Kidd and Marnie Ware. — C. W.

KRAZY & IGNATZ.

by George Herriman.

"Shifting Sands Dusts Its Cheeks In Powdered Beauty."

Compounding the Complete Full-Page Comic Strips,
with some extra Oddities.

1937-38.

Edited by Bill Blackbeard.

Fantagraphics Books, SEATTLE.

Published by Fantagraphics Books.
7563 Lake City Way North East,
Seattle, Washington, 98115, United States of America.

Edited by Bill Blackbeard.
Except where noted, all research materials appear courtesy of the San Francisco Academy of Cartoon Art.
Additional research and cutlines by Jeet Heer.
Design, decoration, and occasional cutlines by Chris Ware.
Production assistance and scanning by Paul Baresh.
Promoted by Eric Reynolds.
Published by Gary Groth and Kim Thompson.

First Fantagraphics Books edition: April 2006.

ISBN10: 1-56097-734-5.
ISBN13: 978-1-56097-734-6.

Printed in Korea through Print Vision.

Special thanks to Peter Merolo of Kokonino Kollectibles,
Lisa Hinzman of the Wisconsin Historical Society,
John Fawcett of the Fawcett Toy Museum,
Tom Bertino, Jeet Heer, and Derya Ataker.

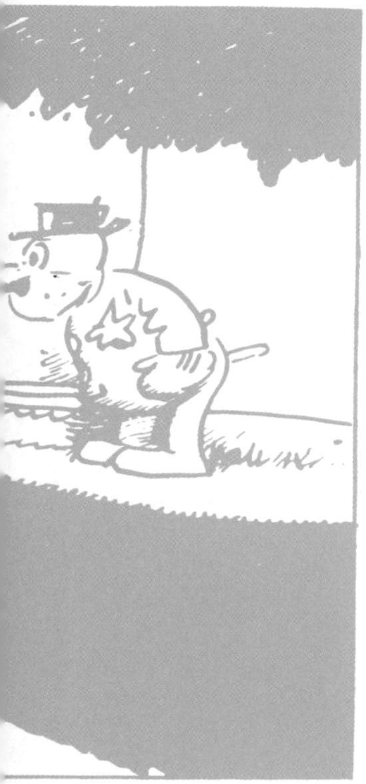

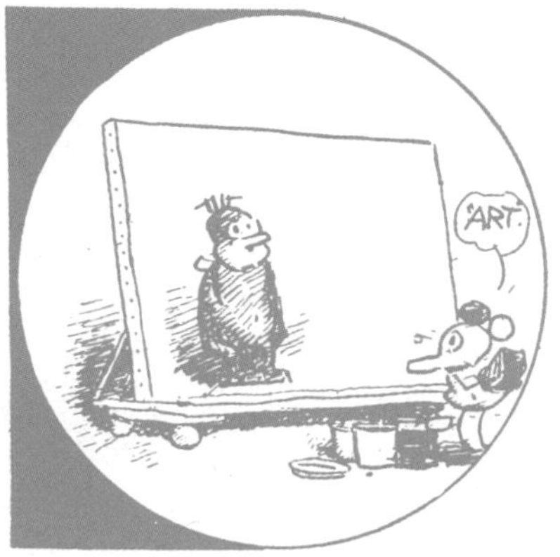
"ART."

KRAZY & IGNATZ.

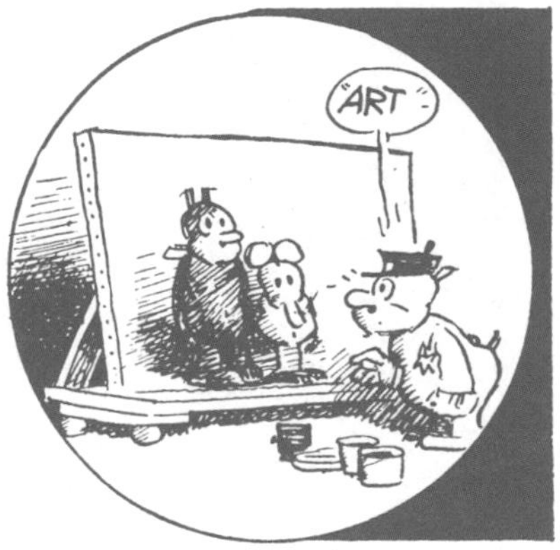
"ART"

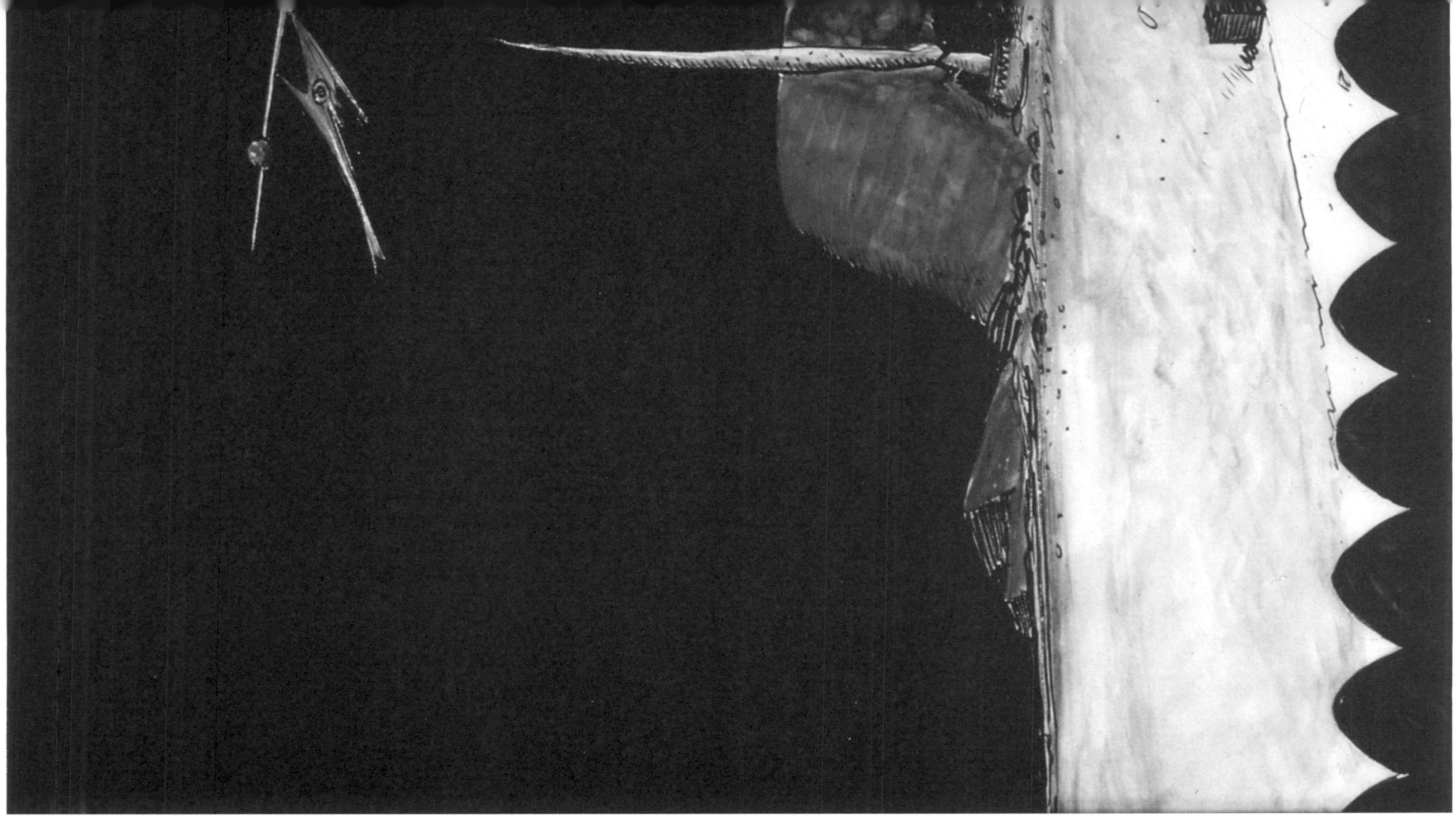

This drawing is inscribed to "Gay" Beaman, who was most likely Gaylord Beaman (1885-1943), a Los Angles insurance executive. Aside from running his own firm, Beaman was a prominent figure in the Southern California cultural scene, frequently mentioned in newspaper columns for his work organizing events and social clubs. An art collector, bon vivant, bibliophile and amateur scholar, Beaman was particularly interested in the history, doing research into the languages of the Southwestern Indians. This last passion, of course, he shared with Herriman, which perhaps explains the origins of this particular drawing. — J.H. (From the collection of, and thanks to, Peter Merolo.)

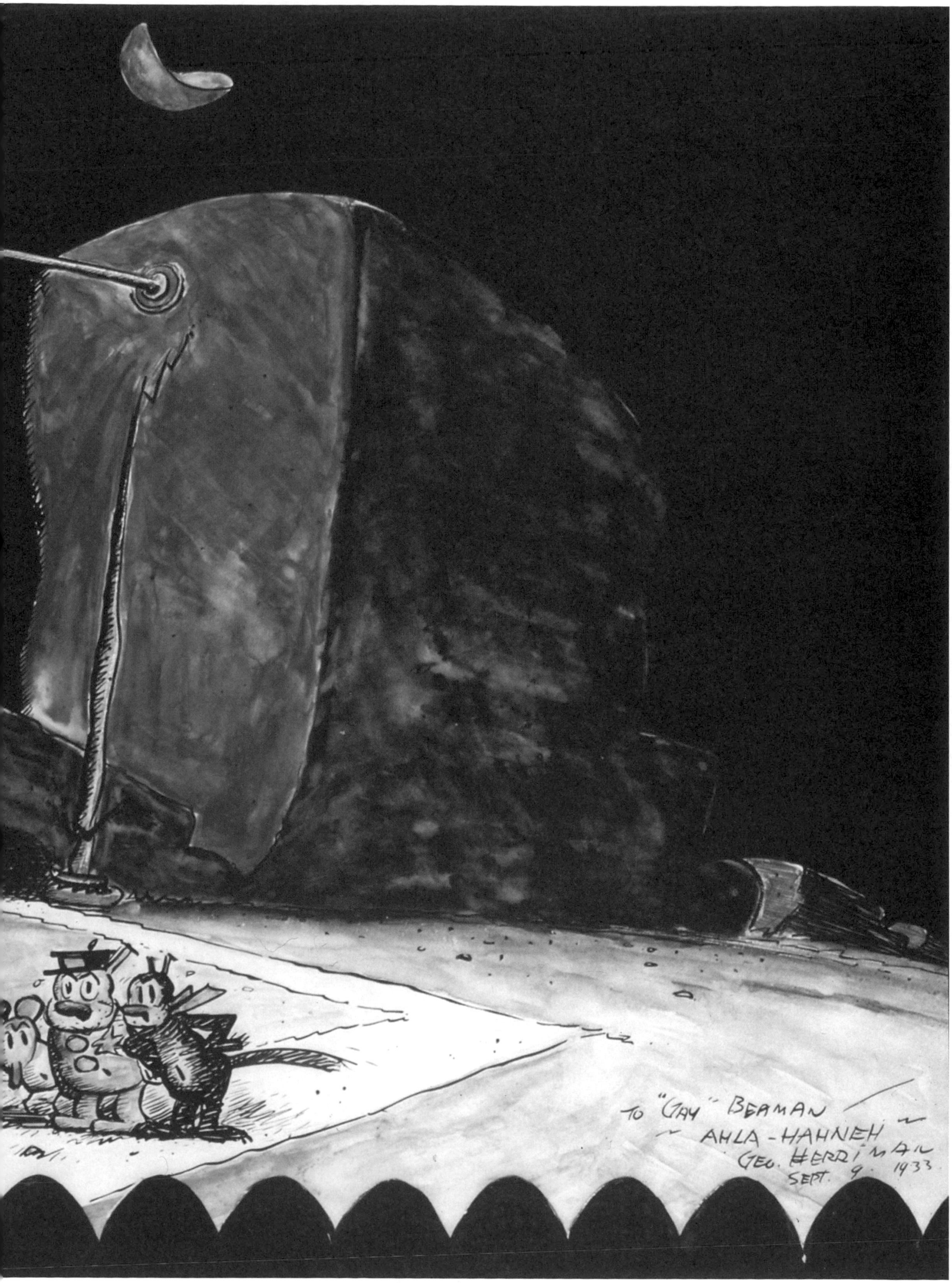
TO "GAY" BEAMAN
AHLA-HAHNEH
GEO. HERRIMAN
SEPT. 9 1933

This drawing was done by George Herriman for John P. O'Farrell, who ran the Trading Post in Red Lake, Arizona. Herriman probably stayed with O'Farrell circa 1920; the places mentioned in this drawing are likely to be an itinerary of Herriman's travels. In this drawing (and also some *Krazy Kat* pages), Herriman exaggerates the size of Red Lake, which is in fact a small pond. Born in 1888, O'Farrell belonged to the first generation of Arizona traders, a tight-knit confederacy that also included John and Louisa Wetherill, who were Herriman's close friends. Aside from Herriman, O'Farrell was also friends with the cartoonist Jimmy Swinnerton. In his old age, Swinnerton asked that after death his ashes be scattered in the Colorado River. By one account, this task fell on O'Farrell. — J.H. (From the collection of, and thanks to, Tom Bertino.)

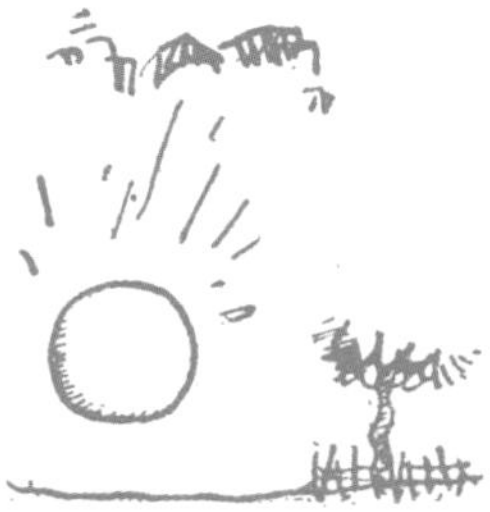

1937.

Readers, please note: an Ignatz "dingbat" placed below a strip indicates a relevant or related footnote at the volume's end for that particular selection, all to be found in the "Ignatz Debaffler" section.

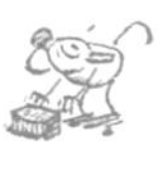

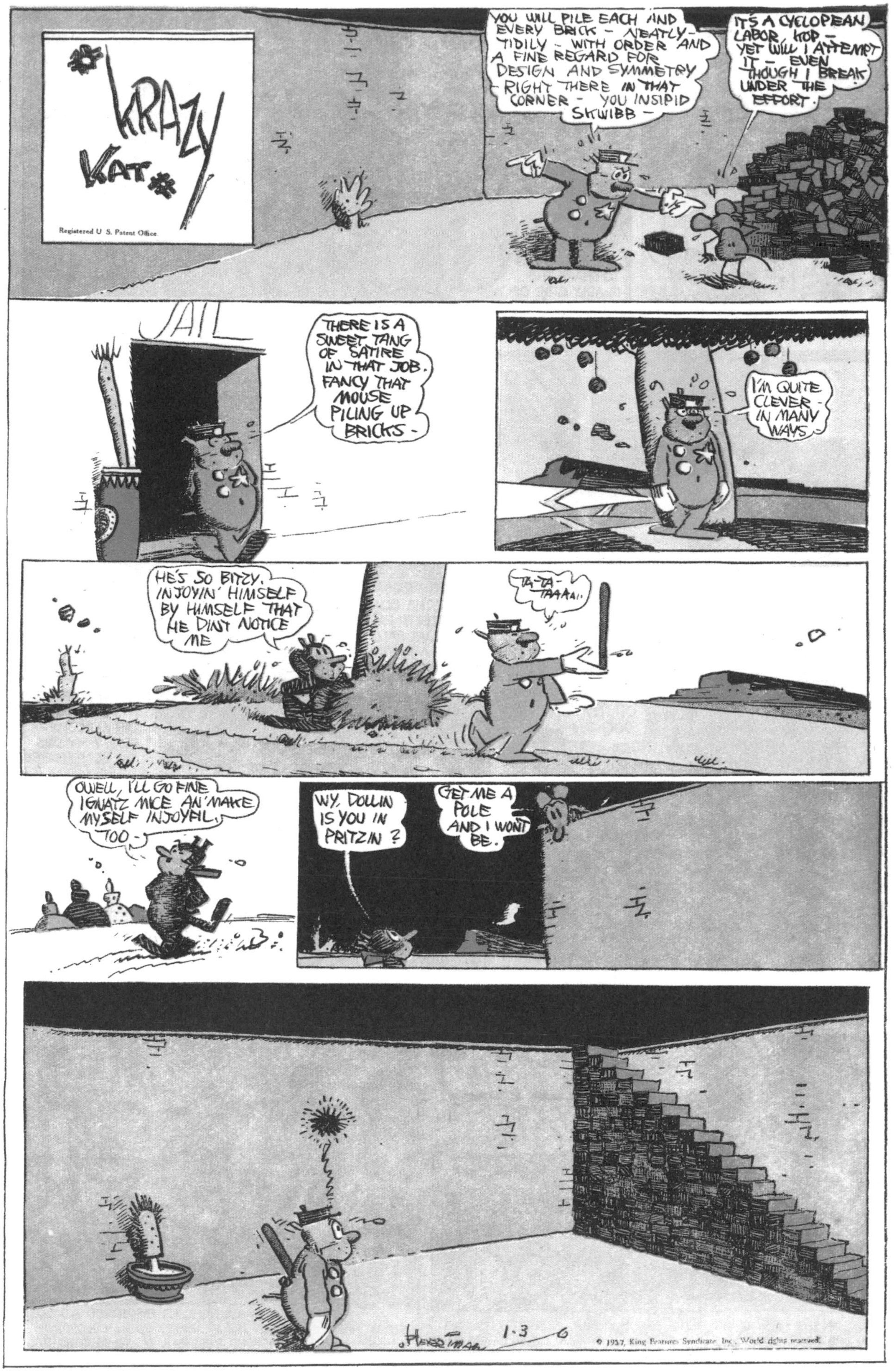
KRAZY KAT
Registered U. S. Patent Office
YOU WILL PILE EACH AND EVERY BRICK - NEATLY- TIDILY - WITH ORDER AND A FINE REGARD FOR DESIGN AND SYMMETRY - RIGHT THERE IN THAT CORNER - YOU INSIPID SKWIBB -
IT'S A CYCLOPEAN LABOR, KOP - YET WILL I ATTEMPT IT - EVEN THOUGH I BREAK UNDER THE EFFORT.
JAIL
THERE IS A SWEET TANG OF SATIRE IN THAT JOB. FANCY THAT MOUSE PILING UP BRICKS -
I'M QUITE CLEVER - IN MANY WAYS -
HE'S SO BITZY, INJOYIN' HIMSELF BY HIMSELF THAT HE DIN'T NOTICE ME
TA-TA-TAAAA!!
O WELL, I'LL GO FINE IGNATZ MICE AN' MAKE MYSELF INJOYFIL, TOO -
WY, DOLLIN IS YOU IN PRITZIN?
GET ME A POLE AND I WON'T BE.
HERRIMAN 1-3 6
© 1937, King Features Syndicate, Inc., World rights reserved.

January 3rd, 1937.

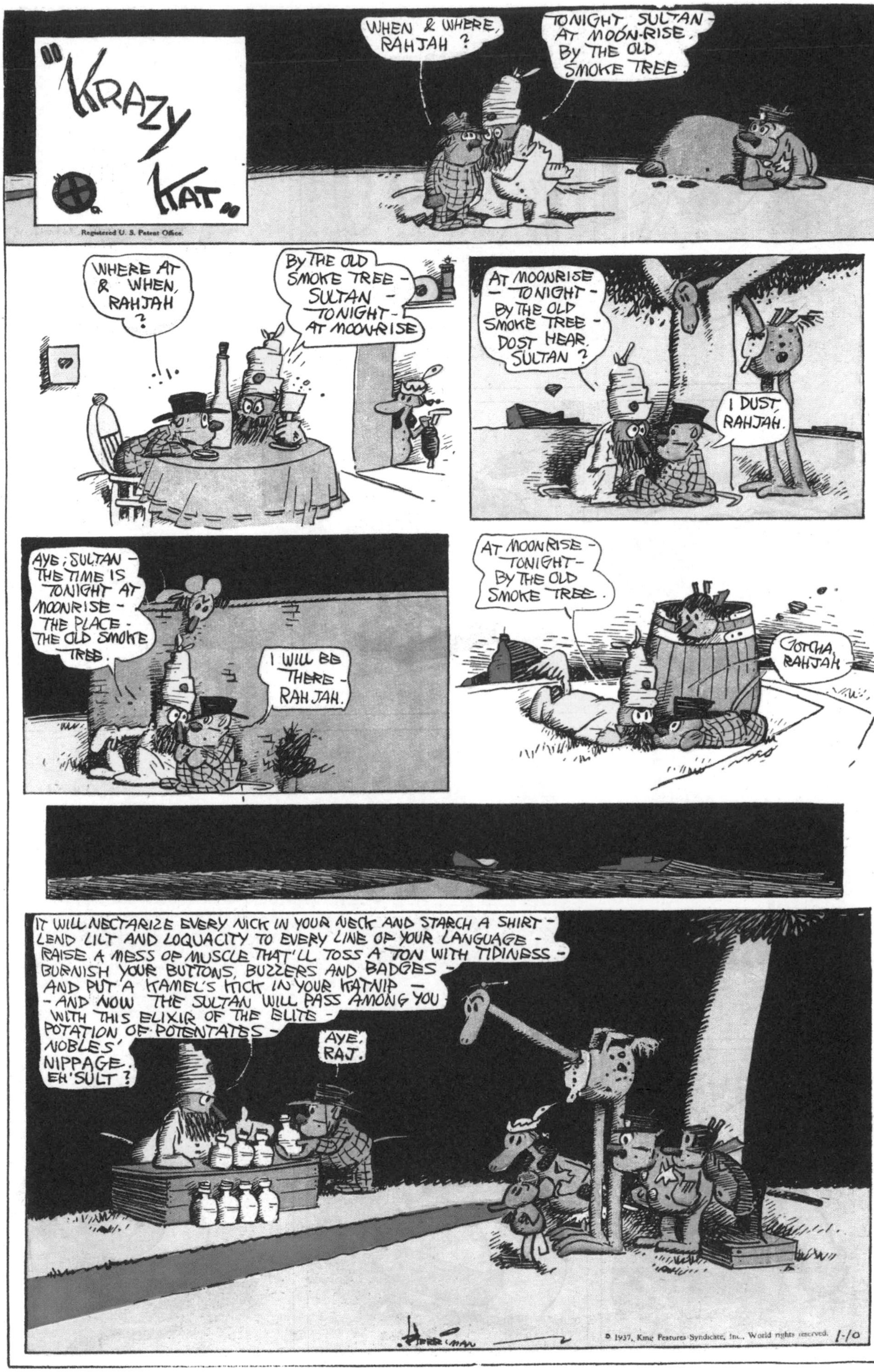
"KRAZY KAT"
Registered U. S. Patent Office.
WHEN & WHERE, RAHJAH ?
TONIGHT, SULTAN - AT MOON-RISE, BY THE OLD SMOKE TREE.
WHERE AT & WHEN, RAHJAH ?
BY THE OLD SMOKE TREE - SULTAN - TONIGHT - AT MOONRISE
AT MOONRISE - TONIGHT - BY THE OLD SMOKE TREE - DOST HEAR, SULTAN ?
I DUST, RAHJAH.
AYE, SULTAN - THE TIME IS TONIGHT AT MOONRISE - THE PLACE - THE OLD SMOKE TREE.
I WILL BE THERE - RAHJAH.
AT MOONRISE - TONIGHT - BY THE OLD SMOKE TREE.
GOTCHA, RAHJAH -
IT WILL NECTARIZE EVERY NICK IN YOUR NECK AND STARCH A SHIRT - LEND LILT AND LOQUACITY TO EVERY LINE OF YOUR LANGUAGE - RAISE A MESS OF MUSCLE THAT'LL TOSS A TON WITH TIDINESS - BURNISH YOUR BUTTONS, BUZZERS AND BADGES - AND PUT A KAMEL'S KICK IN YOUR KATNIP - - AND NOW THE SULTAN WILL PASS AMONG YOU WITH THIS ELIXIR OF THE ELITE - POTATION OF POTENTATES - NOBLES' NIPPAGE. EH SULT ?
AYE, RAJ.
Herriman
© 1937, King Features Syndicate, Inc., World rights reserved. 1-10

January 10th, 1937.

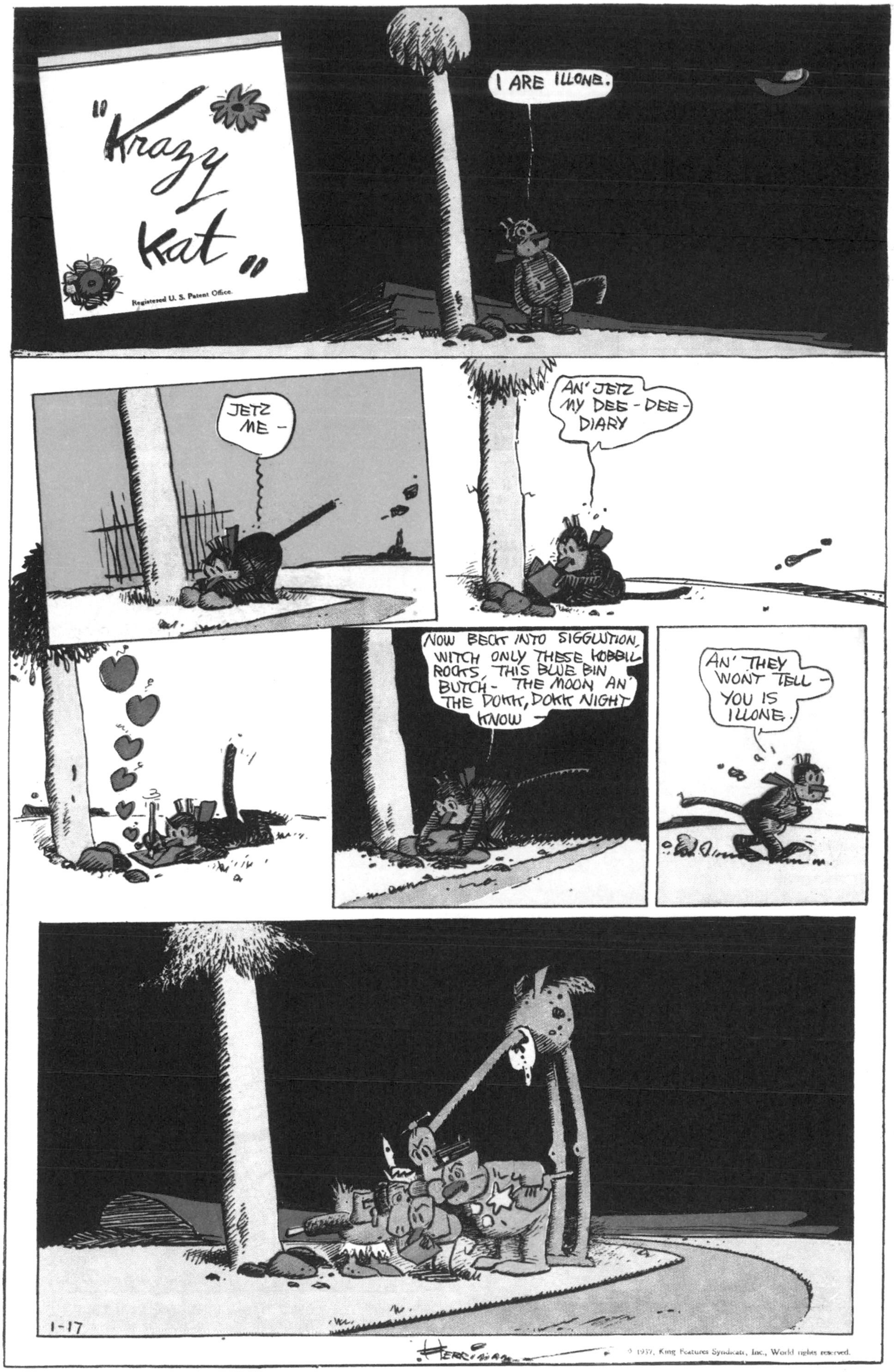
"Krazy Kat"
Registered U. S. Patent Office.
I ARE ILLONE.
JETZ ME –
AN' JETZ MY DEE-DEE-DIARY
NOW BECK INTO SIGGLUTION, WITCH ONLY THESE KOBBIL ROCKS, THIS BLUE BIN BUTCH – THE MOON AN' THE DOKK, DOKK NIGHT KNOW –
AN' THEY WONT TELL – YOU IS ILLONE.
1-17
HERRIMAN
© 1937, King Features Syndicate, Inc., World rights reserved.

January 17th, 1937.

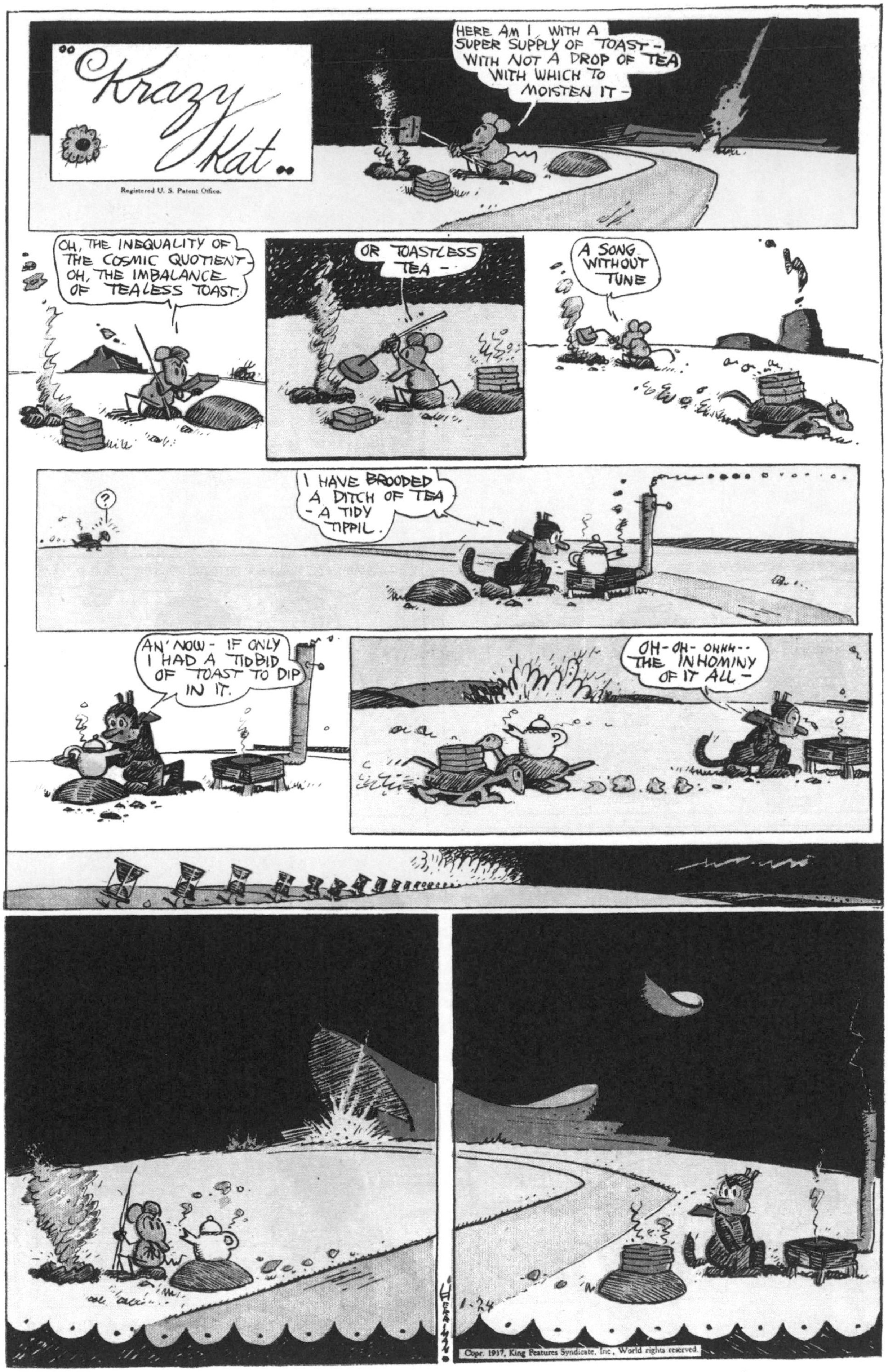

"Krazy Kat"
Registered U. S. Patent Office.
HERE AM I WITH A SUPER SUPPLY OF TOAST - WITH NOT A DROP OF TEA WITH WHICH TO MOISTEN IT -
OH, THE INEQUALITY OF THE COSMIC QUOTIENT - OH, THE IMBALANCE OF TEALESS TOAST.
OR TOASTLESS TEA -
A SONG WITHOUT TUNE
?
I HAVE BROODED A DITCH OF TEA - A TIDY TIPPIL.
AN' NOW - IF ONLY I HAD A TIDBID OF TOAST TO DIP IN IT.
OH - OH - OHHH - - THE INHOMINY OF IT ALL -
1-24
Copr. 1937, King Features Syndicate, Inc., World rights reserved.

January 24th, 1937.

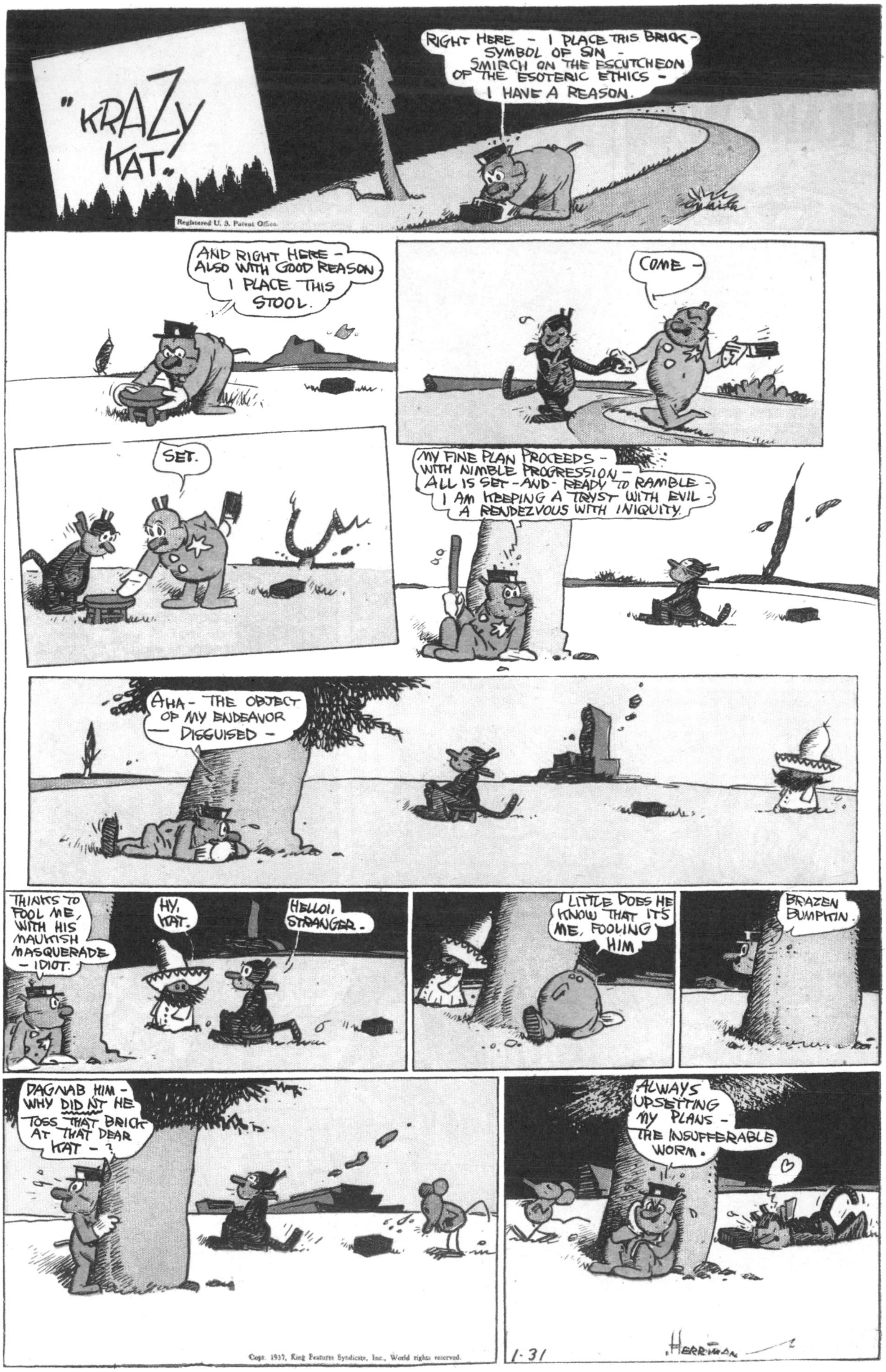
"KRAZY KAT."
Registered U. S. Patent Office.
RIGHT HERE - I PLACE THIS BRICK - SYMBOL OF SIN - SMIRCH ON THE ESCUTCHEON OF THE ESOTERIC ETHICS - I HAVE A REASON.
AND RIGHT HERE - ALSO WITH GOOD REASON I PLACE THIS STOOL.
COME -
SET.
MY FINE PLAN PROCEEDS - WITH NIMBLE PROGRESSION - ALL IS SET - AND - READY TO RAMBLE - I AM KEEPING A TRYST WITH EVIL - A RENDEZVOUS WITH INIQUITY.
AHA - THE OBJECT OF MY ENDEAVOR - DISGUISED -
THINKS TO FOOL ME, WITH HIS MAUKISH MASQUERADE - IDIOT.
HY, KAT.
HELLO, STRANGER.
LITTLE DOES HE KNOW THAT IT'S ME, FOOLING HIM
BRAZEN BUMPKIN.
DAGNAB HIM - WHY DID NT HE TOSS THAT BRICK AT THAT DEAR KAT - ?
ALWAYS UPSETTING MY PLANS - THE INSUFFERABLE WORM.
Copr. 1937, King Features Syndicate, Inc., World rights reserved.
1-31
HERRIMAN

January 31st, 1937.

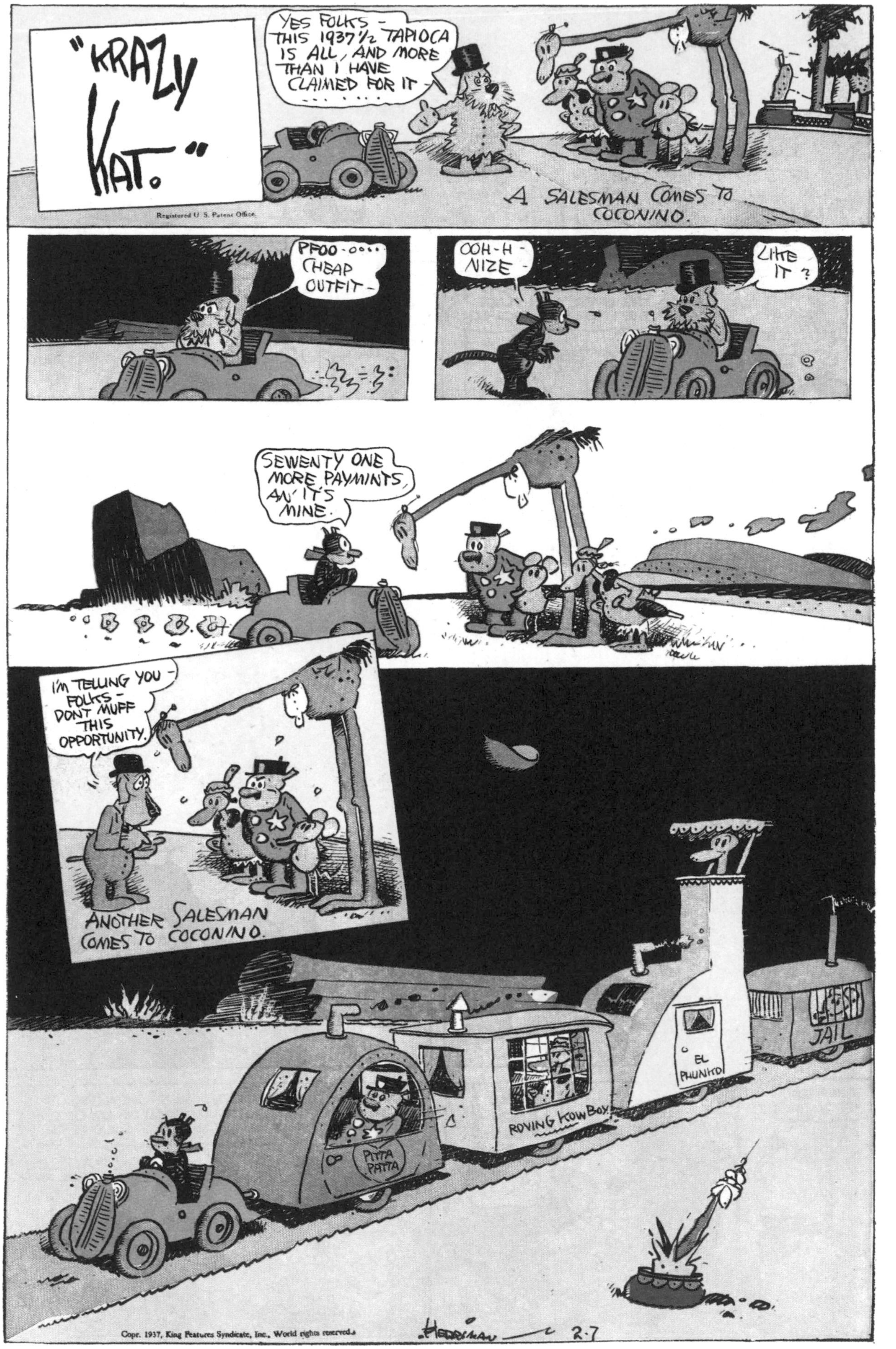

"KRAZY KAT."
Registered U. S. Patent Office.
YES FOLKS - THIS 1937½ TAPIOCA IS ALL, AND MORE THAN I HAVE CLAIMED FOR IT - ......
A SALESMAN COMES TO COCONINO.
PFOO-O.... CHEAP OUTFIT -
OOH-H NIZE -
LIKE IT ?
SEWENTY ONE MORE PAYMINTS, AN' IT'S MINE.
I'M TELLING YOU FOLKS - DONT MUFF THIS OPPORTUNITY.
ANOTHER SALESMAN COMES TO COCONINO.
JAIL
EL PHUNITO
ROVING KOW BOY
PITTA PATTA
Copr. 1937, King Features Syndicate, Inc., World rights reserved.
HERRIMAN 2-7

February 7th, 1937.

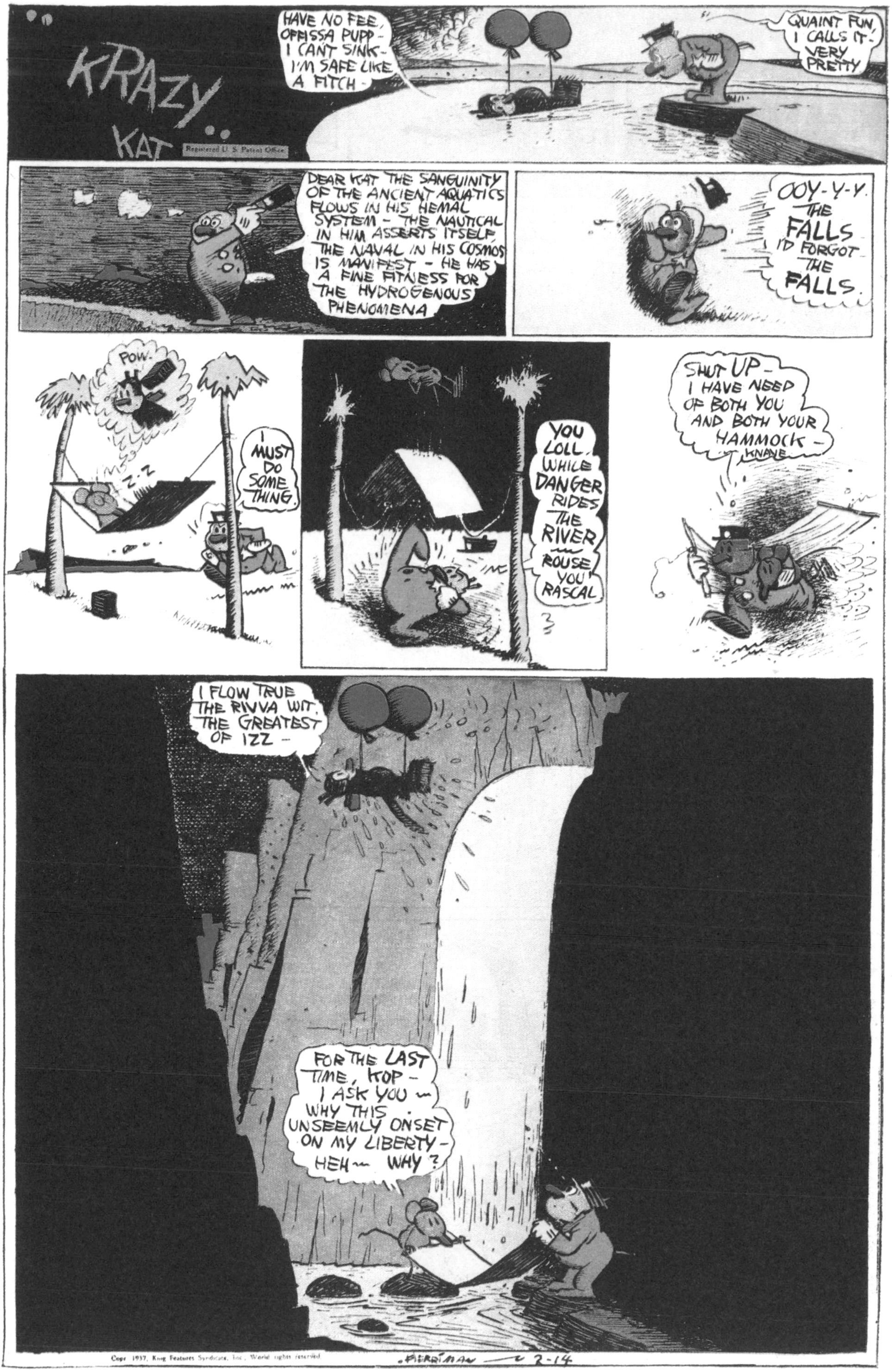
KRAZY KAT
Registered U. S. Patent Office
HAVE NO FEE, OFFISSA PUPP - I CAN'T SINK - I'M SAFE LIKE A FITCH -
QUAINT FUN, I CALLS IT - VERY PRETTY
DEAR KAT THE SANGUINITY OF THE ANCIENT AQUATICS FLOWS IN HIS HEMAL SYSTEM - THE NAUTICAL IN HIM ASSERTS ITSELF, THE NAVAL IN HIS COSMOS IS MANIFEST - HE HAS A FINE FITNESS FOR THE HYDROGENOUS PHENOMENA
OOY-Y-Y. THE FALLS I'D FORGOT THE FALLS.
POW.
Z-Z
I MUST DO SOME THING.
YOU LOLL, WHILE DANGER RIDES THE RIVER - ROUSE, YOU RASCAL
SHUT UP - I HAVE NEED OF BOTH YOU AND BOTH YOUR HAMMOCK - KNAVE
I FLOW TRUE THE RIVVA WIT, THE GREATEST OF IZZ -
FOR THE LAST TIME, KOP - I ASK YOU - WHY THIS UNSEEMLY ONSET ON MY LIBERTY - HEH - WHY?
Copr. 1937, King Features Syndicate, Inc., World rights reserved
HERRIMAN 2-14

February 14th, 1937.

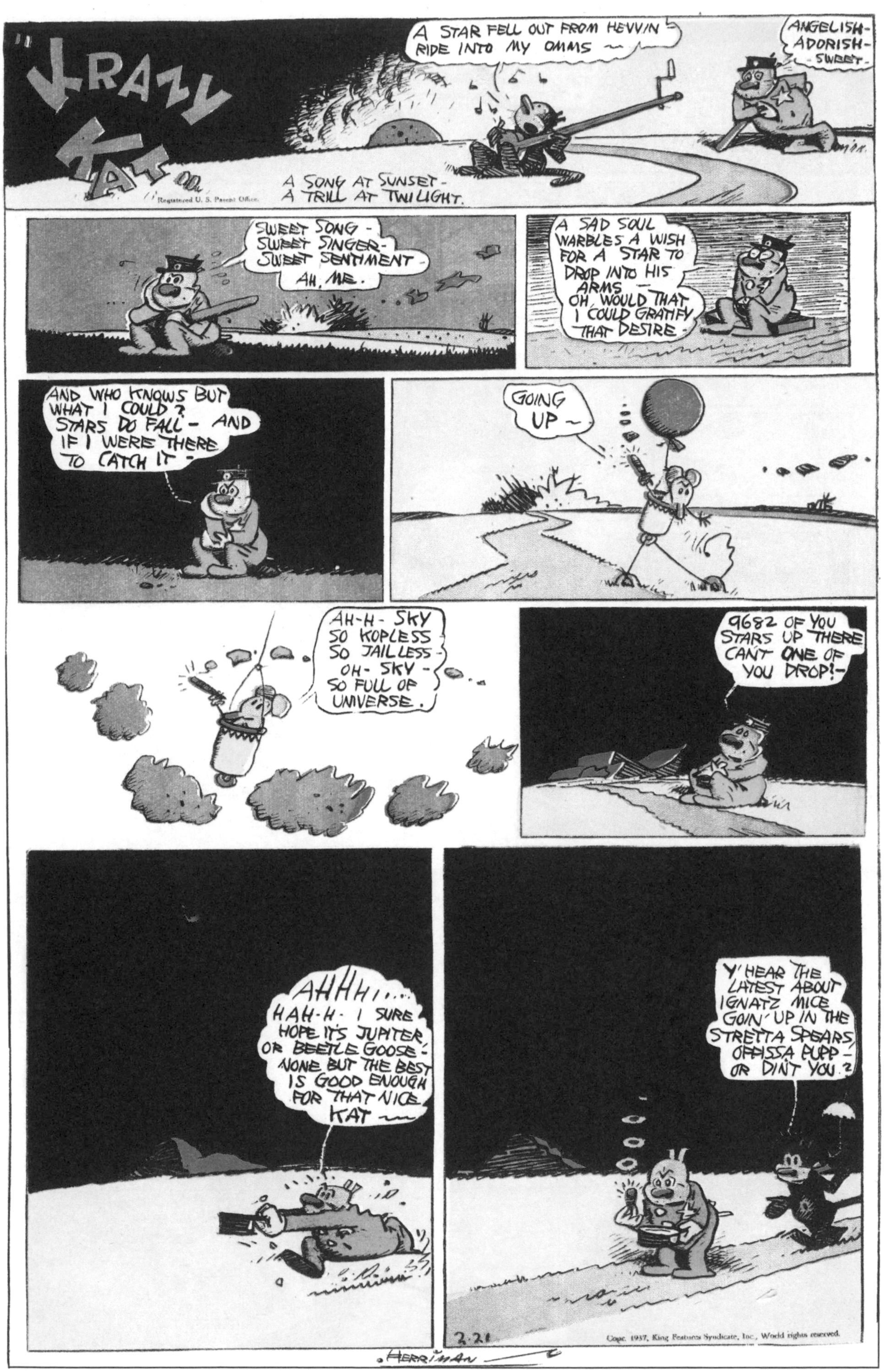
"Krazy Kat"
Registered U. S. Patent Office.
A STAR FELL OUT FROM HEVVIN RIDE INTO MY OMMS ~
ANGELISH - ADORISH - SWEET -
A SONG AT SUNSET - A TRILL AT TWILIGHT.
SWEET SONG - SWEET SINGER - SWEET SENTIMENT - AH, ME.
A SAD SOUL WARBLES A WISH FOR A STAR TO DROP INTO HIS ARMS - OH, WOULD THAT I COULD GRATIFY THAT DESIRE -
AND WHO KNOWS BUT WHAT I COULD? STARS DO FALL - AND IF I WERE THERE TO CATCH IT -
GOING UP ~
AH-H - SKY SO KOPLESS SO JAILLESS - OH - SKY - SO FULL OF UNIVERSE.
9682 OF YOU STARS UP THERE CAN'T ONE OF YOU DROP! -
AHHH!... HAH-H - I SURE HOPE IT'S JUPITER OR BEETLE GOOSE - NONE BUT THE BEST IS GOOD ENOUGH FOR THAT NICE KAT ~
Y' HEAR THE LATEST ABOUT IGNATZ MICE GOIN' UP IN THE STRETTA SPEARS, OFFISSA PUPP - OR DIN'T YOU?
2-21
Copr. 1937, King Features Syndicate, Inc., World rights reserved.
HERRIMAN

February 21st, 1937.

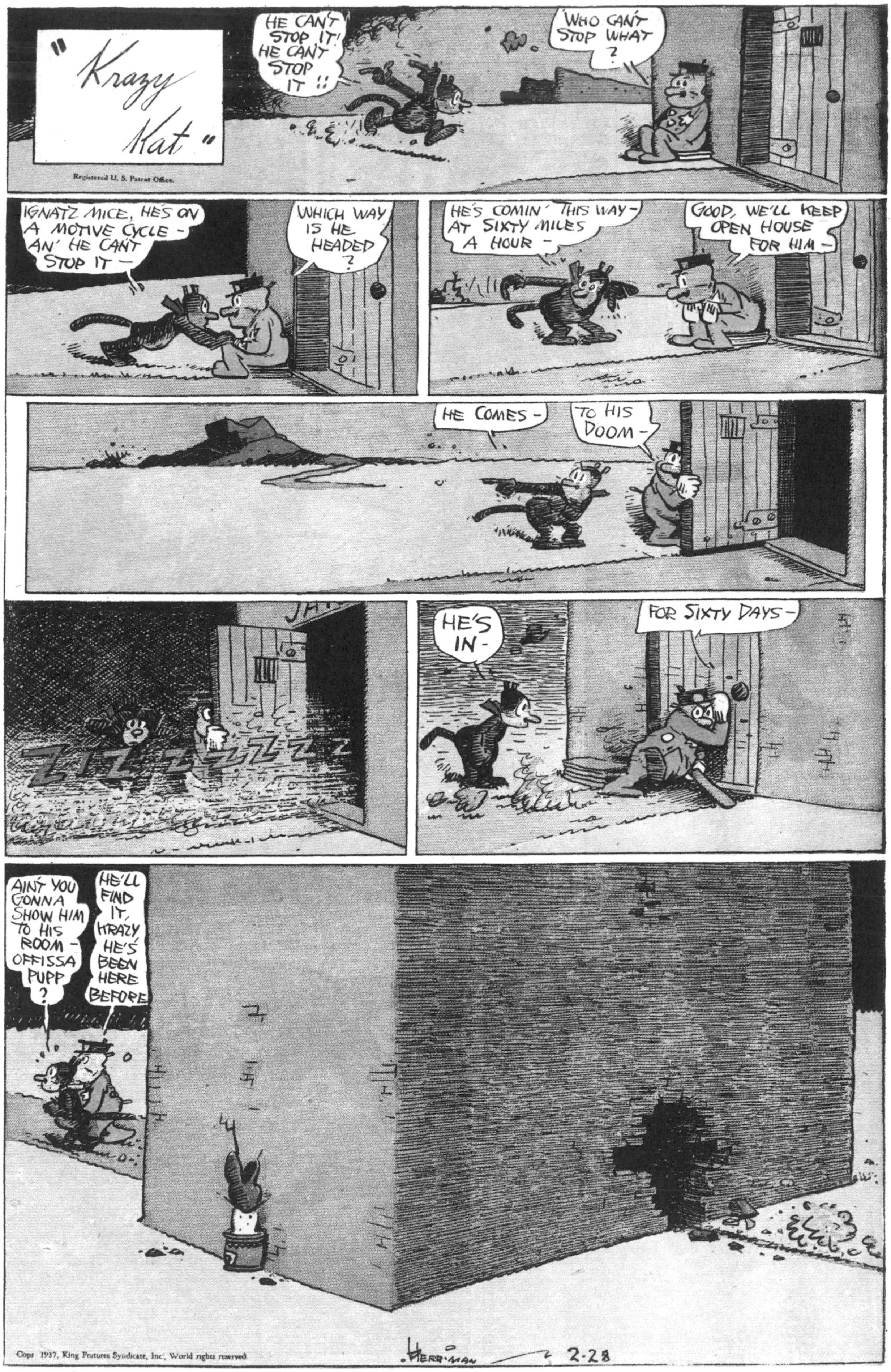
"Krazy Kat"
Registered U. S. Patent Office.
HE CAN'T STOP IT! HE CAN'T STOP IT !!
WHO CAN'T STOP WHAT ?
IGNATZ MICE, HE'S ON A MOTIVE CYCLE - AN' HE CAN'T STOP IT -
WHICH WAY IS HE HEADED ?
HE'S COMIN' THIS WAY - AT SIXTY MILES A HOUR -
GOOD, WE'LL KEEP OPEN HOUSE FOR HIM -
HE COMES -
TO HIS DOOM -
HE'S IN -
FOR SIXTY DAYS -
AIN'T YOU GONNA SHOW HIM TO HIS ROOM - OFFISSA PUPP ?
HE'LL FIND IT, KRAZY HE'S BEEN HERE BEFORE
Copr 1937, King Features Syndicate, Inc, World rights reserved.
HERRIMAN
2-28

February 28th, 1937.

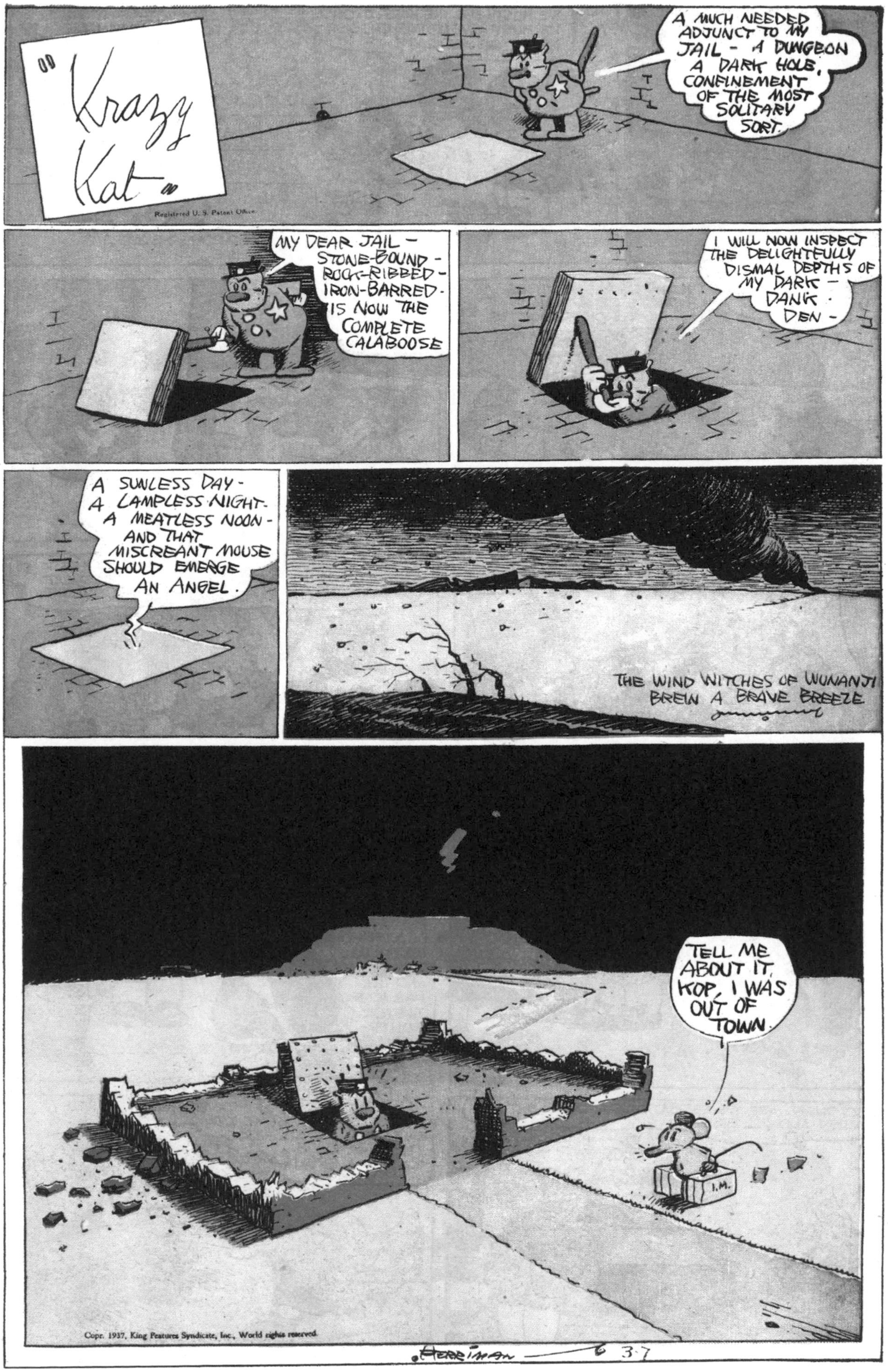
"Krazy Kat"
Registered U. S. Patent Office
A MUCH NEEDED ADJUNCT TO MY JAIL - A DUNGEON A DARK HOLE. CONFINEMENT OF THE MOST SOLITARY SORT.
MY DEAR JAIL - STONE-BOUND - ROCK-RIBBED - IRON-BARRED - IS NOW THE COMPLETE CALABOOSE
I WILL NOW INSPECT THE DELIGHTFULLY DISMAL DEPTHS OF MY DARK - DANK - DEN -
A SUNLESS DAY - A LAMPLESS NIGHT - A MEATLESS NOON - AND THAT MISCREANT MOUSE SHOULD EMERGE AN ANGEL.
THE WIND WITCHES OF WUNANJI BREW A BRAVE BREEZE
TELL ME ABOUT IT, KOP, I WAS OUT OF TOWN.
I.M.
Copr. 1937, King Features Syndicate, Inc., World rights reserved.
HERRIMAN 3-7

March 7th, 1937.

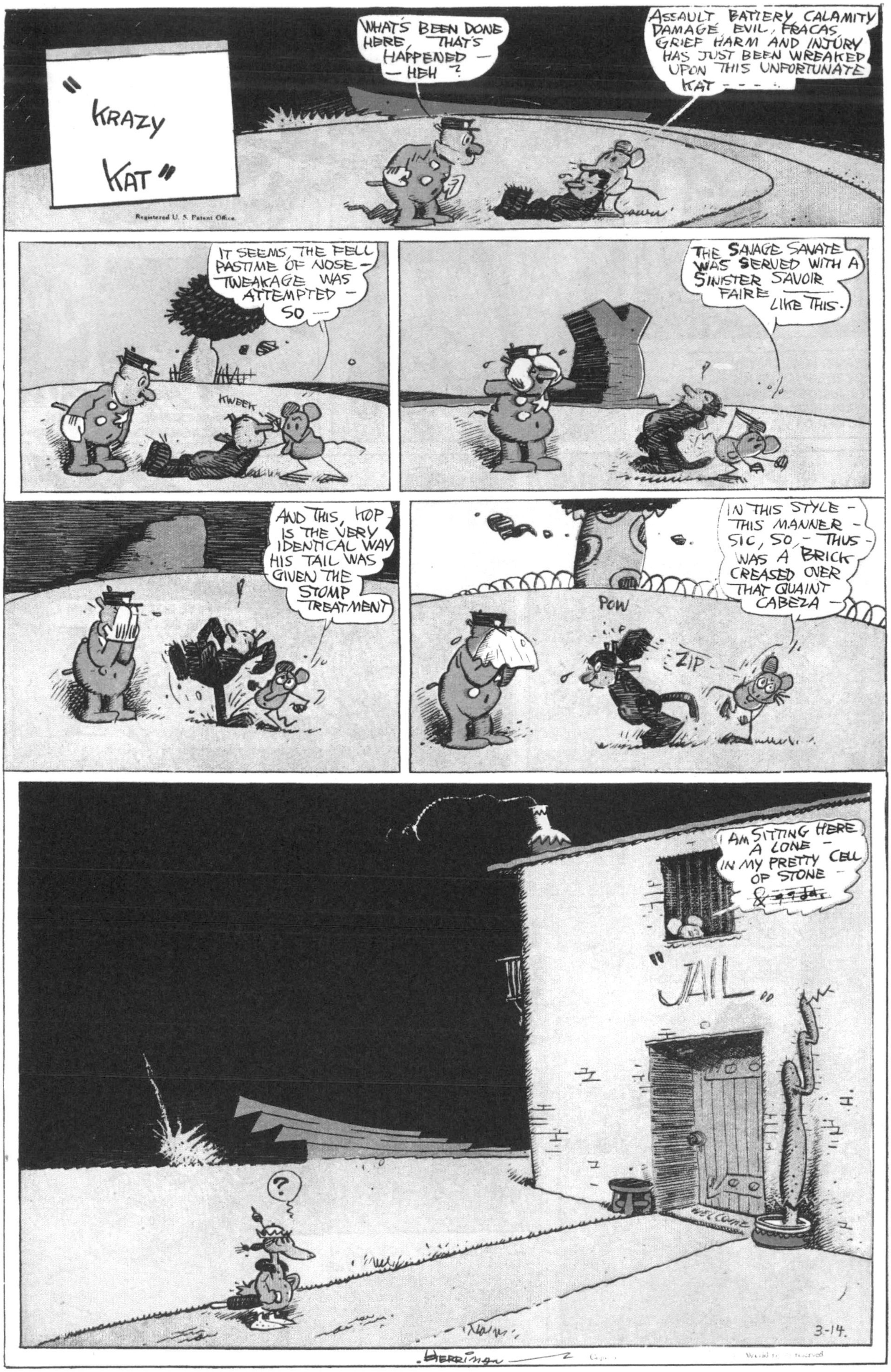
"KRAZY KAT"
Registered U. S. Patent Office.
WHAT'S BEEN DONE HERE, THAT'S HAPPENED — — HEH ?
ASSAULT, BATTERY, CALAMITY, DAMAGE, EVIL, FRACAS, GRIEF, HARM AND INJURY HAS JUST BEEN WREAKED UPON THIS UNFORTUNATE KAT - - -.
IT SEEMS, THE FELL PASTIME OF NOSE-TWEAKAGE WAS ATTEMPTED - SO —
KWEEK
THE SAVAGE SAVATE WAS SERVED WITH A SINISTER SAVOIR FAIRE — LIKE THIS.
AND THIS, KOP IS THE VERY IDENTICAL WAY HIS TAIL WAS GIVEN THE STOMP TREATMENT
IN THIS STYLE - THIS MANNER - SIC, SO, - THUS - WAS A BRICK CREASED OVER THAT QUAINT CABEZA -
POW
ZIP
I AM SITTING HERE A LONE - IN MY PRETTY CELL OF STONE -
"JAIL"
WELCOME
3-14.
HERRIMAN

March 14th, 1937.

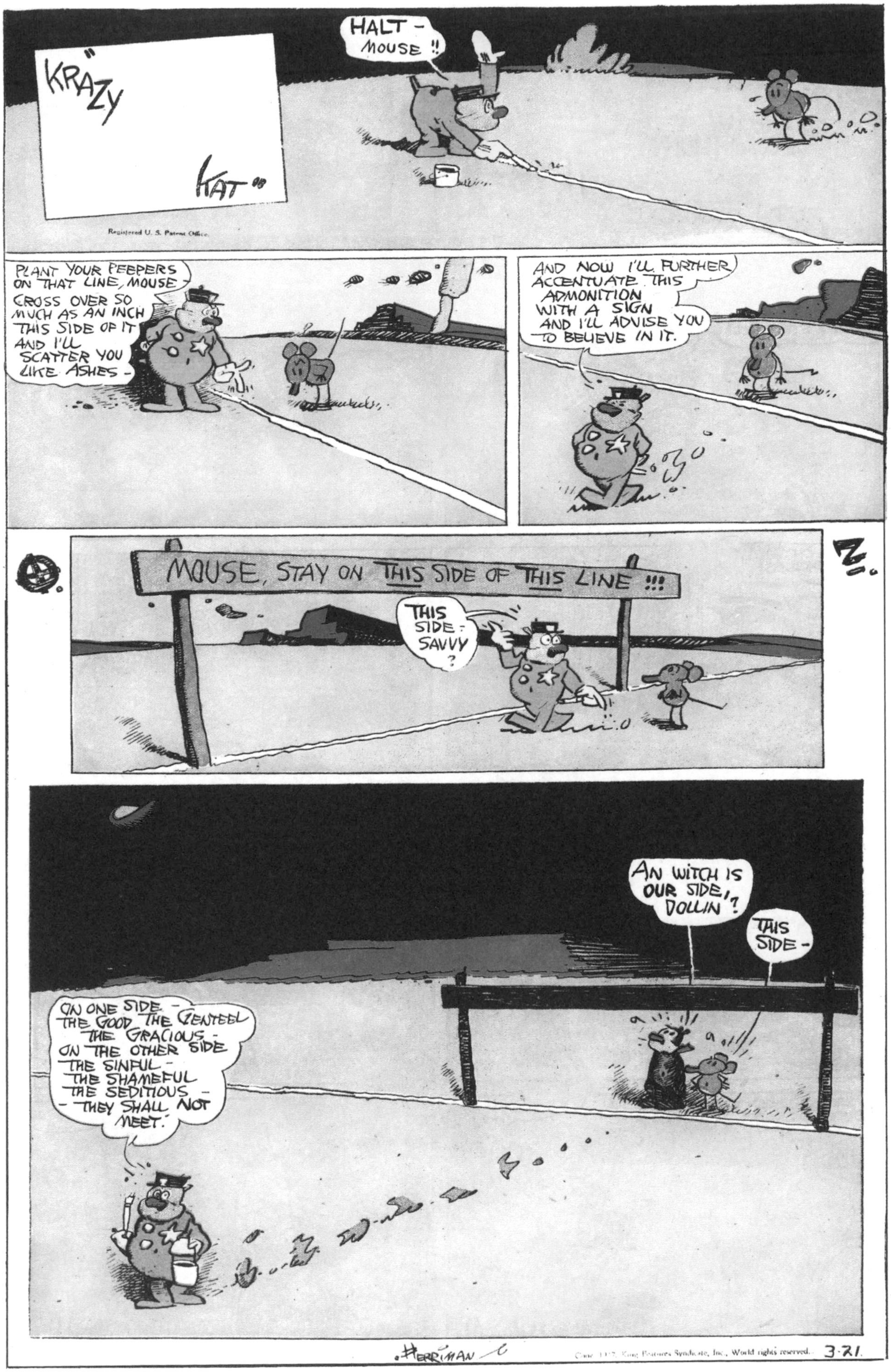
"KRAZY KAT"
Registered U. S. Patent Office.
HALT - MOUSE !!
PLANT YOUR PEEPERS ON THAT LINE, MOUSE - CROSS OVER SO MUCH AS AN INCH THIS SIDE OF IT AND I'LL SCATTER YOU LIKE ASHES -
AND NOW I'LL FURTHER ACCENTUATE THIS ADMONITION WITH A SIGN AND I'LL ADVISE YOU TO BELIEVE IN IT.
MOUSE, STAY ON THIS SIDE OF THIS LINE !!!
THIS SIDE: SAVVY ?
AN WITCH IS OUR SIDE, DOLLIN ?
THIS SIDE -
ON ONE SIDE - THE GOOD THE GENTEEL THE GRACIOUS - ON THE OTHER SIDE THE SINFUL - THE SHAMEFUL THE SEDITIOUS - - THEY SHALL NOT MEET.
HERRIMAN
World rights reserved.
3-21.

March 21st, 1937.

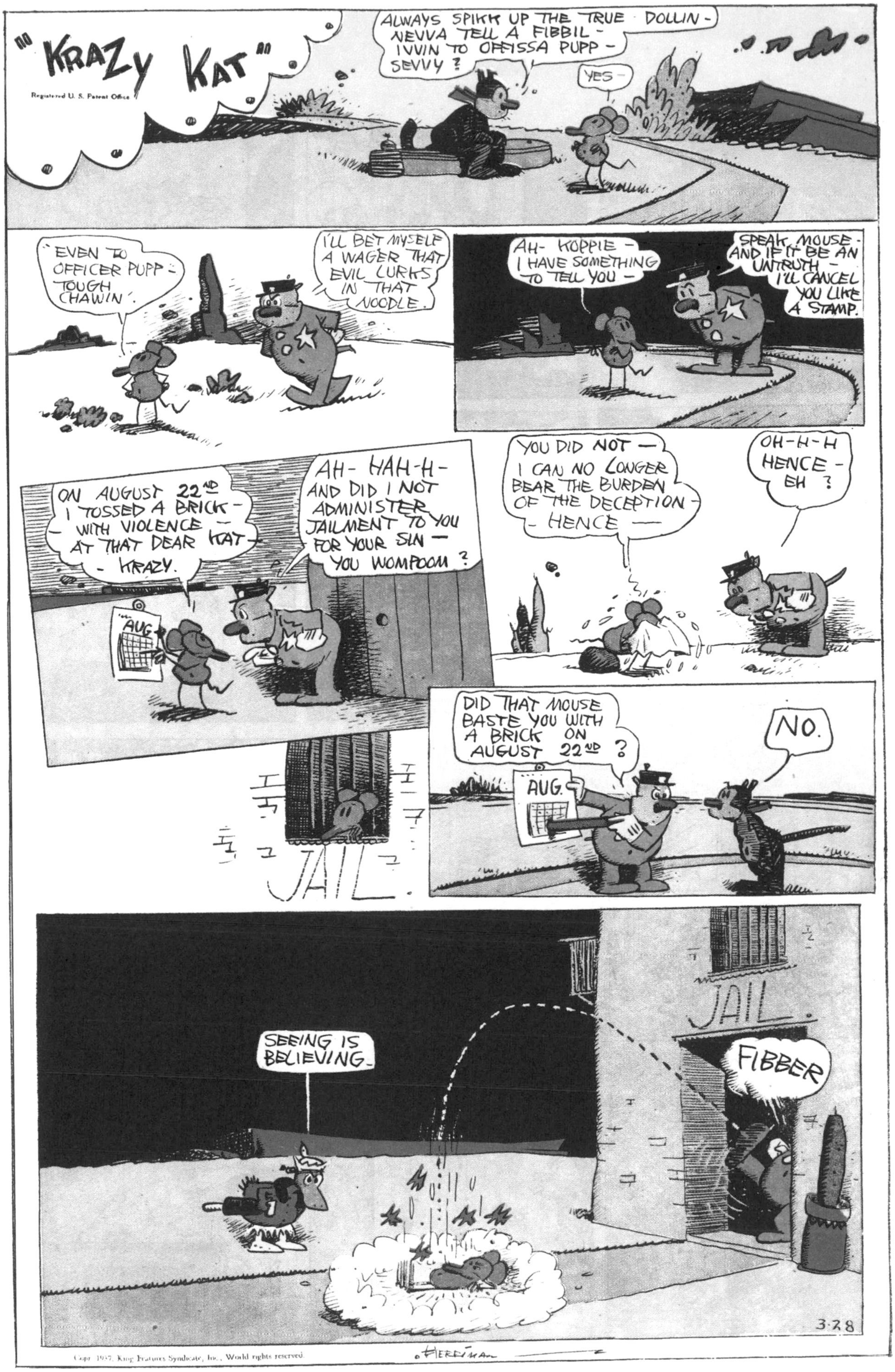

"KRAZY KAT"
Registered U. S. Patent Office
ALWAYS SPIKK UP THE TRUE DOLLIN - NEVVA TELL A FIBBIL - IVVIN TO OFFISSA PUPP - SEVVY ?
YES -
EVEN TO OFFICER PUPP - TOUGH CHAWIN'.
I'LL BET MYSELF A WAGER THAT EVIL LURKS IN THAT NOODLE.
AH- KOPPIE - I HAVE SOMETHING TO TELL YOU -
SPEAK, MOUSE - AND IF IT BE AN UNTRUTH - I'LL CANCEL YOU LIKE A STAMP.
ON AUGUST 22ND I TOSSED A BRICK - WITH VIOLENCE - AT THAT DEAR KAT - KRAZY.
AH- HAH-H- AND DID I NOT ADMINISTER JAILMENT TO YOU FOR YOUR SIN - YOU WOMPOOM ?
AUG
YOU DID NOT - I CAN NO LONGER BEAR THE BURDEN OF THE DECEPTION - HENCE —
OH-H-H HENCE - EH ?
JAIL
DID THAT MOUSE BASTE YOU WITH A BRICK ON AUGUST 22ND ?
NO.
AUG.
SEEING IS BELIEVING.
JAIL.
FIBBER
3-28
Copr. 1937, King Features Syndicate, Inc., World rights reserved.
HERRIMAN

March 28th, 1937.

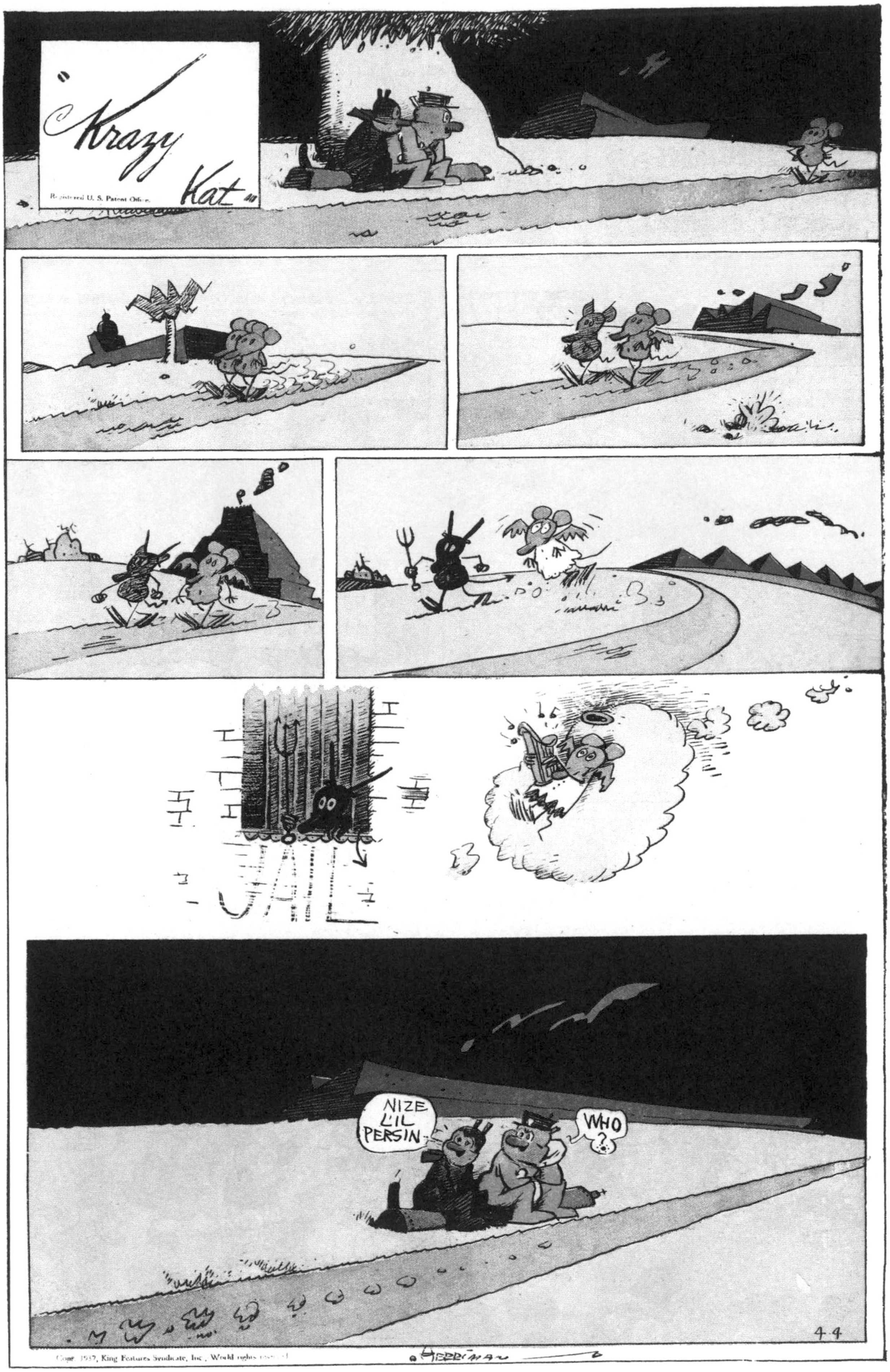
Krazy Kat
Registered U. S. Patent Office.
JAIL
NIZE LI'L PERSIN
WHO ?
4-4
HERRIMAN

April 4th, 1937.

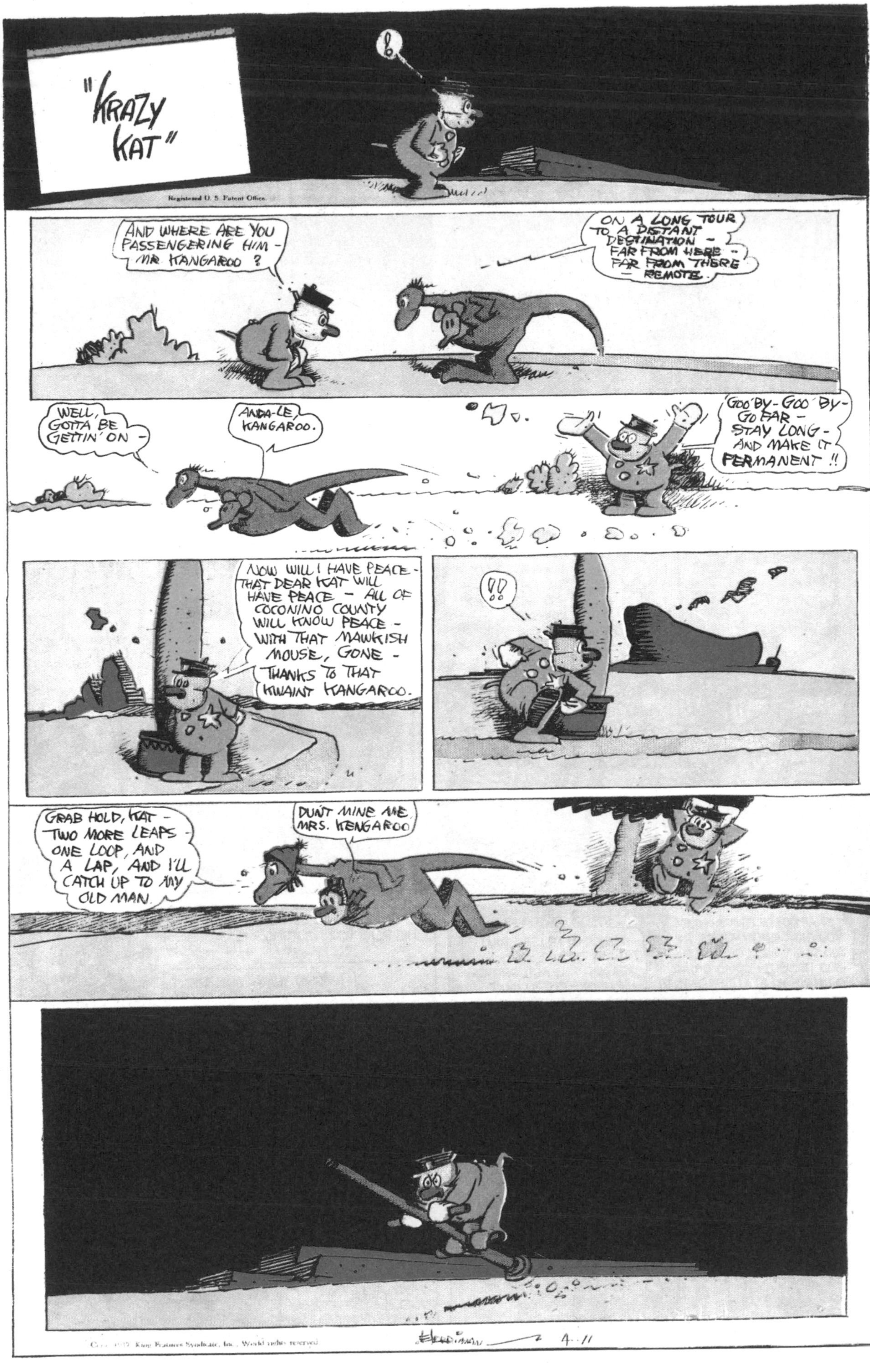
"KRAZY KAT"
Registered U. S. Patent Office.
AND WHERE ARE YOU PASSENGERING HIM - MR KANGAROO ?
ON A LONG TOUR TO A DISTANT DESTINATION - FAR FROM HERE - FAR FROM THERE - REMOTE.
WELL, GOTTA BE GETTIN' ON -
ANDA-LE KANGAROO.
GOO'BY-GOO'BY-GO FAR - STAY LONG - AND MAKE IT PERMANENT !!
NOW WILL I HAVE PEACE - THAT DEAR KAT WILL HAVE PEACE - ALL OF COCONINO COUNTY WILL KNOW PEACE - WITH THAT MAWKISH MOUSE, GONE - THANKS TO THAT KWAINT KANGAROO.
!!
GRAB HOLD, KAT - TWO MORE LEAPS - ONE LOOP, AND A LAP, AND I'LL CATCH UP TO MY OLD MAN.
DUNT MINE ME MRS. KENGAROO

April 11th, 1937.

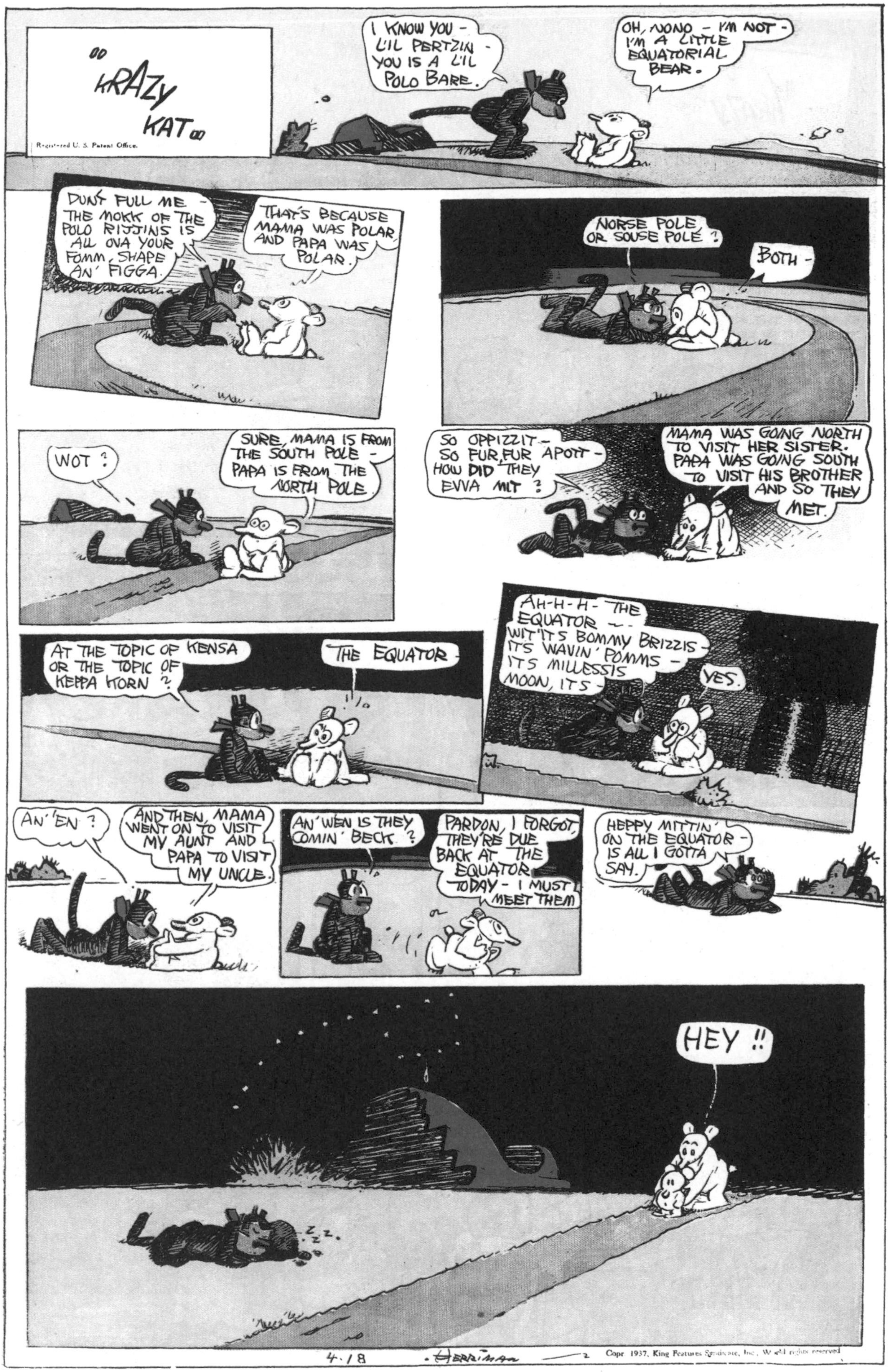
"KRAZY KAT"
Registered U. S. Patent Office.
I KNOW YOU - LIL PERTZIN - YOU IS A L'IL POLO BARE.
OH, NONO - I'M NOT - I'M A LITTLE EQUATORIAL BEAR.
DON'T FULL ME - THE MOKK OF THE POLO RIJJINS IS ALL OVA YOUR FOMM, SHAPE AN' FIGGA.
THAT'S BECAUSE MAMA WAS POLAR, AND PAPA WAS POLAR.
NORSE POLE OR SOUSE POLE ?
BOTH -
WOT ?
SURE, MAMA IS FROM THE SOUTH POLE - PAPA IS FROM THE NORTH POLE
SO OPPIZZIT - SO FUR, FUR APOTT - HOW DID THEY EVVA MIT ?
MAMA WAS GOING NORTH TO VISIT HER SISTER. PAPA WAS GOING SOUTH TO VISIT HIS BROTHER AND SO THEY MET.
AT THE TOPIC OF KENSA OR THE TOPIC OF KEPPA KORN ?
THE EQUATOR
AH-H-H - THE EQUATOR - - WIT IT'S BOMMY BRIZZIS - ITS WAVIN' POMMS - ITS MILLESSIS MOON, ITS -
YES.
AN' EN ?
AND THEN, MAMA WENT ON TO VISIT MY AUNT AND PAPA TO VISIT MY UNCLE.
AN' WEN IS THEY COMIN' BECK ?
PARDON, I FORGOT, THEY'RE DUE BACK AT THE EQUATOR TODAY - I MUST MEET THEM
HEPPY MITTIN' ON THE EQUATOR - IS ALL I GOTTA SAY.
HEY !!
Z Z Z.
4.18
HERRIMAN
Copr 1937, King Features Syndicate, Inc., World rights reserved

April 18th, 1937.

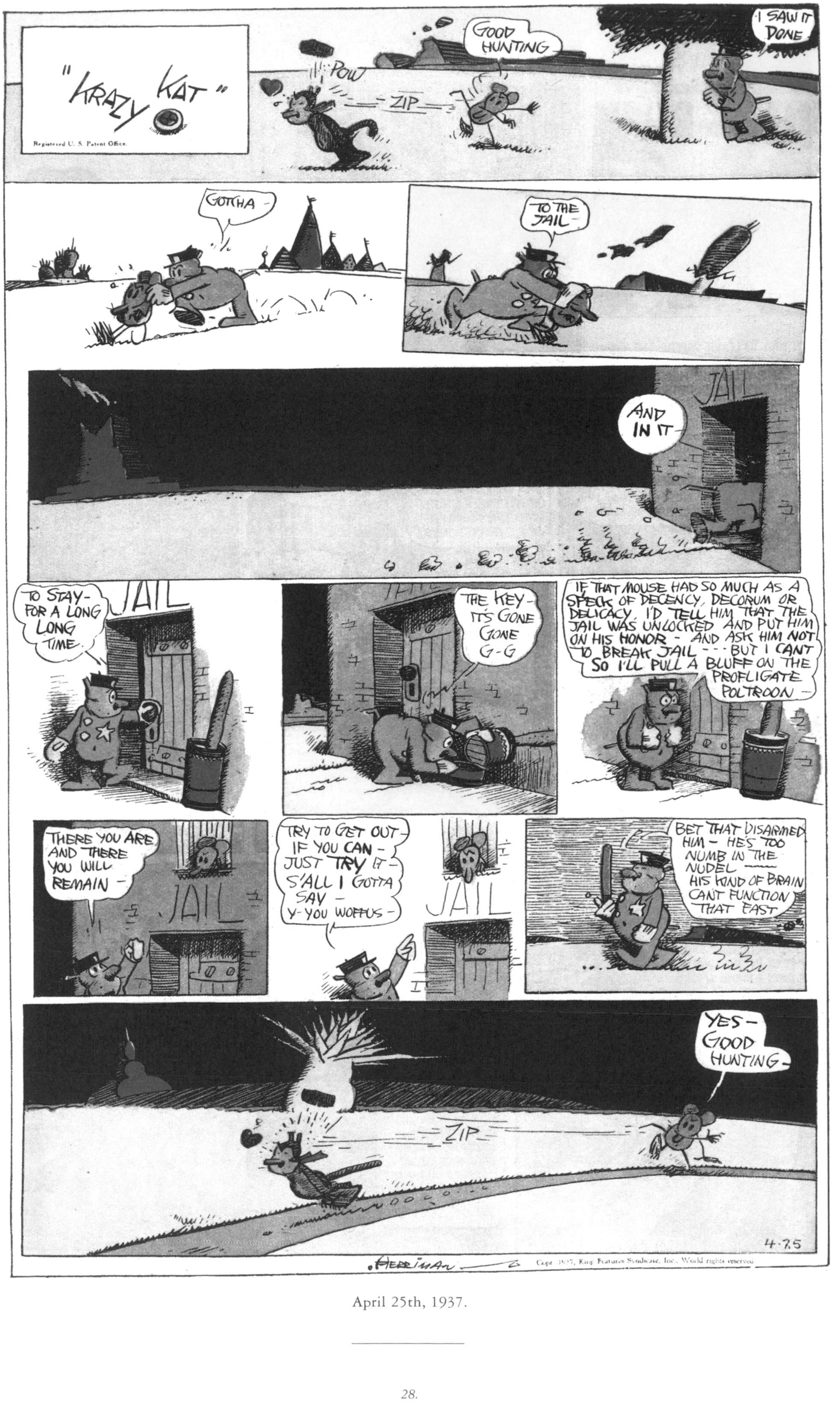
"KRAZY KAT"
Registered U. S. Patent Office.
POW
ZIP
GOOD HUNTING
I SAW IT DONE
GOTCHA
TO THE JAIL
AND IN IT
TO STAY- FOR A LONG LONG TIME.
JAIL
THE KEY- IT'S GONE GONE G-G
IF THAT MOUSE HAD SO MUCH AS A SPECK OF DECENCY, DECORUM OR DELICACY, I'D TELL HIM THAT THE JAIL WAS UNLOCKED AND PUT HIM ON HIS HONOR - AND ASK HIM NOT TO BREAK JAIL --- BUT I CANT SO I'LL PULL A BLUFF ON THE PROFLIGATE POLTROON -
THERE YOU ARE AND THERE YOU WILL REMAIN -
JAIL
TRY TO GET OUT - IF YOU CAN - JUST TRY IT - S'ALL I GOTTA SAY - Y-YOU WOFFUS -
JAIL
BET THAT DISARMED HIM - HE'S TOO NUMB IN THE NUDEL --- HIS KIND OF BRAIN CANT FUNCTION THAT FAST
YES - GOOD HUNTING -
ZIP
4-25
HERRIMAN
Copr. 1937, King Features Syndicate, Inc., World rights reserved.

April 25th, 1937.

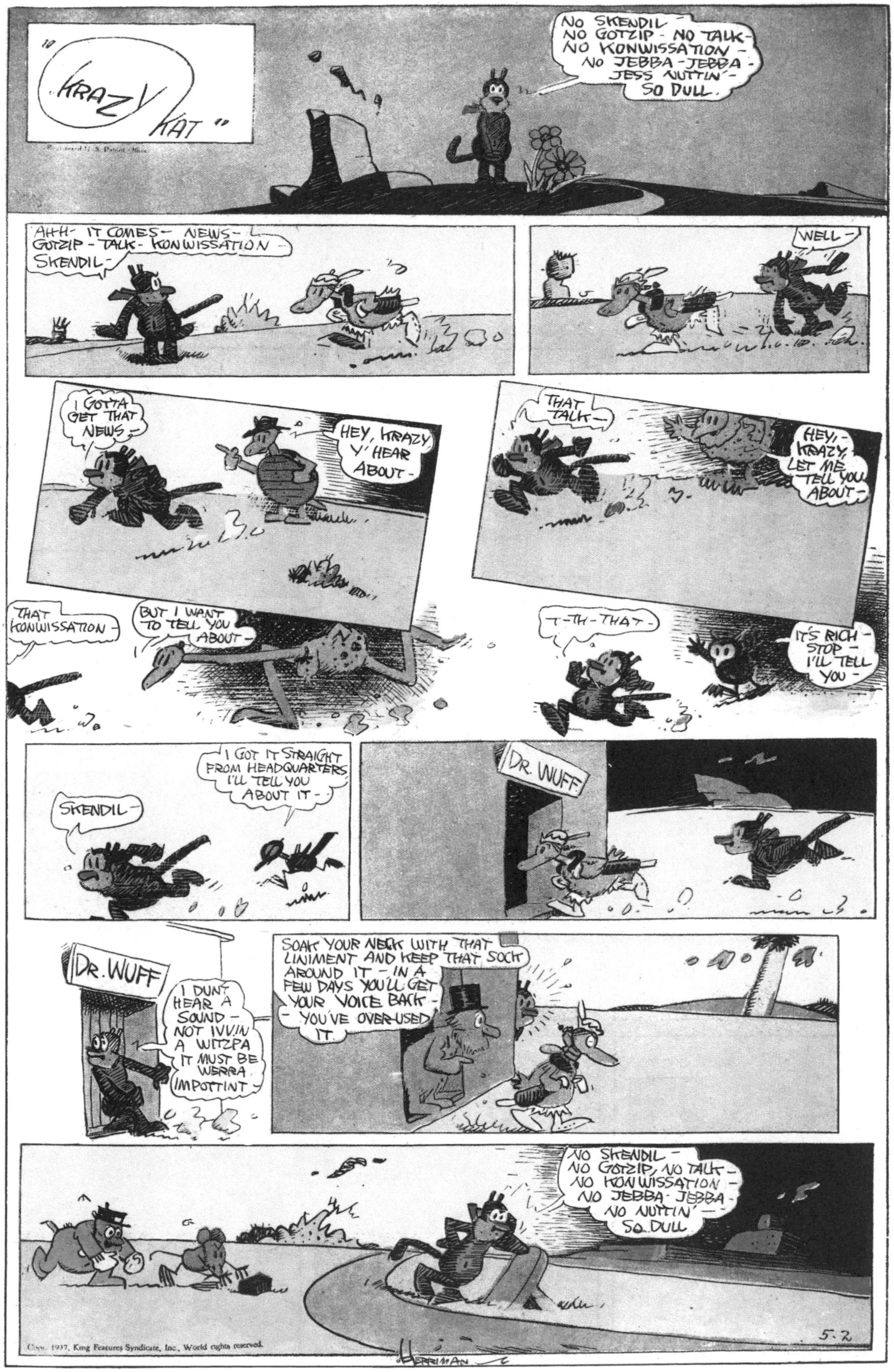
"KRAZY KAT"
NO SKENDIL - NO GOTZIP - NO TALK - NO KONWISSATION - NO JEBBA-JEBBA - JESS NUTTIN' - SO DULL.
AHH- IT COMES - NEWS - GOTZIP - TALK - KONWISSATION - SKENDIL -
WELL -
I GOTTA GET THAT NEWS -
HEY, KRAZY, Y' HEAR ABOUT -
THAT TALK -
HEY, - KRAZY, LET ME TELL YOU ABOUT -
THAT KONWISSATION -
BUT I WANT TO TELL YOU ABOUT -
T-TH-THAT -
IT'S RICH - STOP - I'LL TELL YOU -
SKENDIL -
I GOT IT STRAIGHT FROM HEADQUARTERS I'LL TELL YOU ABOUT IT -
DR. WUFF
DR. WUFF
I DUNT HEAR A SOUND - NOT IVV'IN A WITZPA IT MUST BE WERRA IMPOTTINT -
SOAK YOUR NECK WITH THAT LINIMENT AND KEEP THAT SOCK AROUND IT - IN A FEW DAYS YOU'LL GET YOUR VOICE BACK - YOU'VE OVER-USED IT.
NO SKENDIL - NO GOTZIP, NO TALK - NO KONWISSATION - NO JEBBA-JEBBA - NO NUTTIN' - SO DULL -
5-2
Copr. 1937, King Features Syndicate, Inc., World rights reserved.
HERRIMAN

May 2nd, 1937.

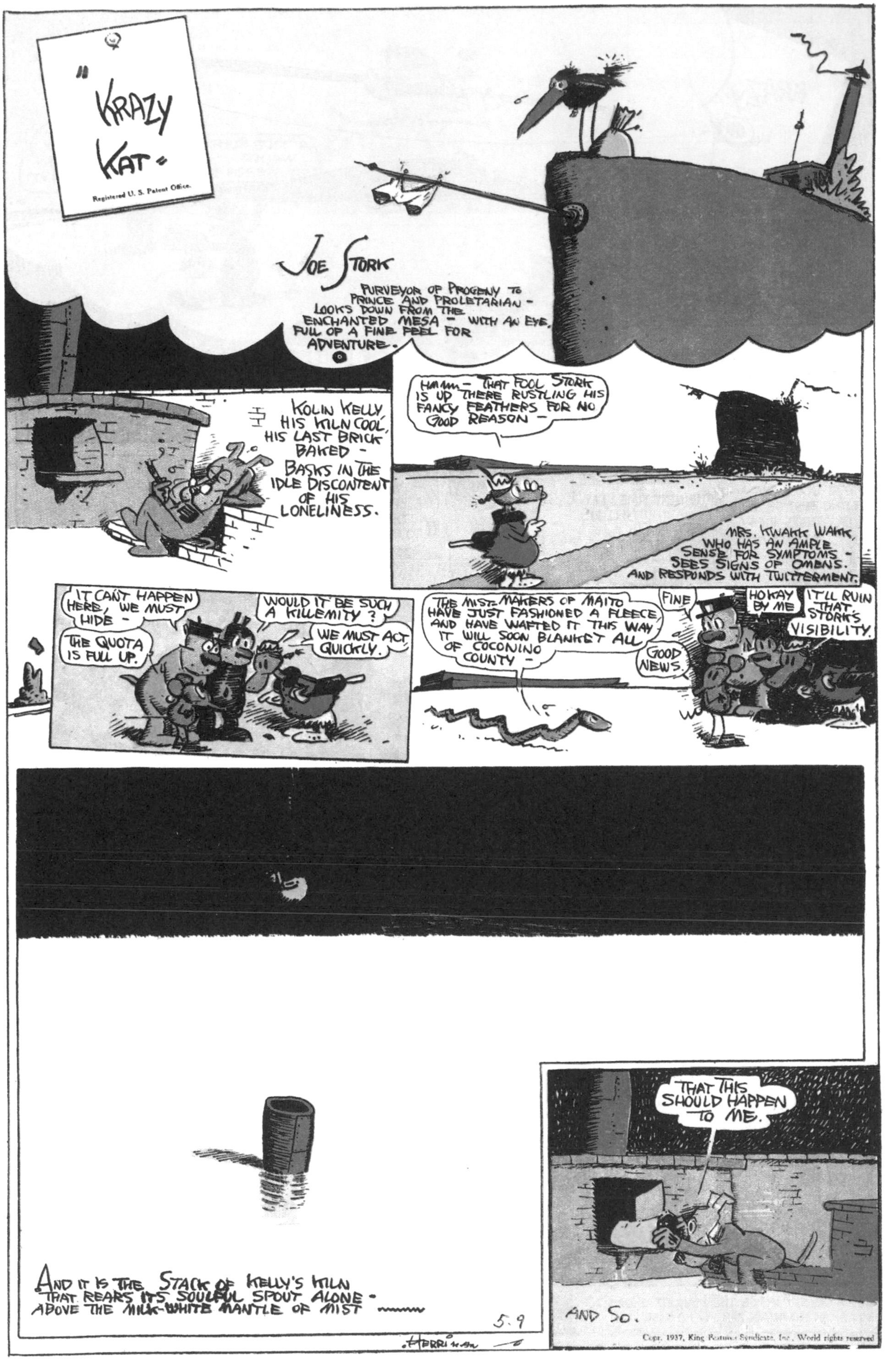
"Krazy Kat"
Registered U. S. Patent Office.
Joe Stork
Purveyor of progeny to prince and proletarian - looks down from the enchanted mesa - with an eye full of a fine feel for adventure.
Kolin Kelly, his kiln cool, his last brick baked - basks in the idle discontent of his loneliness.
Hmm - that fool stork is up there rustling his fancy feathers for no good reason -
Mrs. Kwakk Wakk, who has an ample sense for symptoms - sees signs of omens. and responds with twitterment.
It can't happen here, we must hide -
The quota is full up.
Would it be such a killemity?
We must act quickly.
The mist-makers of Maito have just fashioned a fleece, and have wafted it this way it will soon blanket all of Coconino County -
Fine
Good news.
Ho-kay by me
It'll ruin that stork's visibility.
And it is the stack of Kelly's kiln that rears its soulful spout alone - above the milk-white mantle of mist
5.9
Herriman
That this should happen to me.
And so.
Copr. 1937, King Features Syndicate, Inc., World rights reserved

May 9th, 1937.

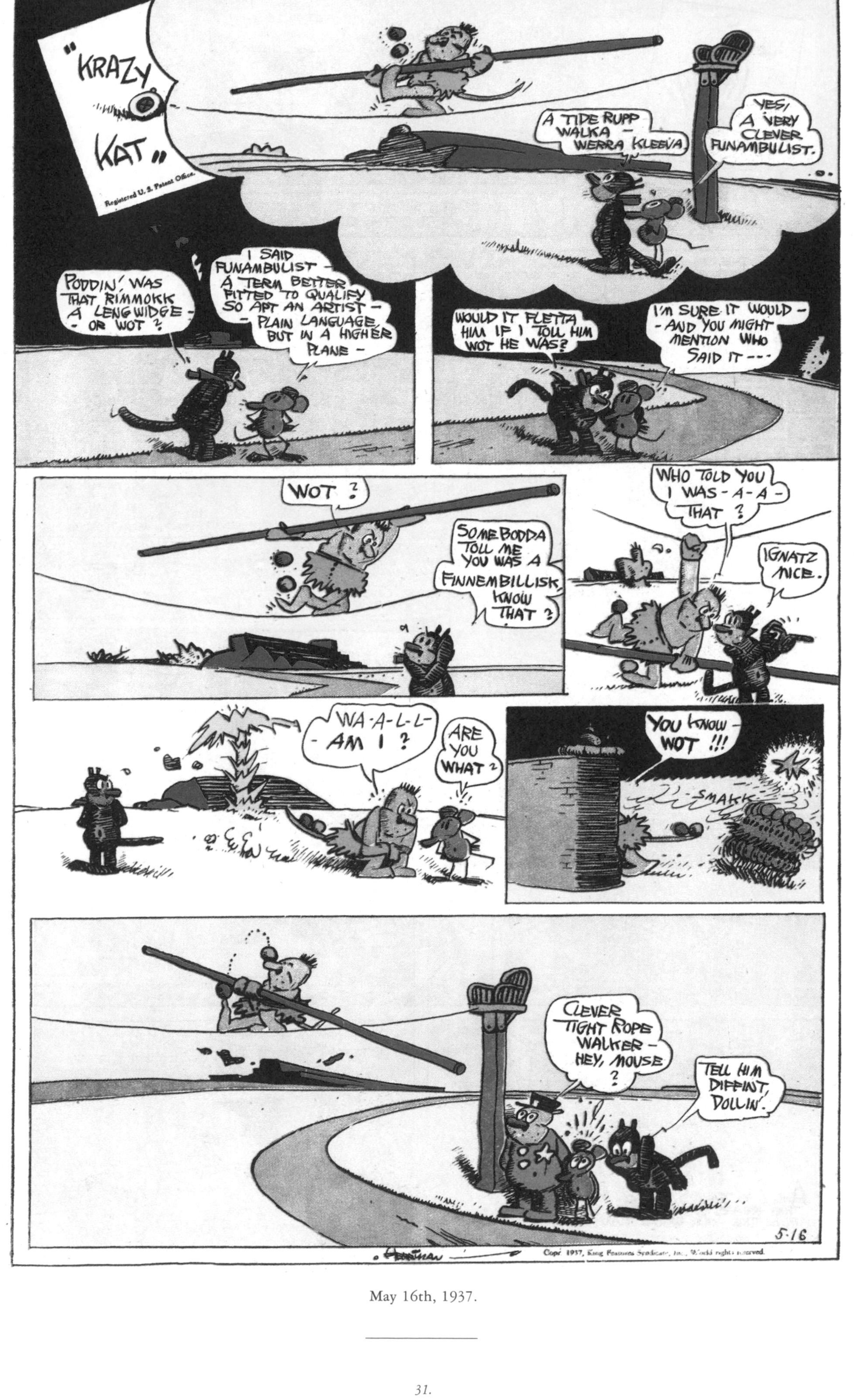
"KRAZY KAT"
Registered U. S. Patent Office.
A TIDE RUPP WALKA - WERRA KLEEVA.
YES, A VERY CLEVER FUNAMBULIST.
PODDIN' WAS THAT RIMMOKK A LENGWIDGE - OR WOT ?
I SAID FUNAMBULIST - A TERM BETTER FITTED TO QUALIFY SO APT AN ARTIST - - PLAIN LANGUAGE, BUT IN A HIGHER PLANE -
WOULD IT FLETTA HIM IF I TOLL HIM WOT HE WAS?
I'M SURE IT WOULD - - AND YOU MIGHT MENTION WHO SAID IT - - -
WOT ?
SOME BODDA TOLL ME YOU WAS A FINNEMBILLISK, KNOW THAT ?
WHO TOLD YOU I WAS - A - A - THAT ?
IGNATZ MICE.
WA-A-L-L - AM I ?
ARE YOU WHAT ?
YOU KNOW WOT !!!
SMAKK
CLEVER TIGHT ROPE WALKER - HEY, MOUSE ?
TELL HIM DIFFINT, DOLLIN'.
5-16
Copr. 1937, King Features Syndicate, Inc., World rights reserved.

May 16th, 1937.

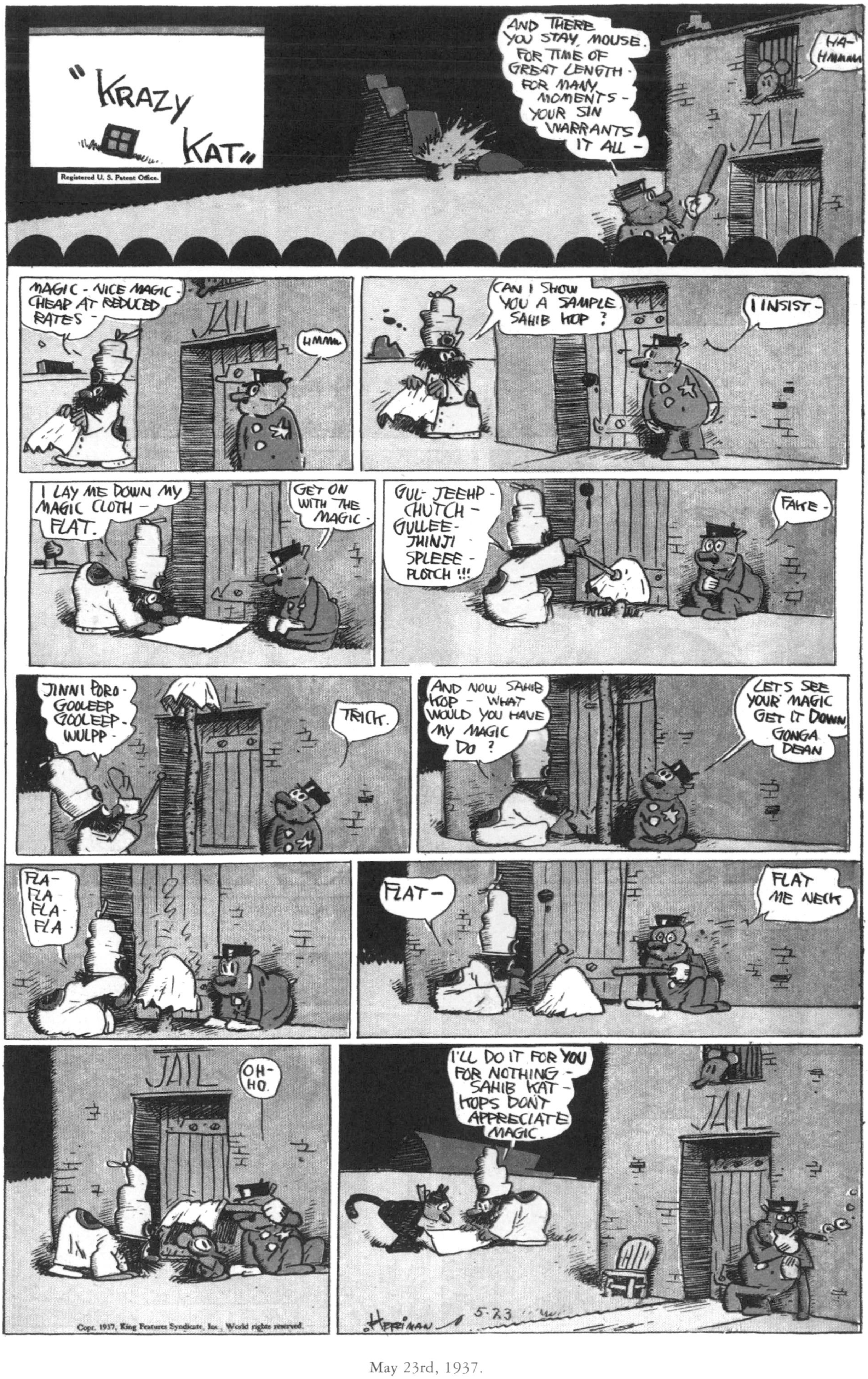
"KRAZY KAT"
Registered U. S. Patent Office.
AND THERE YOU STAY, MOUSE. FOR TIME OF GREAT LENGTH - FOR MANY MOMENTS - YOUR SIN WARRANTS IT ALL -
HA-HMMM
JAIL
MAGIC - NICE MAGIC - CHEAP AT REDUCED RATES -
HMMM
JAIL
CAN I SHOW YOU A SAMPLE SAHIB KOP ?
I INSIST -
I LAY ME DOWN MY MAGIC CLOTH - FLAT.
GET ON WITH THE MAGIC -
GUL- JEEHP - CHUTCH - GULLEE - JHINJI - SPLEEE - PLOTCH !!!
FAKE -
JINNI PORO - GOOLEEP - GOOLEEP - WULPP -
TRICK.
AND NOW SAHIB KOP - WHAT WOULD YOU HAVE MY MAGIC DO ?
LET'S SEE YOUR MAGIC GET IT DOWN, GONGA DEAN
FLA - FLA - FLA - FLA
FLAT -
FLAT ME NECK
JAIL
OH - HO.
I'LL DO IT FOR YOU FOR NOTHING - SAHIB KAT - KOPS DON'T APPRECIATE MAGIC.
JAIL
Copr. 1937, King Features Syndicate, Inc., World rights reserved.
Herriman 5-23

May 23rd, 1937.

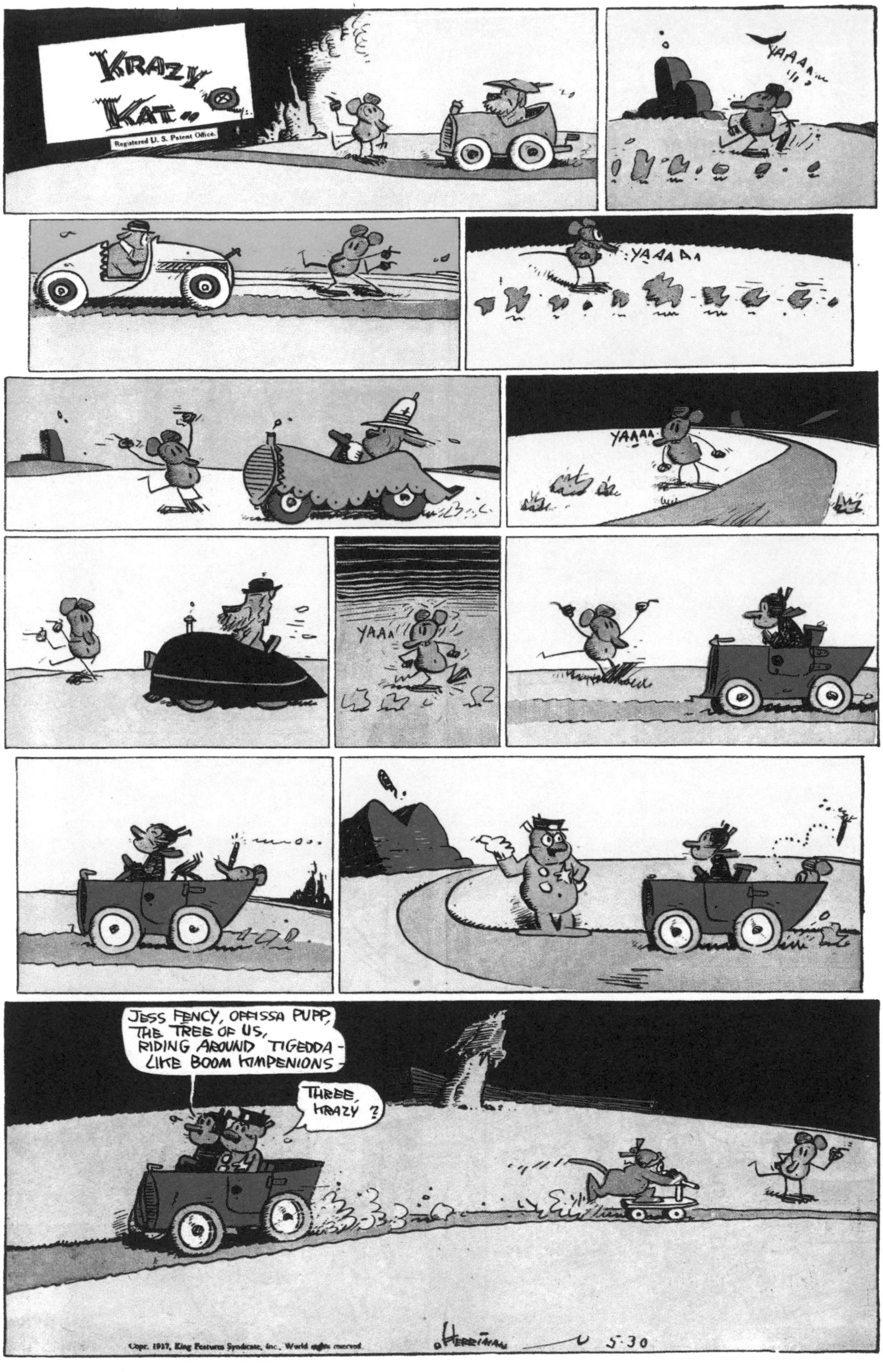
KRAZY KAT
Registered U. S. Patent Office.
YAAAA
YAAAA
YAAAA
YAAA
JESS FENCY, OFFISSA PUPP, THE TREE OF US, RIDING AROUND TIGEDDA - LIKE BOOM KIMPENIONS -
THREE, KRAZY ?
Copr. 1937, King Features Syndicate, Inc., World rights reserved.
Herriman
5-30

May 30th, 1937.

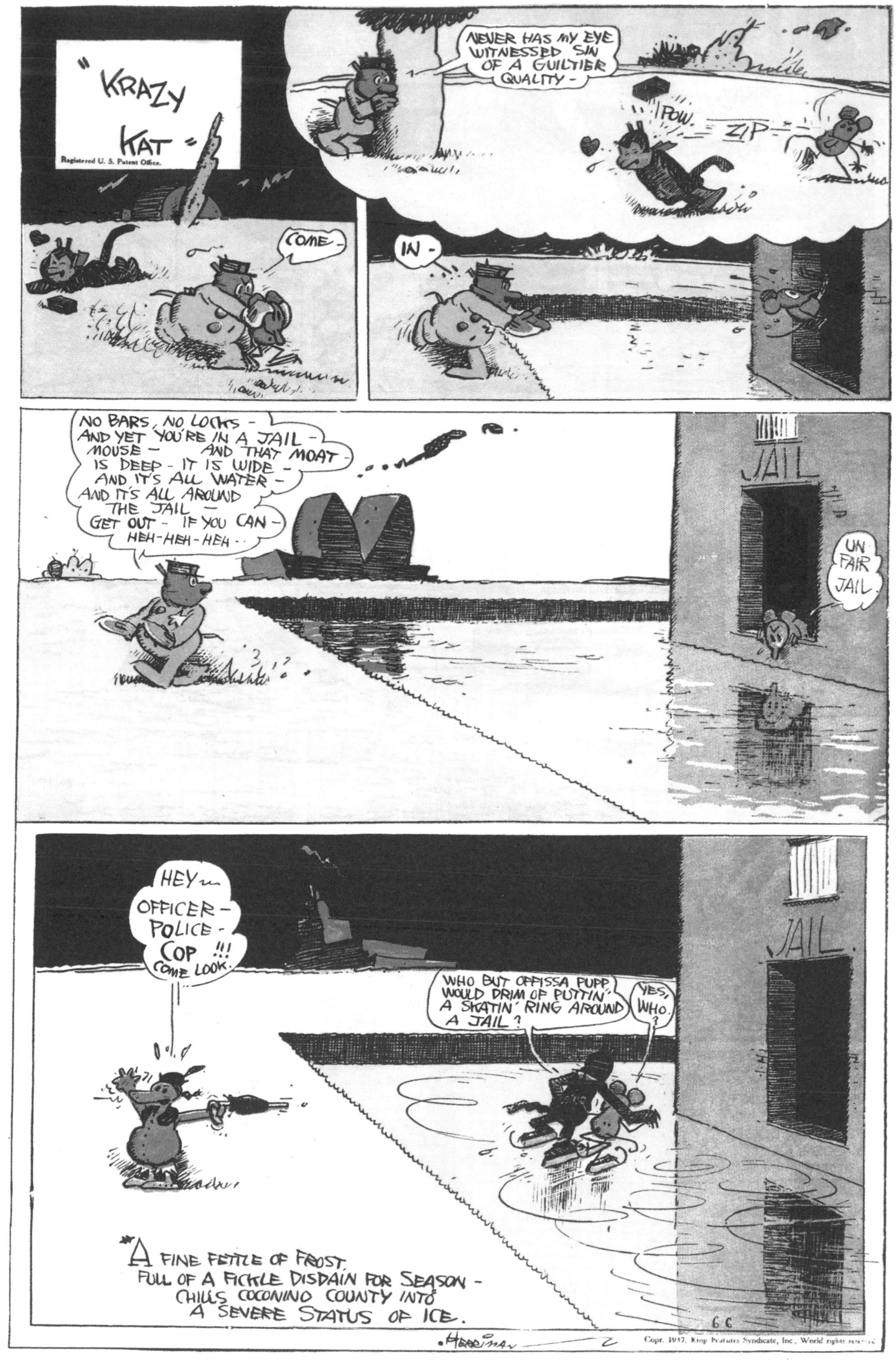
"KRAZY KAT"
Registered U. S. Patent Office.
NEVER HAS MY EYE WITNESSED SIN OF A GUILTIER QUALITY -
POW
ZIP
COME -
IN -
NO BARS, NO LOCKS - AND YET YOU'RE IN A JAIL - MOUSE - AND THAT MOAT IS DEEP - IT IS WIDE - AND IT'S ALL WATER - AND IT'S ALL AROUND THE JAIL - GET OUT - IF YOU CAN - HEH-HEH-HEH..
JAIL
UN FAIR JAIL.
HEY - OFFICER - POLICE - COP !!! COME LOOK.
JAIL.
WHO BUT OFFISSA PUPP WOULD DRIM OF PUTTIN' A SKATIN' RING AROUND A JAIL?
YES, WHO.?
*A FINE FETTLE OF FROST FULL OF A FICKLE DISDAIN FOR SEASON - CHILLS COCONINO COUNTY INTO A SEVERE STATUS OF ICE.
6-6
HERRIMAN

June 6th, 1937.

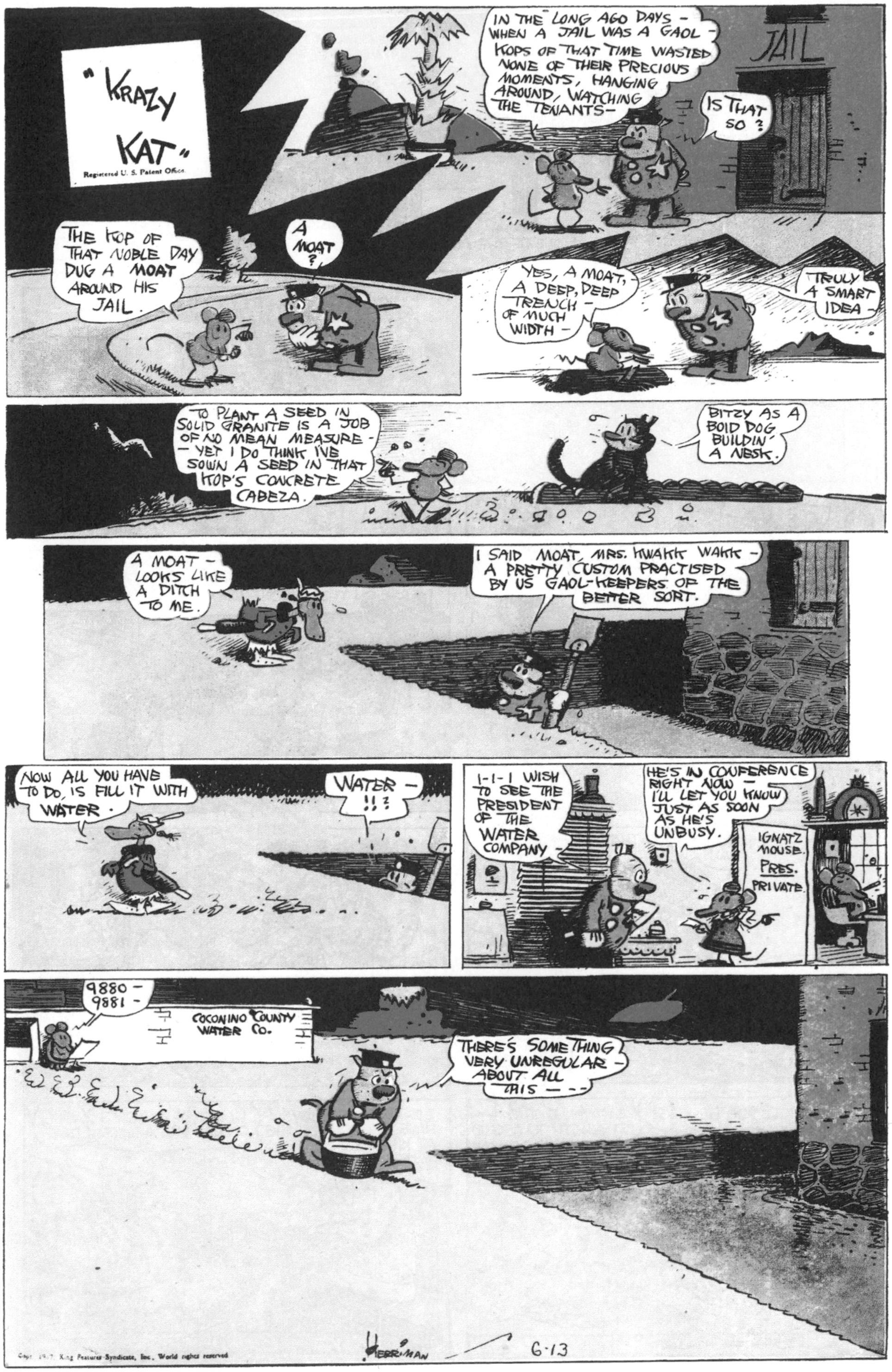
"KRAZY KAT"
Registered U. S. Patent Office
IN THE "LONG AGO DAYS - WHEN A JAIL WAS A GAOL - KOPS OF THAT TIME WASTED NONE OF THEIR PRECIOUS MOMENTS, HANGING AROUND, WATCHING THE TENANTS -
JAIL
IS THAT SO?
THE KOP OF THAT NOBLE DAY DUG A MOAT AROUND HIS JAIL.
A MOAT?
YES, A MOAT, A DEEP, DEEP TRENCH - OF MUCH WIDTH -
TRULY A SMART IDEA -
TO PLANT A SEED IN SOLID GRANITE IS A JOB OF NO MEAN MEASURE - YET I DO THINK I'VE SOWN A SEED IN THAT KOP'S CONCRETE CABEZA.
BITZY AS A BOID DOG BUILDIN' A NESK.
A MOAT - LOOKS LIKE A DITCH TO ME.
I SAID MOAT, MRS. KWAKK WAKK - A PRETTY CUSTOM PRACTISED BY US GAOL-KEEPERS OF THE BETTER SORT.
NOW ALL YOU HAVE TO DO, IS FILL IT WITH WATER.
WATER - !!?
I-I-I WISH TO SEE THE PRESIDENT OF THE WATER COMPANY -
HE'S IN CONFERENCE RIGHT NOW - I'LL LET YOU KNOW JUST AS SOON AS HE'S UNBUSY.
IGNATZ MOUSE PRES. PRIVATE
9880 - 9881 -
COCONINO COUNTY WATER CO.
THERE'S SOMETHING VERY UNREGULAR - ABOUT ALL THIS - - -
HERRIMAN 6-13

June 13th, 1937.

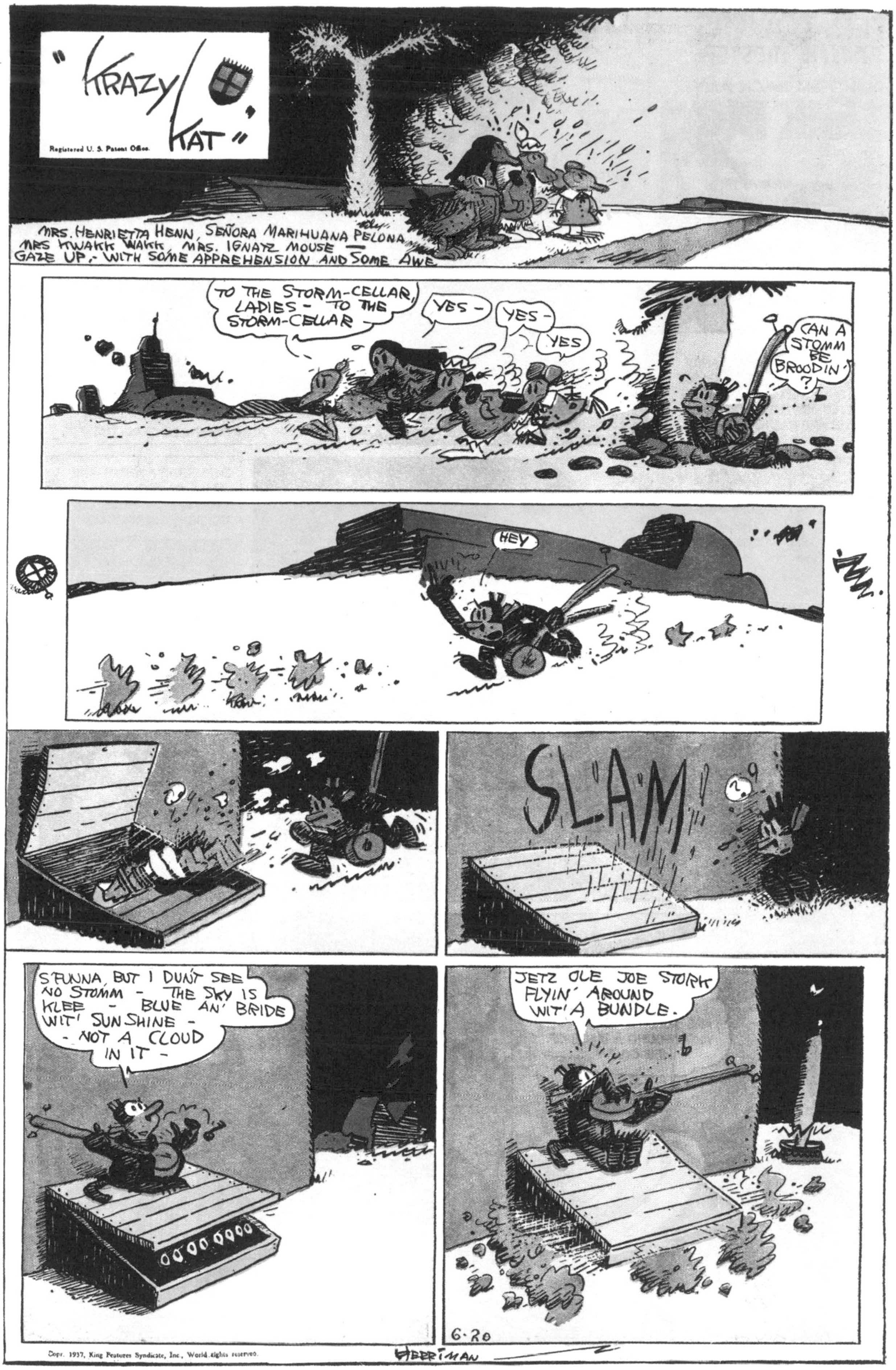
"Krazy Kat"
Registered U. S. Patent Office.
MRS. HENRIETTA HENN, SEÑORA MARIHUANA PELONA, MRS KWAKK WAKK, MRS. IGNATZ MOUSE — GAZE UP, - WITH SOME APPREHENSION AND SOME AWE.
TO THE STORM-CELLAR, LADIES - TO THE STORM-CELLAR -
YES -
YES -
YES
CAN A STOMM BE BROODIN' ?
HEY
SLAM
S'FUNNA, BUT I DUN'T SEE NO STOMM - THE SKY IS KLEE - BLUE AN' BRIDE WIT' SUNSHINE - - NOT A CLOUD IN IT -
JETZ OLE JOE STORK FLYIN' AROUND WIT' A BUNDLE.
6-20
Copr. 1937, King Features Syndicate, Inc., World rights reserved.
HERRIMAN

June 20th, 1937.

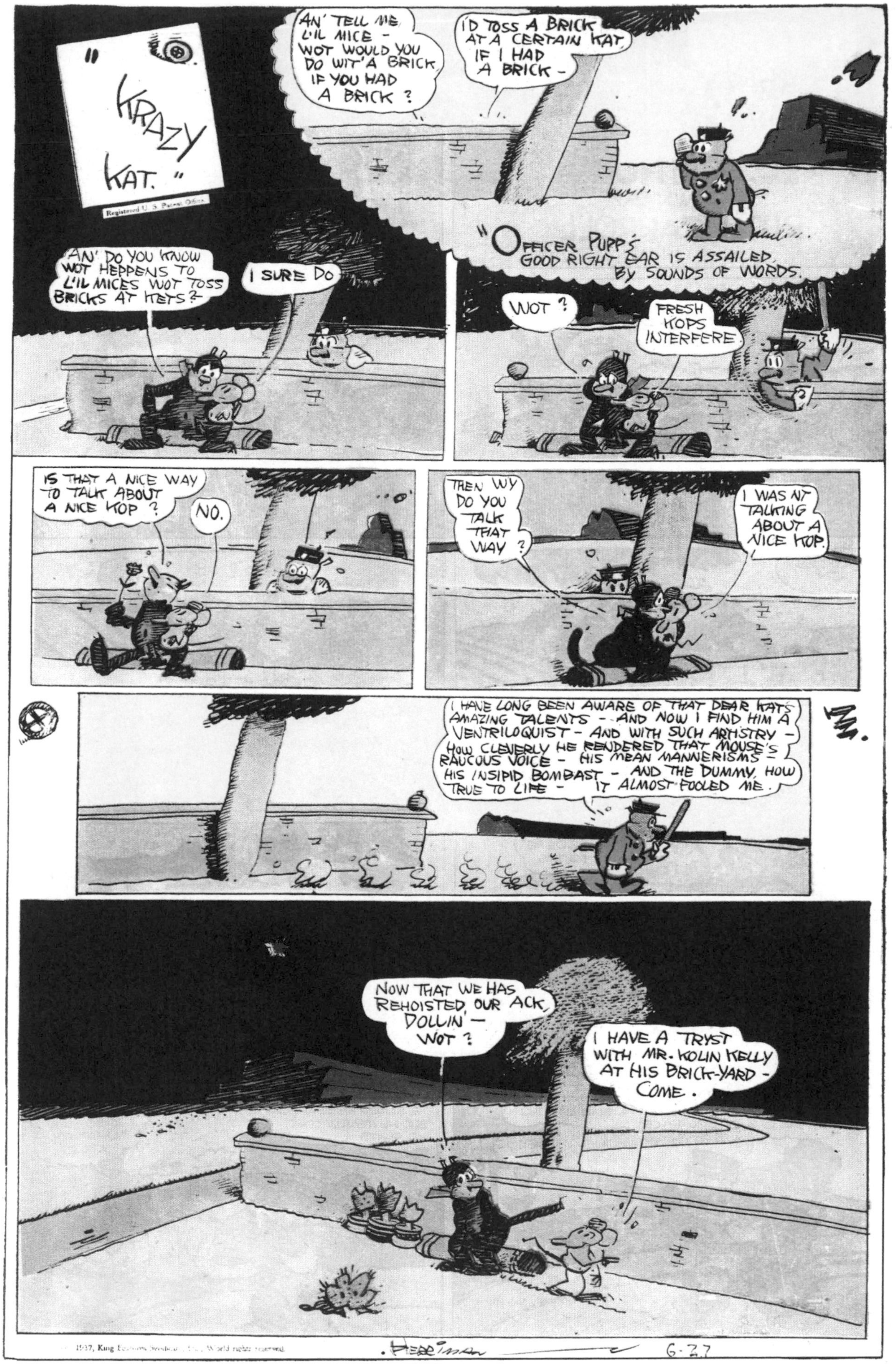
"KRAZY KAT."
Registered U. S. Patent Office
AN' TELL ME L'IL MICE - WOT WOULD YOU DO WIT A BRICK IF YOU HAD A BRICK ?
I'D TOSS A BRICK AT A CERTAIN KAT IF I HAD A BRICK -
"OFFICER PUPP'S GOOD RIGHT EAR IS ASSAILED BY SOUNDS OF WORDS.
AN' DO YOU KNOW WOT HEPPENS TO L'IL MICES WOT TOSS BRICKS AT KETS ?
I SURE DO
WOT ?
FRESH KOPS INTERFERE
IS THAT A NICE WAY TO TALK ABOUT A NICE KOP ?
NO.
THEN WY DO YOU TALK THAT WAY ?
I WAS N'T TALKING ABOUT A NICE KOP.
I HAVE LONG BEEN AWARE OF THAT DEAR KAT'S AMAZING TALENTS - AND NOW I FIND HIM A VENTRILOQUIST - AND WITH SUCH ARTISTRY - HOW CLEVERLY HE RENDERED THAT MOUSE'S RAUCOUS VOICE - HIS MEAN MANNERISMS - HIS INSIPID BOMBAST - AND THE DUMMY, HOW TRUE TO LIFE - IT ALMOST FOOLED ME.
NOW THAT WE HAS REHOISTED OUR ACK, DOLLIN' - WOT ?
I HAVE A TRYST WITH MR. KOLIN KELLY AT HIS BRICK-YARD - COME.
1937, King Features Syndicate, Inc., World rights reserved.
HERRIMAN
6-27

June 27th, 1937.

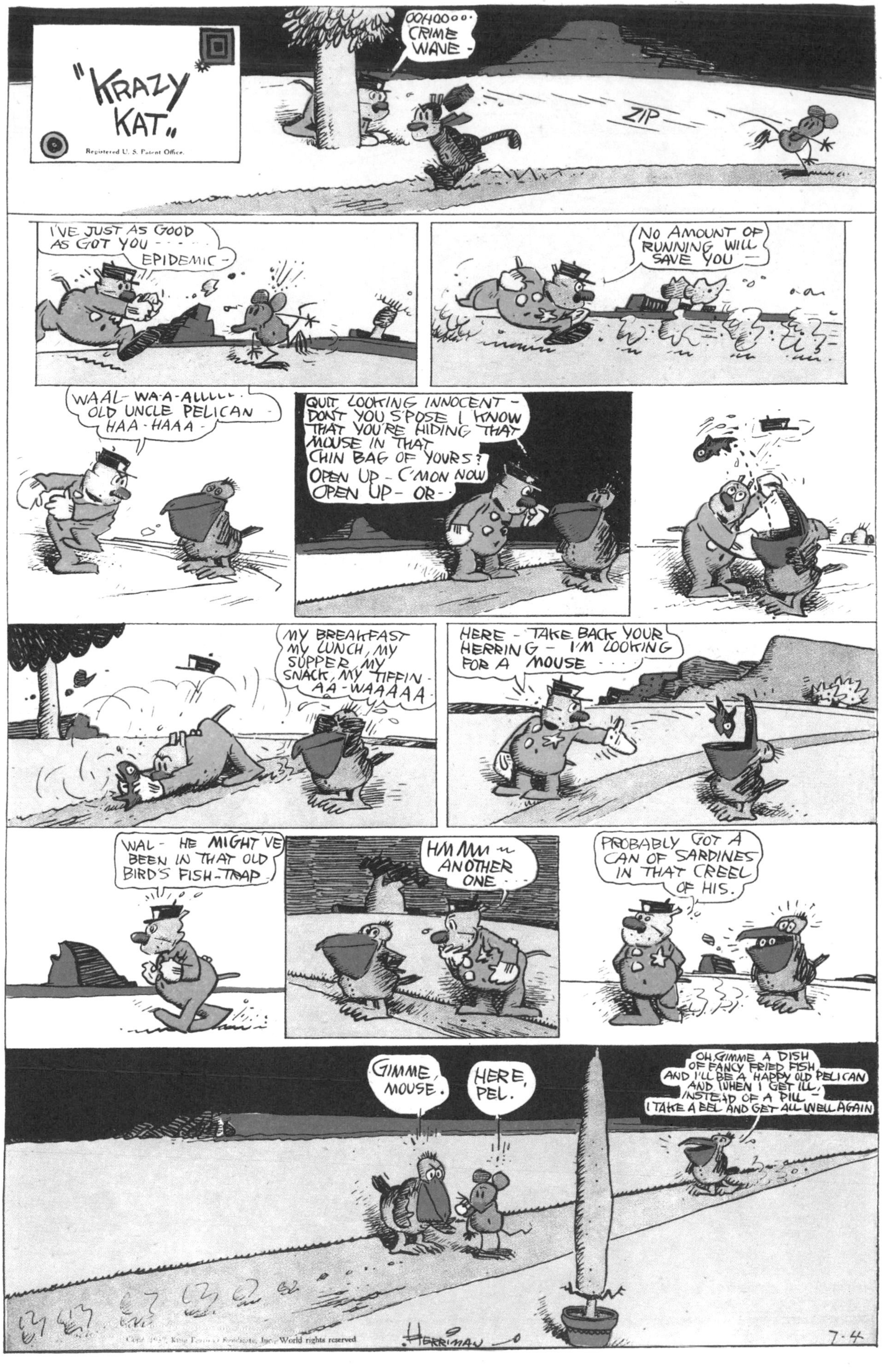
"KRAZY KAT"
Registered U. S. Patent Office.
OOHOO°°° CRIME WAVE -
ZIP
I'VE JUST AS GOOD AS GOT YOU - - - EPIDEMIC -
NO AMOUNT OF RUNNING WILL SAVE YOU -
WAAL-WA-A-ALLLLL OLD UNCLE PELICAN HAA-HAAA -
QUIT LOOKING INNOCENT - DON'T YOU S'POSE I KNOW THAT YOU'RE HIDING THAT MOUSE IN THAT CHIN BAG OF YOURS? OPEN UP - C'MON NOW OPEN UP - OR -
MY BREAKFAST MY LUNCH, MY SUPPER, MY SNACK, MY TIFFIN - AA-WAAAAA
HERE - TAKE BACK YOUR HERRING - I'M LOOKING FOR A MOUSE - - -
WAL - HE MIGHT'VE BEEN IN THAT OLD BIRD'S FISH-TRAP -
HMMM - ANOTHER ONE -
PROBABLY GOT A CAN OF SARDINES IN THAT CREEL OF HIS.
GIMME, MOUSE.
HERE, PEL.
OH, GIMME A DISH OF FANCY FRIED FISH AND I'LL BE A HAPPY OLD PELICAN AND WHEN I GET ILL, INSTEAD OF A PILL - I TAKE A EEL AND GET ALL WELL AGAIN
World rights reserved
HERRIMAN
7-4

July 4th, 1937.

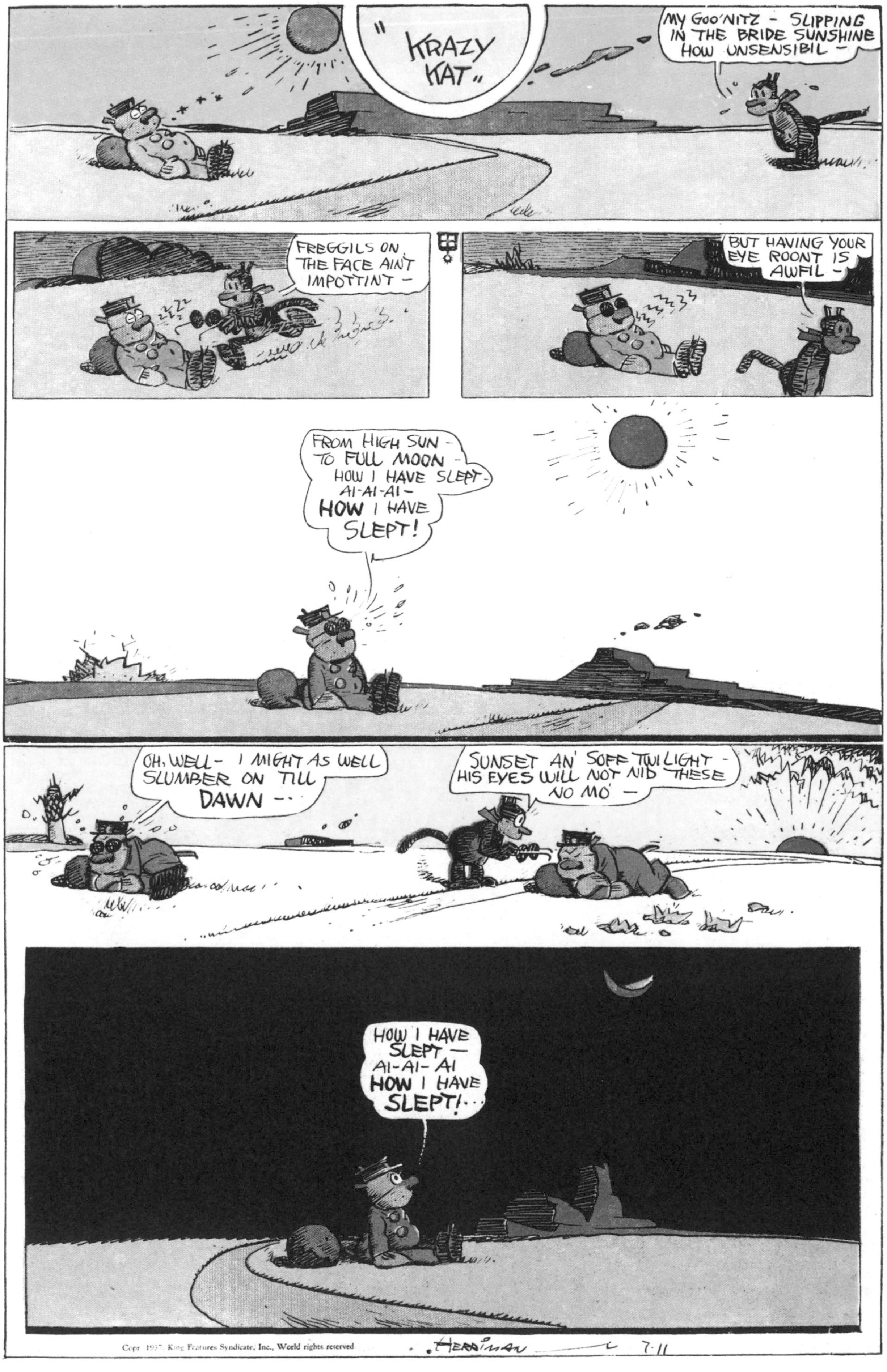
"KRAZY KAT"
MY GOO'NITZ - SLIPPING IN THE BRIDE SUNSHINE HOW UNSENSIBIL -
FREGGILS ON THE FACE AIN'T IMPOTTINT -
BUT HAVING YOUR EYE ROONT IS AWFIL -
FROM HIGH SUN - TO FULL MOON - HOW I HAVE SLEPT - AI-AI-AI - HOW I HAVE SLEPT!
OH, WELL - I MIGHT AS WELL SLUMBER ON TILL DAWN - -
SUNSET AN' SOFF TWILIGHT - HIS EYES WILL NOT NID THESE NO MO' -
HOW I HAVE SLEPT - AI-AI- AI HOW I HAVE SLEPT! . .
Copr 1937, King Features Syndicate, Inc., World rights reserved
HERRIMAN
7-11

July 11th, 1937.

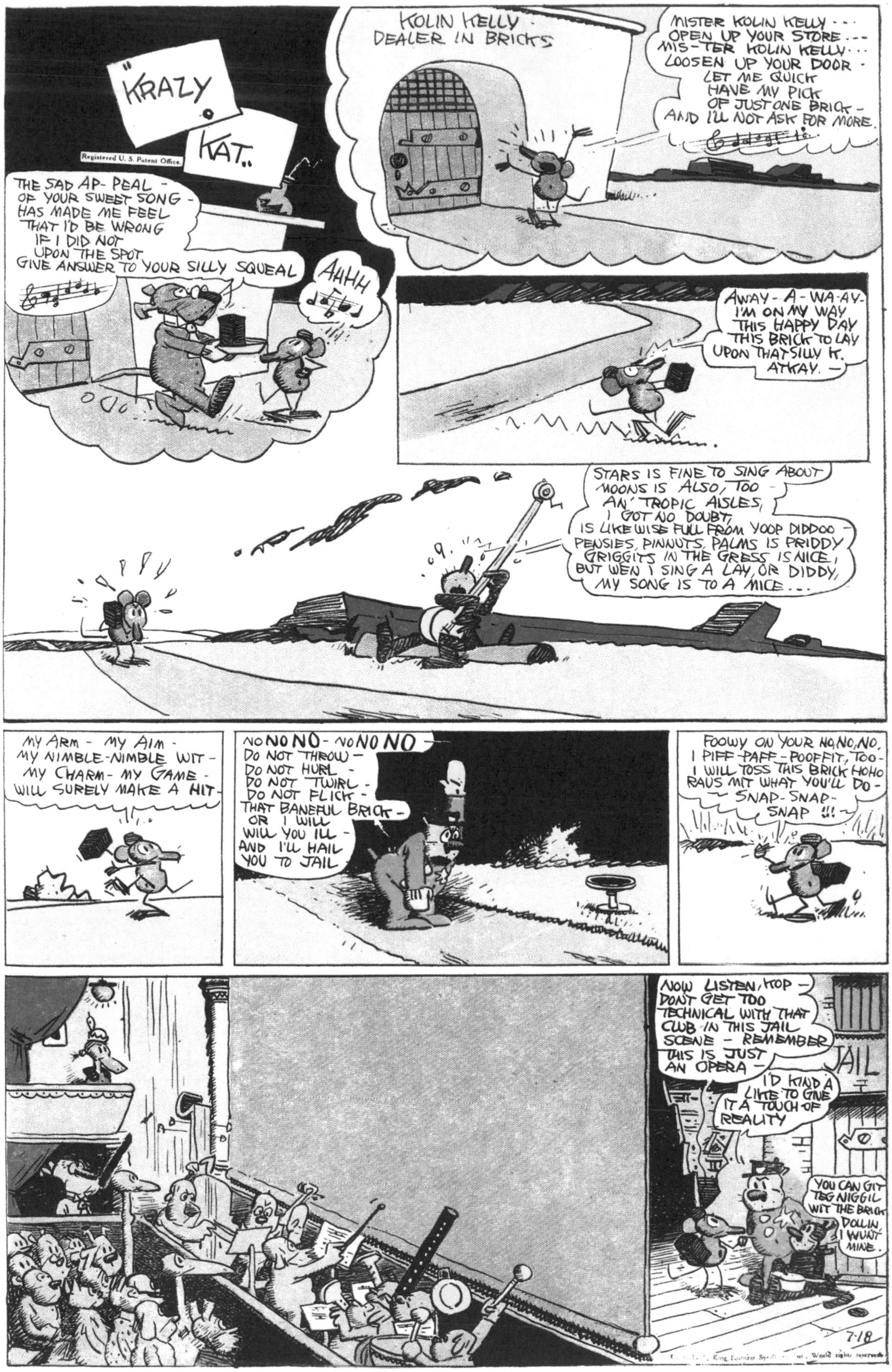
"KRAZY KAT"
Registered U. S. Patent Office.
KOLIN KELLY DEALER IN BRICKS
MISTER KOLIN KELLY - - - OPEN UP YOUR STORE - - - MIS-TER KOLIN KELLY - - LOOSEN UP YOUR DOOR - LET ME QUICK HAVE MY PICK OF JUST ONE BRICK - AND I'LL NOT ASK FOR MORE.
THE SAD AP-PEAL - OF YOUR SWEET SONG - HAS MADE ME FEEL THAT I'D BE WRONG IF I DID NOT UPON THE SPOT GIVE ANSWER TO YOUR SILLY SQUEAL
AHHH
AWAY - A - WA-AY - I'M ON MY WAY THIS HAPPY DAY THIS BRICK TO LAY UPON THAT SILLY K. ATKAY. -
STARS IS FINE TO SING ABOUT MOONS IS ALSO, TOO - AN' TROPIC AISLES, I GOT NO DOUBT, IS LIKEWISE FULL FROM YOOP DIDDOO - PENSIES, PINNUTS, PALMS IS PRIDDY GRIGGITS IN THE GRESS IS NICE, BUT WEN I SING A LAY, OR DIDDY, MY SONG IS TO A MICE - - -
MY ARM - MY AIM - MY NIMBLE-NIMBLE WIT - MY CHARM - MY GAME - WILL SURELY MAKE A HIT -
NO NO NO - NO NO NO - DO NOT THROW - DO NOT HURL - DO NOT TWIRL - DO NOT FLICK THAT BANEFUL BRICK - OR I WILL WILL YOU ILL AND I'LL HAIL YOU TO JAIL
FOOWY ON YOUR NO, NO, NO, I PIFF-PAFF-POOFFIT, TOO - I WILL TOSS THIS BRICK HOHO RAUS MIT WHAT YOU'LL DO - SNAP-SNAP-SNAP !!! -
NOW LISTEN, KOP - DONT GET TOO TECHNICAL WITH THAT CLUB IN THIS JAIL SCENE - REMEMBER THIS IS JUST AN OPERA -
JAIL
I'D KIND A LIKE TO GIVE IT A TOUCH OF REALITY
YOU CAN GIT TEG NIGGIL WIT THE BRICK DOLLIN, I WUNT MINE.
7-18

July 18th, 1937.

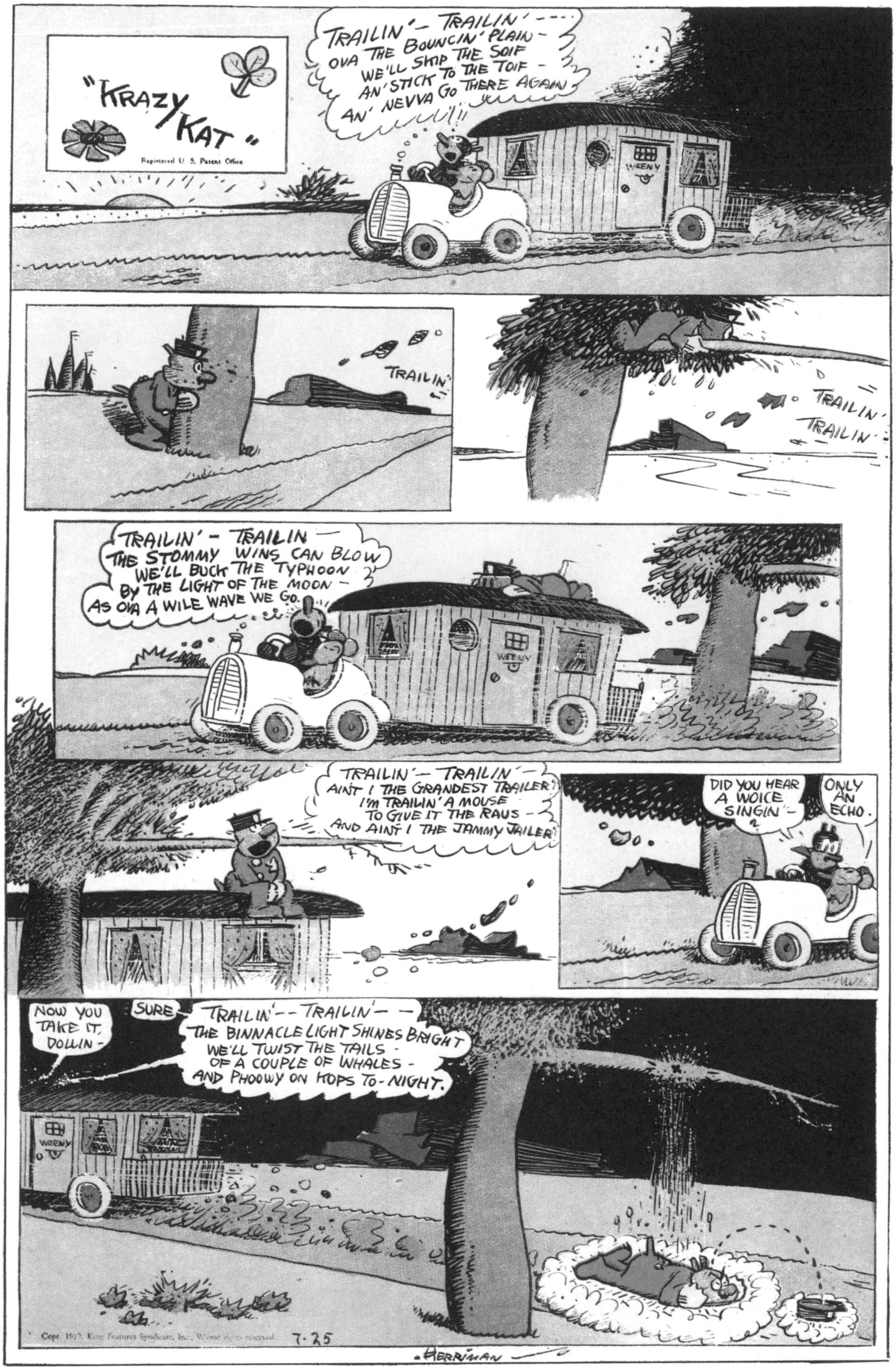
"KRAZY KAT"
Registered U. S. Patent Office
TRAILIN' - TRAILIN' --- OVA THE BOUNCIN' PLAIN - WE'LL SKIP THE SOIF AN' STICK TO THE TOIF - AN' NEVVA GO THERE AGAIN
WEENY
TRAILIN'
TRAILIN' TRAILIN'
TRAILIN' - TRAILIN - THE STOMMY WINS CAN BLOW WE'LL BUCK THE TYPHOON BY THE LIGHT OF THE MOON AS OVA A WILE WAVE WE GO.
WEENY
TRAILIN' -- TRAILIN' - AIN'T I THE GRANDEST TRAILER? I'M TRAILIN' A MOUSE TO GIVE IT THE RAUS - AND AIN'T I THE JAMMY JAILER?
DID YOU HEAR A WOICE SINGIN' - ?
ONLY AN ECHO.
NOW YOU TAKE IT, DOLLIN -
SURE
TRAILIN' -- TRAILIN' -- THE BINNACLE LIGHT SHINES BRIGHT WE'LL TWIST THE TAILS - OF A COUPLE OF WHALES - AND PHOOWY ON HOPS TO-NIGHT.
WEENY
Copr. 1937, King Features Syndicate, Inc., World rights reserved
7-25
HERRIMAN

July 25th, 1937.

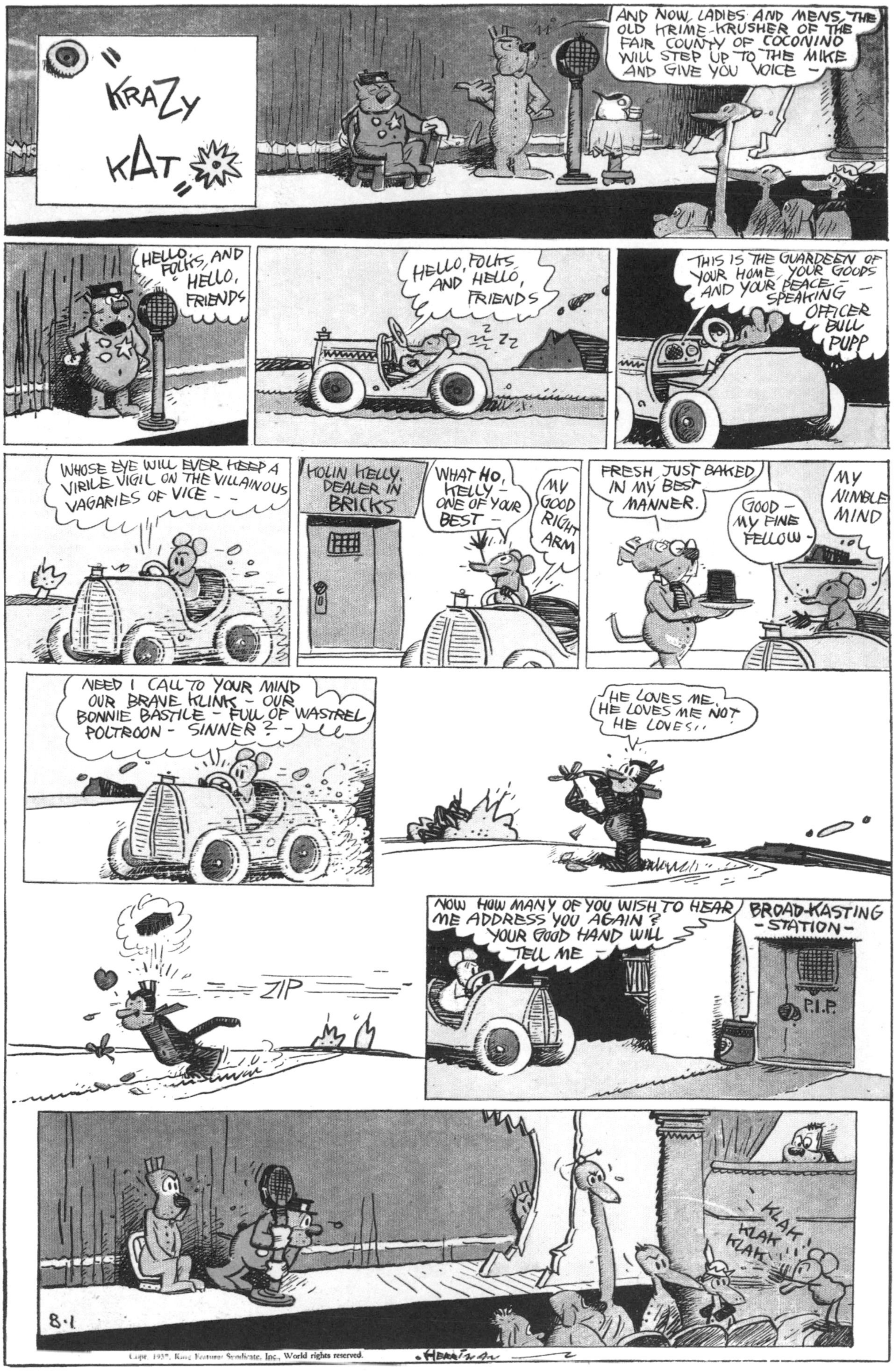
KRAZY KAT
AND NOW, LADIES AND MENS, THE OLD KRIME-KRUSHER OF THE FAIR COUNTY OF COCONINO WILL STEP UP TO THE MIKE AND GIVE YOU VOICE -
HELLO, FOLKS, AND HELLO, FRIENDS
HELLO, FOLKS AND HELLO, FRIENDS
THIS IS THE GUARDEEN OF YOUR HOME, YOUR GOODS AND YOUR PEACE - SPEAKING - OFFICER BULL PUPP
WHOSE EYE WILL EVER KEEP A VIRILE VIGIL ON THE VILLAINOUS VAGARIES OF VICE - -
KOLIN KELLY, DEALER IN BRICKS
WHAT HO, KELLY - ONE OF YOUR BEST -
MY GOOD RIGHT ARM
FRESH, JUST BAKED IN MY BEST MANNER.
GOOD - MY FINE FELLOW -
MY NIMBLE MIND
NEED I CALL TO YOUR MIND OUR BRAVE KLINK - OUR BONNIE BASTILE - FULL OF WASTREL POLTROON - SINNER ? - -
HE LOVES ME, HE LOVES ME NOT HE LOVES,,,
ZIP
NOW HOW MANY OF YOU WISH TO HEAR ME ADDRESS YOU AGAIN ? YOUR GOOD HAND WILL TELL ME -
BROAD-KASTING - STATION -
P.I.P.
KLAK KLAK KLAK
8.1
Copr. 1937, King Features Syndicate, Inc., World rights reserved.
HERRIMAN

August 1st, 1937.

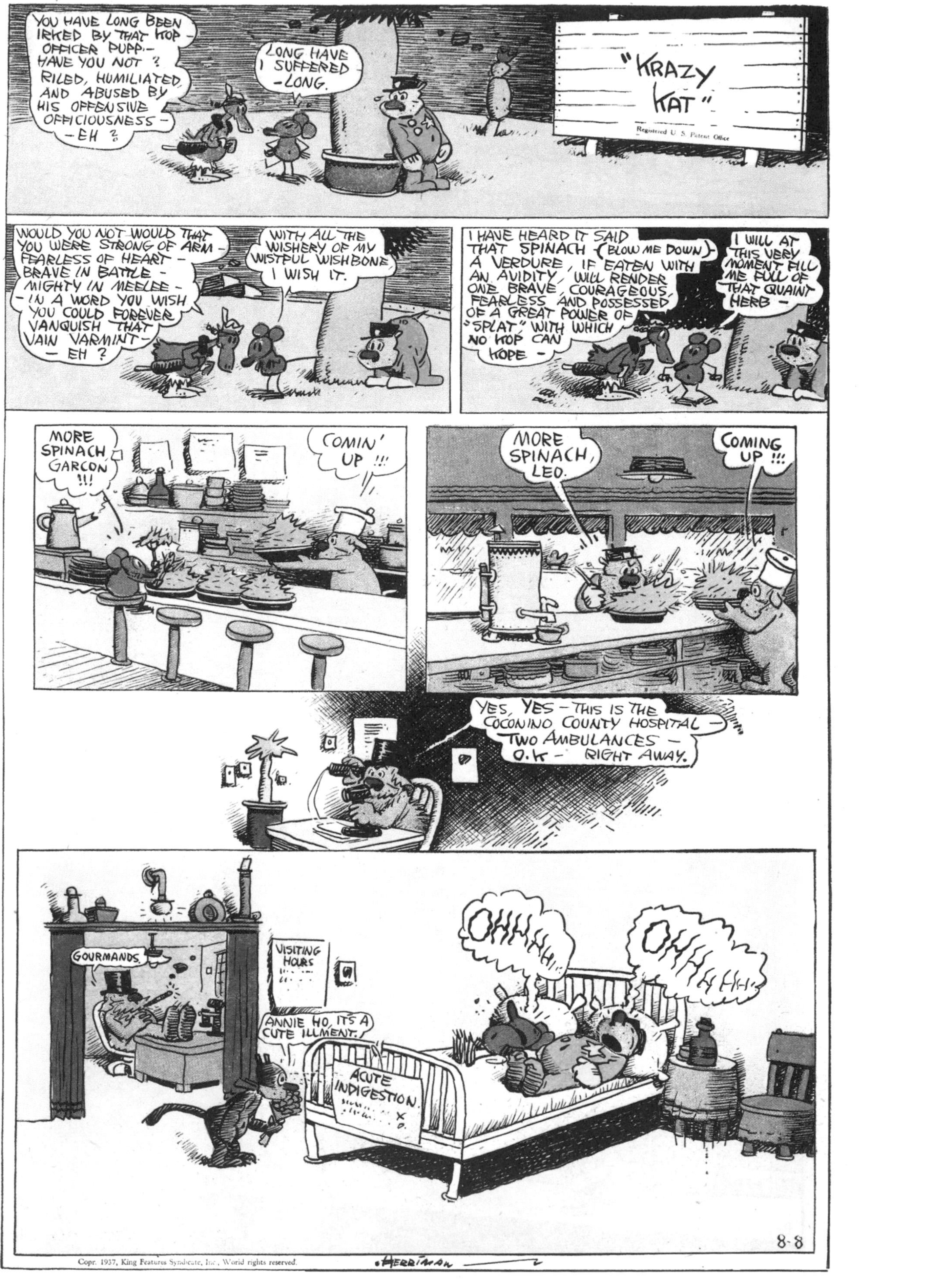

YOU HAVE LONG BEEN IRKED BY THAT KOP - OFFICER PUPP - HAVE YOU NOT ? RILED, HUMILIATED AND ABUSED BY HIS OFFENSIVE OFFICIOUSNESS - - EH ?
LONG HAVE I SUFFERED - LONG.
"KRAZY KAT"
Registered U. S. Patent Office
WOULD YOU NOT WOULD THAT YOU WERE STRONG OF ARM - FEARLESS OF HEART - BRAVE IN BATTLE - MIGHTY IN MEELEE - - IN A WORD YOU WISH YOU COULD FOREVER VANQUISH THAT VAIN VARMINT - - EH ?
WITH ALL THE WISHERY OF MY WISTFUL WISHBONE I WISH IT.
I HAVE HEARD IT SAID THAT SPINACH - (BLOW ME DOWN) - A VERDURE, IF EATEN WITH AN AVIDITY, WILL RENDER ONE BRAVE, COURAGEOUS, FEARLESS AND POSSESSED OF A GREAT POWER OF "SPLAT," WITH WHICH NO KOP CAN HOPE -
I WILL AT THIS VERY MOMENT FILL ME FULL OF THAT QUAINT HERB -
MORE SPINACH GARCON !!!
COMIN' UP !!!
MORE SPINACH, LEO.
COMING UP !!!
YES, YES - THIS IS THE COCONINO COUNTY HOSPITAL - TWO AMBULANCES - O.K - RIGHT AWAY.
GOURMANDS.
VISITING HOURS
ANNIE HO, ITS A CUTE ILLMENT.
ACUTE INDIGESTION
OHHHH!
OHHHH!
8-8
Copr. 1937, King Features Syndicate, Inc., World rights reserved.
HERRIMAN

August 8th, 1937.

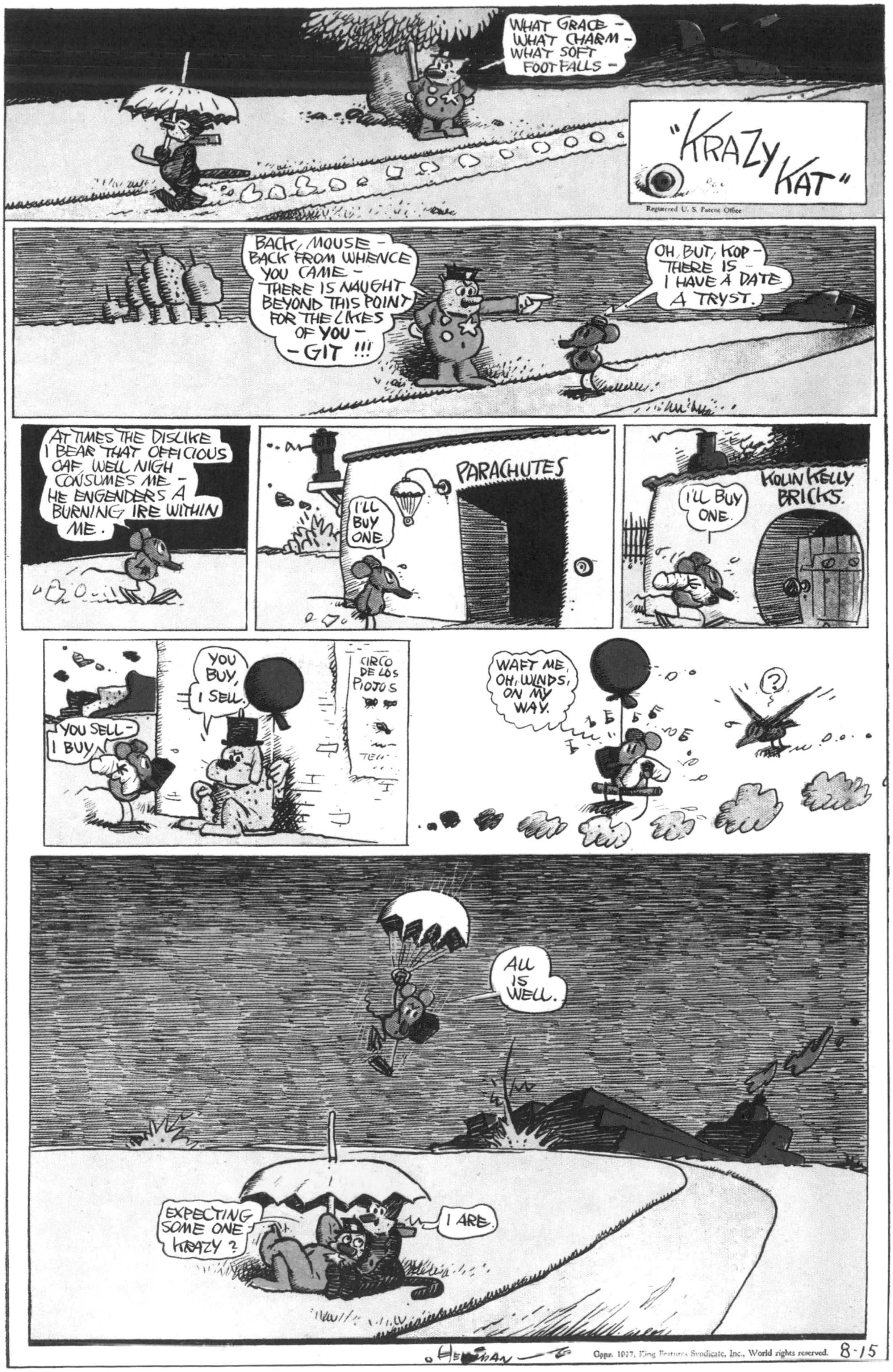
WHAT GRACE - WHAT CHARM - WHAT SOFT FOOT FALLS -
"KRAZY KAT"
Registered U. S. Patent Office
BACK, MOUSE - BACK FROM WHENCE YOU CAME - THERE IS NAUGHT BEYOND THIS POINT FOR THE LIKES OF YOU - GIT !!!
OH, BUT, KOP - THERE IS - I HAVE A DATE A TRYST.
AT TIMES THE DISLIKE I BEAR THAT OFFICIOUS OAF WELL NIGH CONSUMES ME - HE ENGENDERS A BURNING IRE WITHIN ME.
PARACHUTES
I'LL BUY ONE
KOLIN KELLY BRICKS
I'LL BUY ONE.
YOU SELL - I BUY.
YOU BUY, I SELL.
CIRCO DE LOS PIOJOS
WAFT ME, OH, WINDS, ON MY WAY.
?
ALL IS WELL.
EXPECTING SOME ONE KRAZY ?
I ARE.
Copr. 1937, King Features Syndicate, Inc., World rights reserved.
8-15

August 15th, 1937.

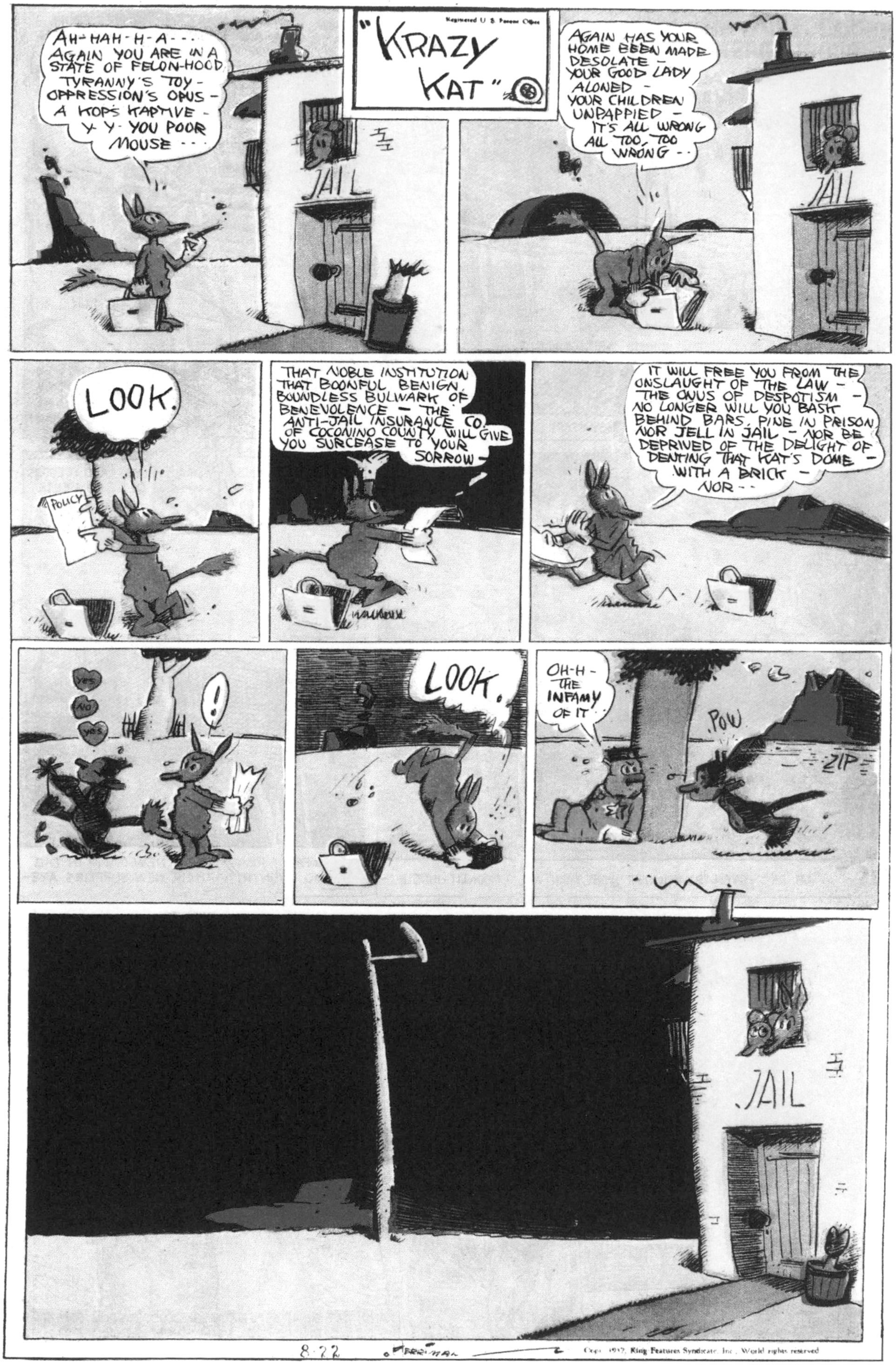
Registered U. S. Patent Office
"KRAZY KAT"
AH-HAH-H-A--- AGAIN YOU ARE IN A STATE OF FELON-HOOD TYRANNY'S TOY - OPPRESSION'S OPUS - A KOP'S KAPTIVE - Y-Y- YOU POOR MOUSE ---
JAIL
AGAIN HAS YOUR HOME BEEN MADE DESOLATE - YOUR GOOD LADY ALONED - YOUR CHILDREN UNPAPPIED - IT'S ALL WRONG ALL TOO, TOO WRONG --
JAIL
LOOK.
POLICY
THAT NOBLE INSTITUTION THAT BOONFUL BENIGN, BOUNDLESS BULWARK OF BENEVOLENCE - THE ANTI-JAIL INSURANCE CO. OF COCONINO COUNTY WILL GIVE YOU SURCEASE TO YOUR SORROW -
IT WILL FREE YOU FROM THE ONSLAUGHT OF THE LAW - THE ONUS OF DESPOTISM - NO LONGER WILL YOU BASK BEHIND BARS, PINE IN PRISON NOR JELL IN JAIL - NOR BE DEPRIVED OF THE DELIGHT OF DENTING THAT KAT'S DOME - WITH A BRICK - NOR --
YES
NO
YES
!
LOOK.
OH-H THE INFAMY OF IT
POW
ZIP
JAIL
8.22
Copr. 1937, King Features Syndicate, Inc., World rights reserved

August 22nd, 1937.

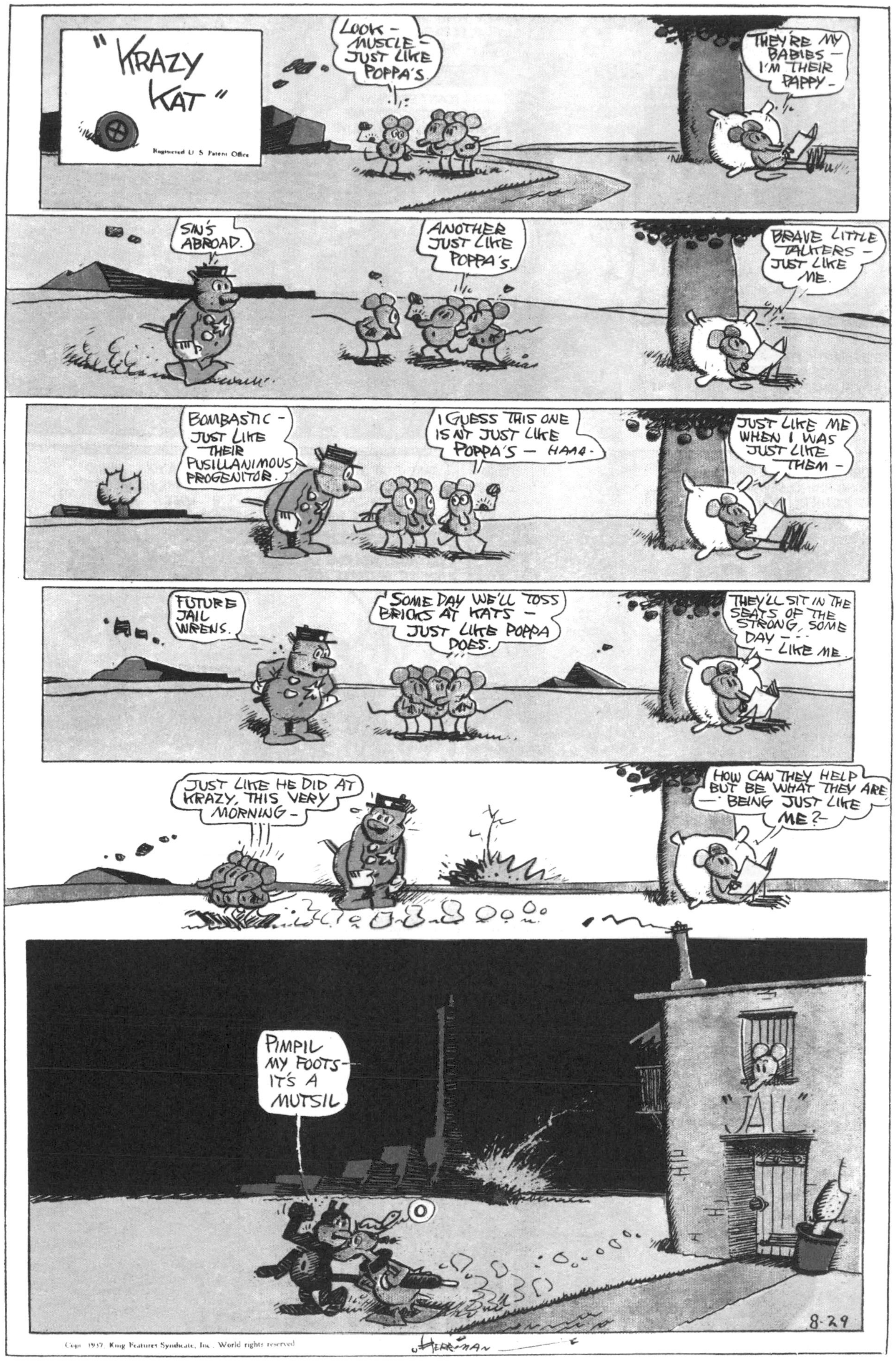
"KRAZY KAT"
Registered U. S. Patent Office
LOOK - MUSCLE - JUST LIKE POPPA'S.
THEY'RE MY BABIES - I'M THEIR PAPPY -
SIN'S ABROAD.
ANOTHER JUST LIKE POPPA'S.
BRAVE LITTLE TALKERS - JUST LIKE ME.
BOMBASTIC - JUST LIKE THEIR PUSILLANIMOUS PROGENITOR.
I GUESS THIS ONE IS'NT JUST LIKE POPPA'S — HAAA.
JUST LIKE ME WHEN I WAS JUST LIKE THEM -
FUTURE JAIL WRENS.
SOME DAY WE'LL TOSS BRICKS AT KATS - JUST LIKE POPPA DOES.
THEY'LL SIT IN THE SEATS OF THE STRONG, SOME DAY - - - LIKE ME.
JUST LIKE HE DID AT KRAZY, THIS VERY MORNING -
HOW CAN THEY HELP BUT BE WHAT THEY ARE - BEING JUST LIKE ME?
PIMPIL MY FOOTS - IT'S A MUTSIL
"JAIL"
8-29
Copr. 1937, King Features Syndicate, Inc., World rights reserved
HERRIMAN

August 29th, 1937.

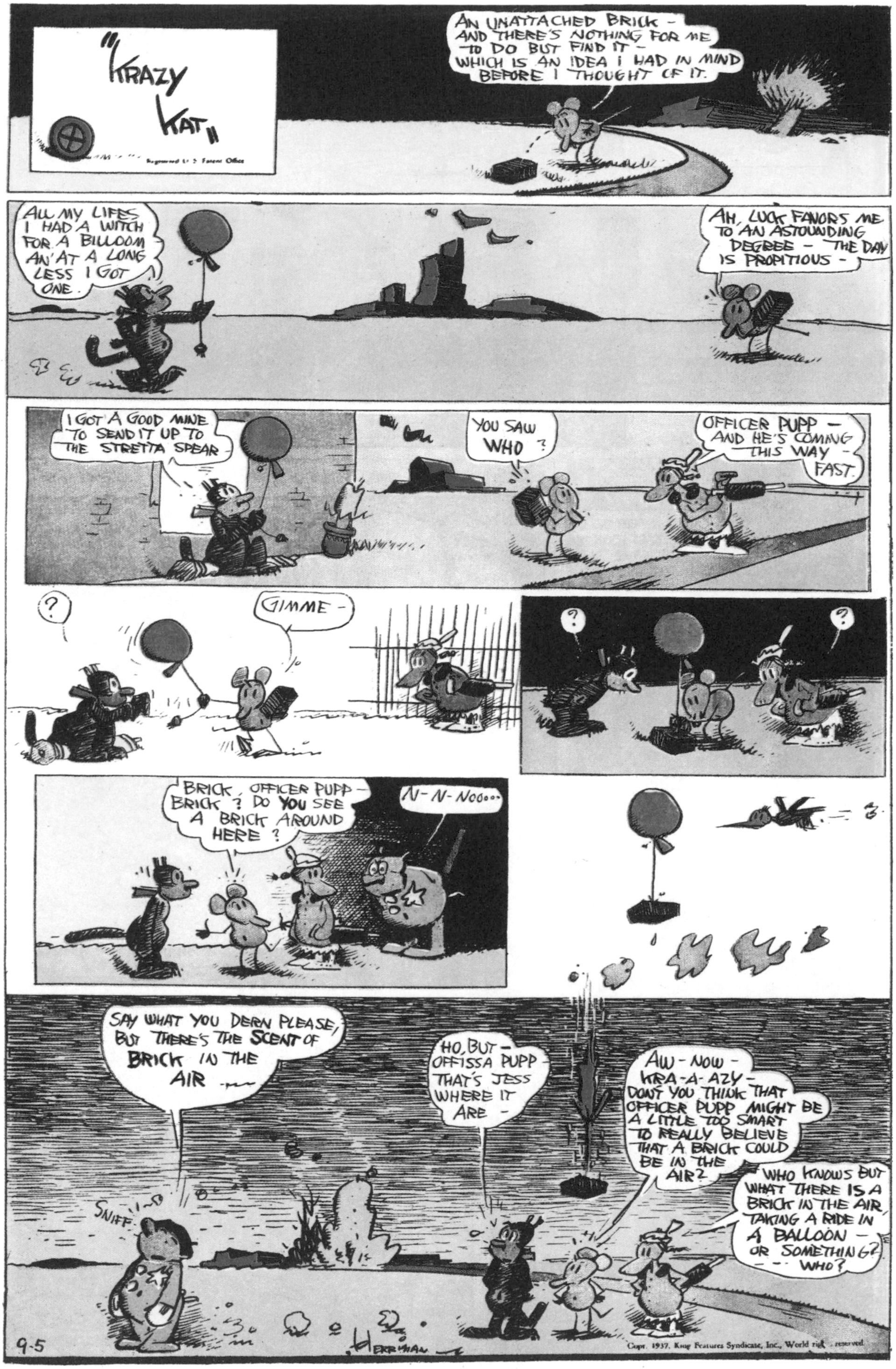
"Krazy Kat"
Registered U. S. Patent Office
AN UNATTACHED BRICK - AND THERE'S NOTHING FOR ME TO DO BUT FIND IT - WHICH IS AN IDEA I HAD IN MIND BEFORE I THOUGHT OF IT.
ALL MY LIFES I HAD A WITCH FOR A BILLOOM AN' AT A LONG LESS I GOT ONE.
AH, LUCK FAVORS ME TO AN ASTOUNDING DEGREE - THE DAY IS PROPITIOUS -
I GOT A GOOD MINE TO SEND IT UP TO THE STRETTA SPEAR -
YOU SAW WHO ?
OFFICER PUPP - AND HE'S COMMING THIS WAY - FAST.
?
GIMME -
?
?
BRICK, OFFICER PUPP - BRICK ? DO YOU SEE A BRICK AROUND HERE ?
N-N-NOOO...
SAY WHAT YOU DERN PLEASE, BUT THERE'S THE SCENT OF BRICK IN THE AIR
HO, BUT - OFFISSA PUPP THAT'S JESS WHERE IT ARE -
AW - NOW - KRA-A-AZY - DON'T YOU THINK THAT OFFICER PUPP MIGHT BE A LITTLE TOO SMART TO REALLY BELIEVE THAT A BRICK COULD BE IN THE AIR?
WHO KNOWS BUT WHAT THERE IS A BRICK IN THE AIR, TAKING A RIDE IN A BALLOON - OR SOMETHING? - - WHO?
SNIFF
9-5
HERRIMAN
Copr. 1937, King Features Syndicate, Inc., World rights reserved.

September 5th, 1937.

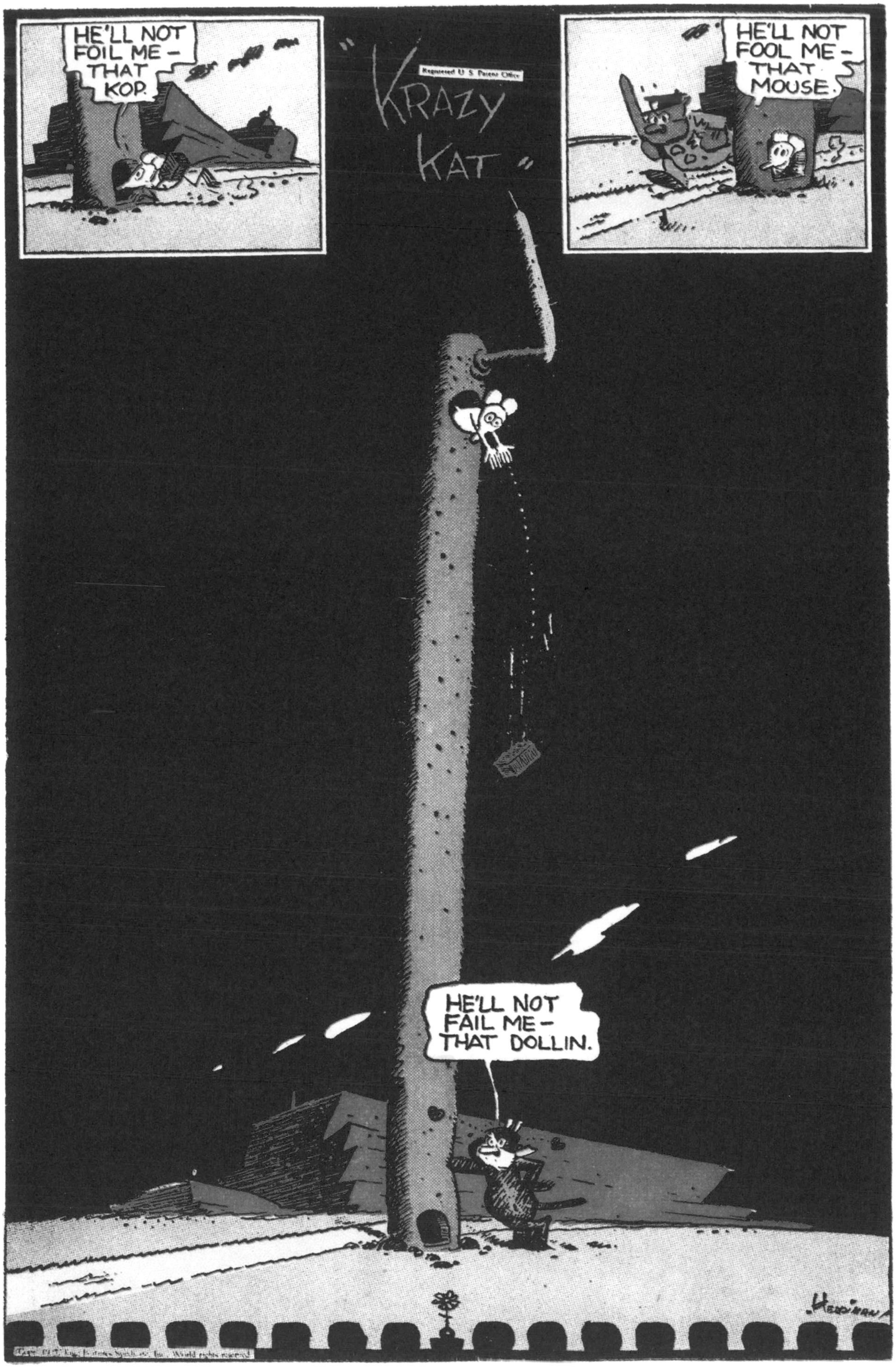
HE'LL NOT FOIL ME – THAT KOP.
"KRAZY KAT"
Registered U. S. Patent Office
HE'LL NOT FOOL ME – THAT MOUSE.
HE'LL NOT FAIL ME – THAT DOLLIN.

September 12th, 1937.

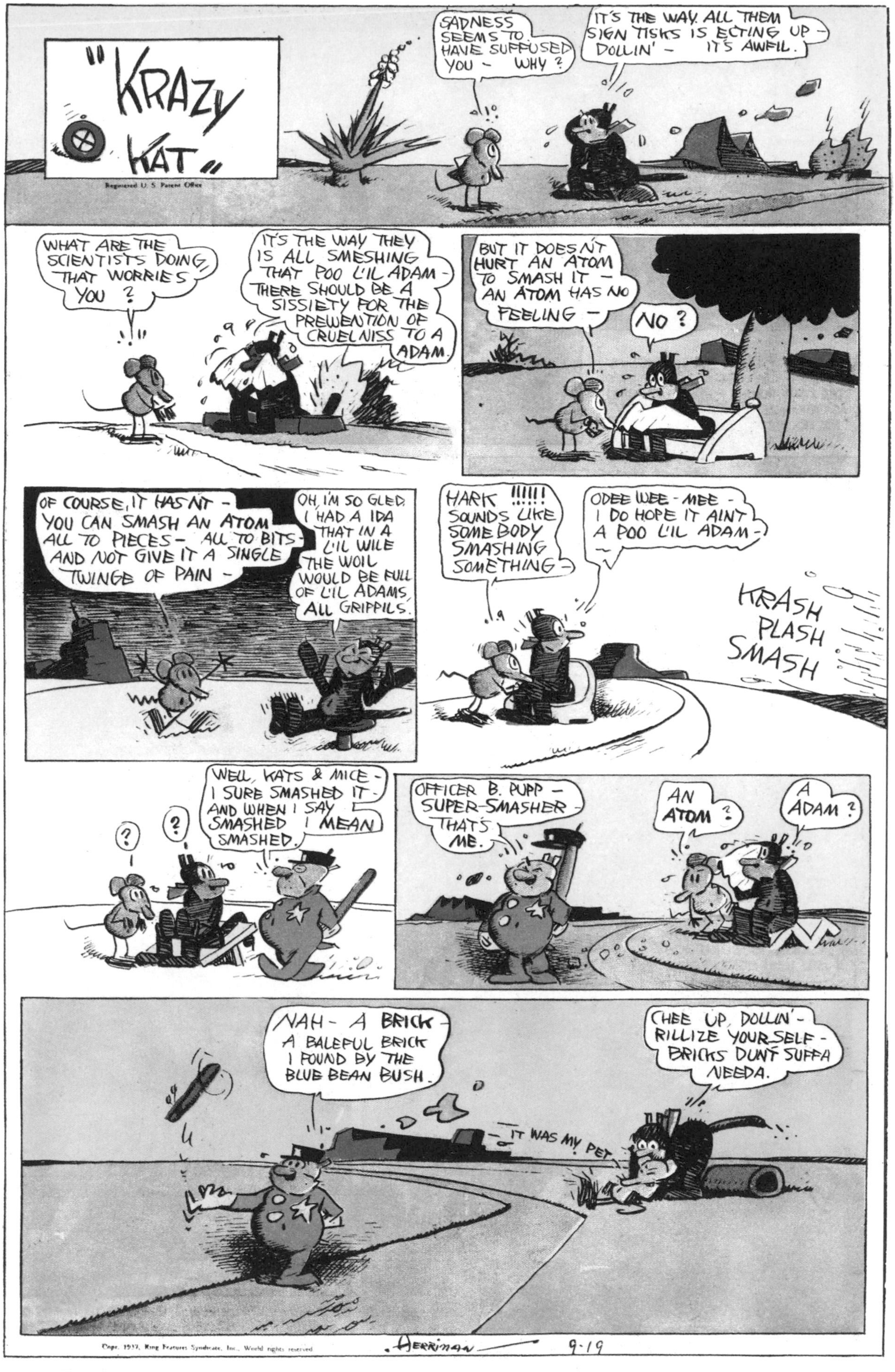
"KRAZY KAT"
Registered U. S. Patent Office
SADNESS SEEMS TO HAVE SUFFUSED YOU - WHY?
IT'S THE WAY ALL THEM SIGN TISKS IS ECTING UP - DOLLIN' - IT'S AWFIL.
WHAT ARE THE SCIENTISTS DOING THAT WORRIES YOU?
IT'S THE WAY THEY IS ALL SMESHING THAT POO L'IL ADAM - THERE SHOULD BE A SISSIETY FOR THE PREWENTION OF CRUELNISS TO A ADAM.
BUT IT DOES'NT HURT AN ATOM TO SMASH IT - AN ATOM HAS NO FEELING -
NO?
OF COURSE, IT HAS'NT - YOU CAN SMASH AN ATOM ALL TO PIECES - ALL TO BITS - AND NOT GIVE IT A SINGLE TWINGE OF PAIN -
OH, I'M SO GLED, I HAD A IDA THAT IN A L'IL WILE THE WOIL WOULD BE FULL OF L'IL ADAMS, ALL GRIPPILS.
HARK !!!!!! SOUNDS LIKE SOMEBODY SMASHING SOMETHING -
ODEE WEE - MEE - I DO HOPE IT AIN'T A POO L'IL ADAM -
KRASH PLASH SMASH
?
?
WELL, KATS & MICE - I SURE SMASHED IT - AND WHEN I SAY SMASHED I MEAN SMASHED.
OFFICER B. PUPP - SUPER-SMASHER - THAT'S ME.
AN ATOM?
A ADAM?
NAH - A BRICK - A BALEFUL BRICK I FOUND BY THE BLUE BEAN BUSH.
IT WAS MY PET
CHEE UP, DOLLIN' - RILLIZE YOUR SELF - BRICKS DON'T SUFFA NEEDA.
Copr. 1937, King Features Syndicate, Inc., World rights reserved.
HERRIMAN 9-19

September 19th, 1937.

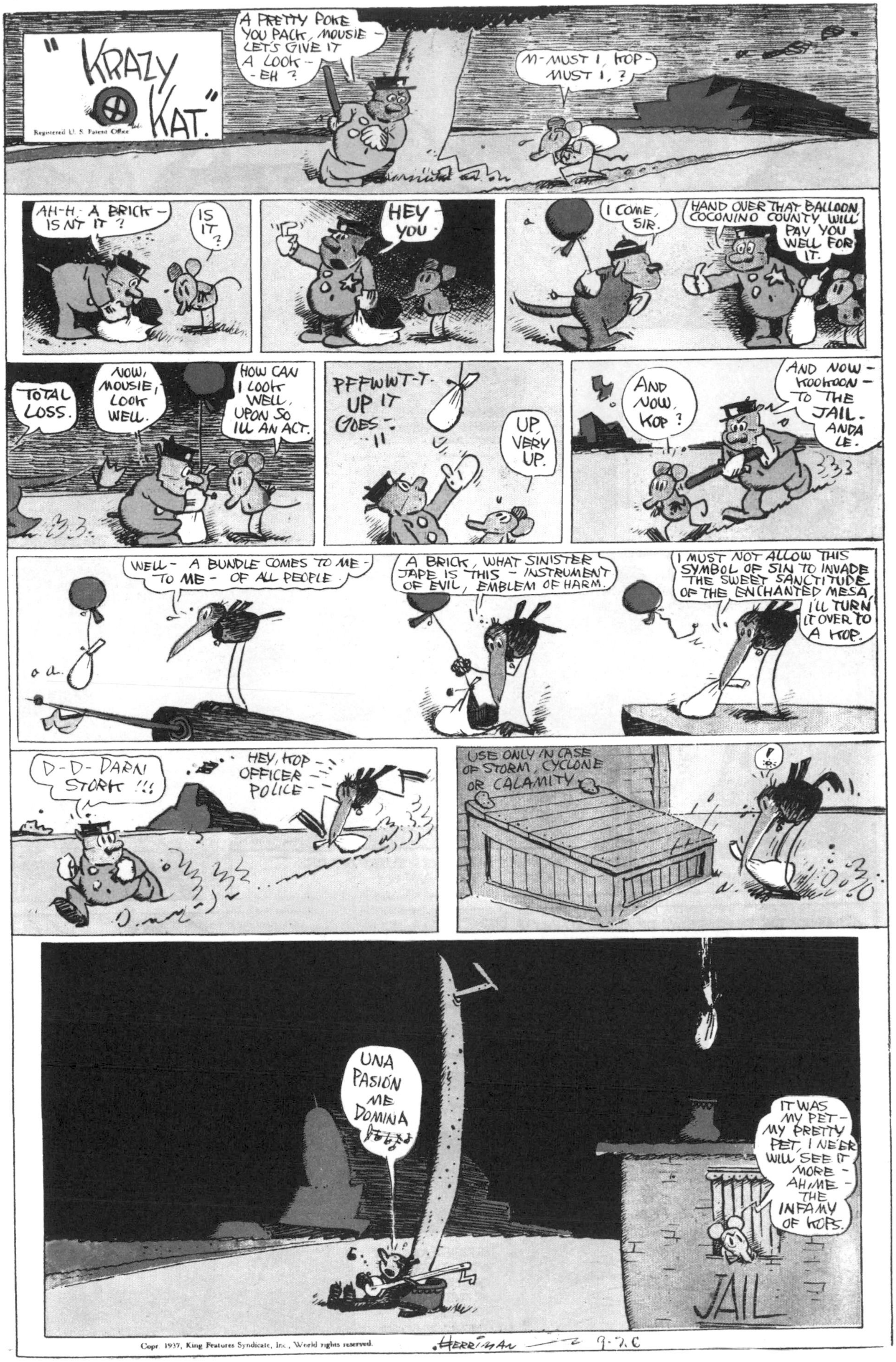
"Krazy Kat."
Registered U. S. Patent Office
A PRETTY POKE YOU PACK, MOUSIE - LET'S GIVE IT A LOOK - - EH ?
M-MUST I, KOP - MUST I, ?
AH-H. A BRICK - IS N'T IT ?
IS IT ?
HEY YOU
I COME, SIR.
HAND OVER THAT BALLOON, COCONINO COUNTY WILL PAY YOU WELL FOR IT.
TOTAL LOSS.
NOW, MOUSIE, LOOK WELL.
HOW CAN I LOOK WELL, UPON SO ILL AN ACT.
PFFWWT-T. UP IT GOES
UP. VERY UP.
AND NOW, KOP ?
AND NOW - KOOHOON - TO THE JAIL. ANDALE.
WELL - A BUNDLE COMES TO ME - TO ME - OF ALL PEOPLE
A BRICK, WHAT SINISTER JAPE IS THIS - INSTRUMENT OF EVIL, EMBLEM OF HARM.
I MUST NOT ALLOW THIS SYMBOL OF SIN TO INVADE THE SWEET SANCTITUDE OF THE ENCHANTED MESA, I'LL TURN IT OVER TO A KOP.
D-D-DARN STORK !!!
HEY, KOP - OFFICER - POLICE -
USE ONLY IN CASE OF STORM, CYCLONE OR CALAMITY.
UNA PASION ME DOMINA
IT WAS MY PET - MY PRETTY PET, I NE'ER WILL SEE IT MORE - AHIME - THE INFAMY OF KOPS.
JAIL
Copr. 1937, King Features Syndicate, Inc., World rights reserved.
HERRIMAN 9-26

September 26th, 1937.

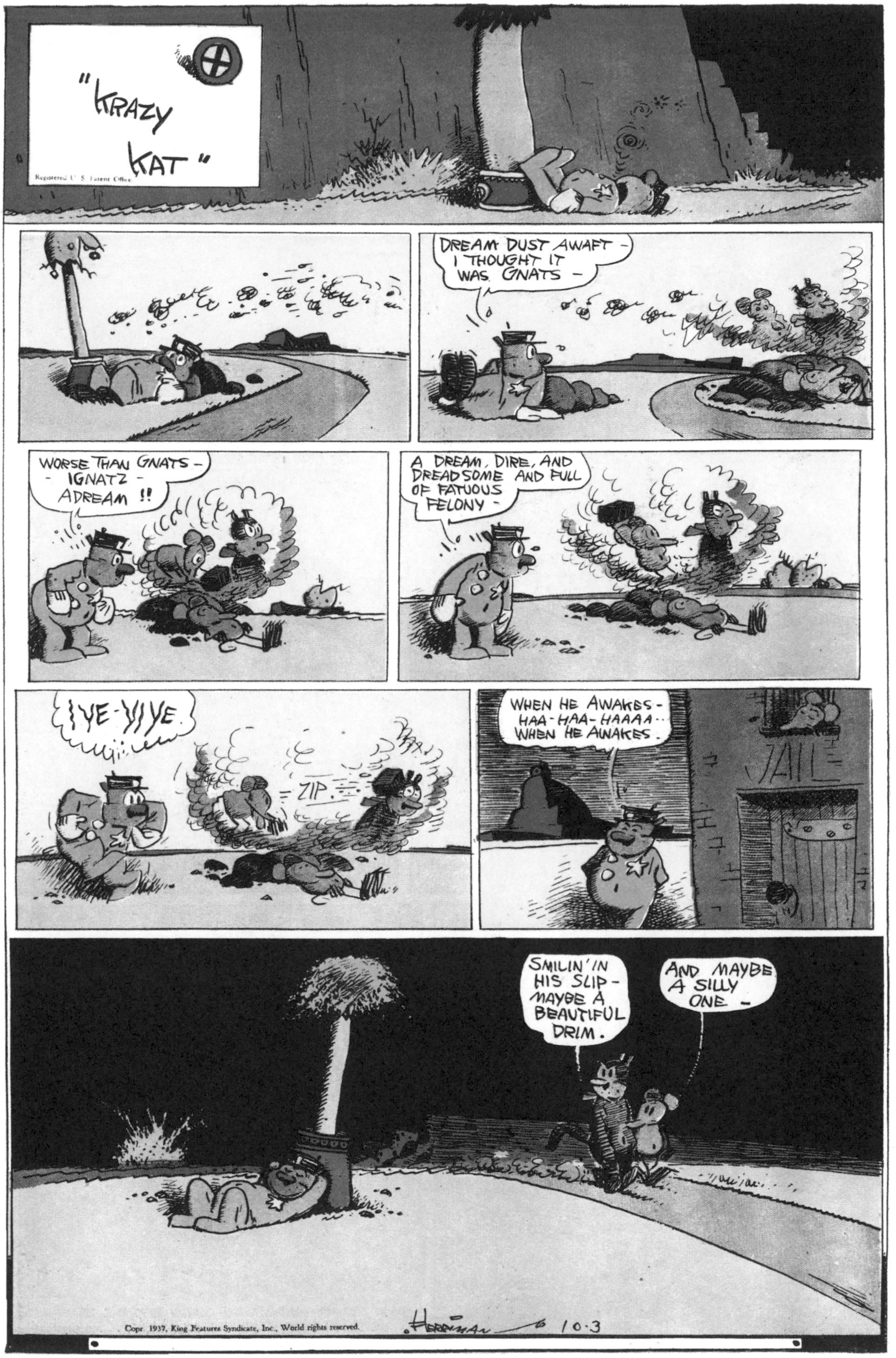
"KRAZY KAT"
Registered U. S. Patent Office
DREAM DUST AWAFT - I THOUGHT IT WAS GNATS -
WORSE THAN GNATS - - IGNATZ - ADREAM !!
A DREAM, DIRE, AND DREADSOME AND FULL OF FATUOUS FELONY -
YE-YI YE.
ZIP.
WHEN HE AWAKES - HAA-HAA-HAAAA... WHEN HE AWAKES.
JAIL
SMILIN' IN HIS SLIP - MAYBE A BEAUTIFUL DRIM.
AND MAYBE A SILLY ONE -
Copr. 1937, King Features Syndicate, Inc., World rights reserved.
HERRIMAN 10-3

October 3rd, 1937.

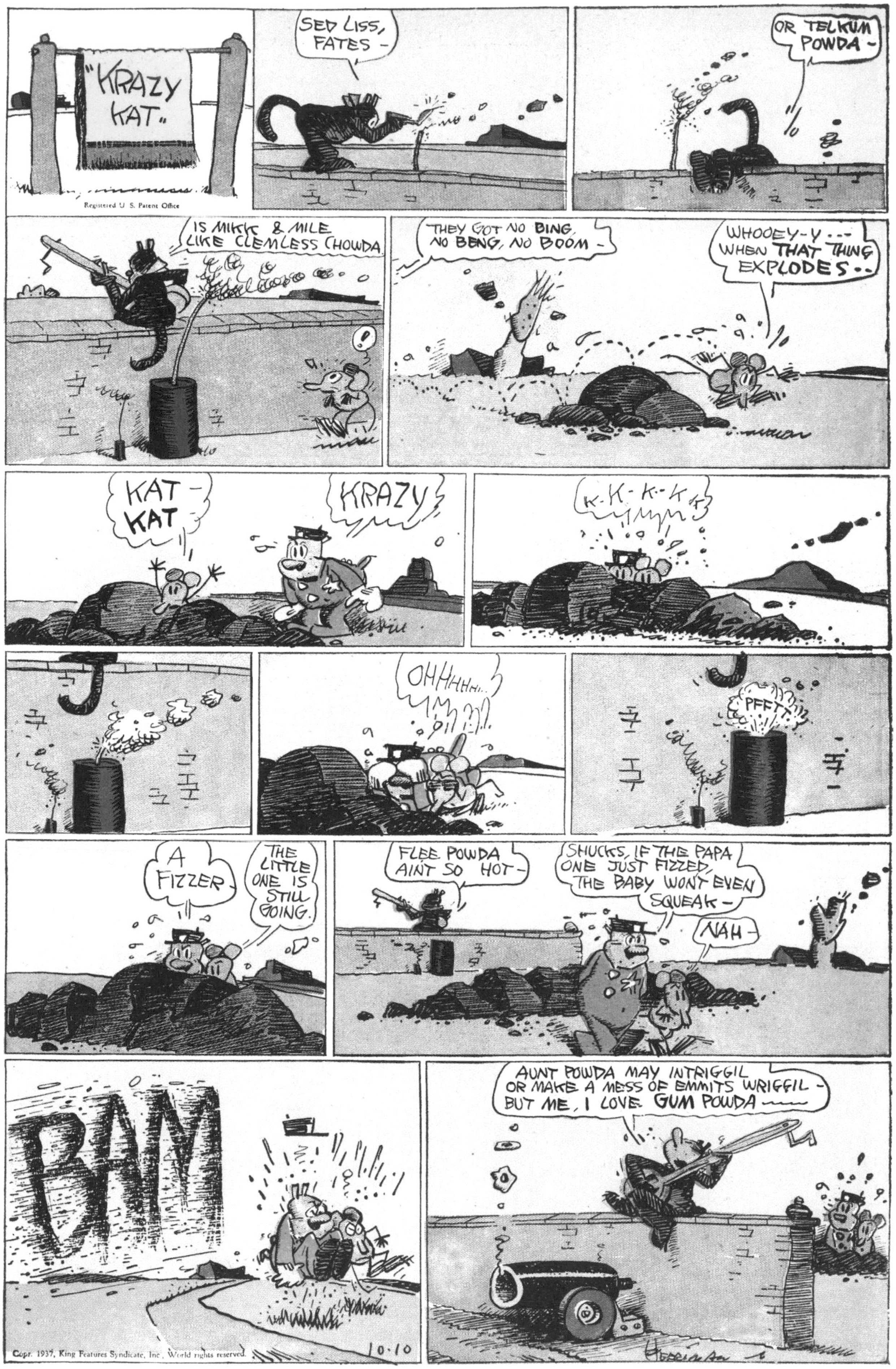
"KRAZY KAT"
Registered U. S. Patent Office
SED LISS, FATES -
OR TELKUM POWDA -
IS MIKK & MILE LIKE CLEMLESS CHOWDA
THEY GOT NO BING, NO BENG, NO BOOM -
WHOOEY-Y --- WHEN THAT THING EXPLODES --
!
KAT - KAT
KRAZY
K-K-K-K-K
OHHHHH...
PFFT
A FIZZER
THE LITTLE ONE IS STILL GOING.
FLEE POWDA AINT SO HOT -
SHUCKS, IF THE PAPA ONE JUST FIZZED, THE BABY WONT EVEN SQUEAK -
NAH -
BAM
AUNT POWDA MAY INTRIGGIL OR MAKE A MESS OF EMMITS WRIGGIL - BUT ME, I LOVE GUM POWDA
Copr. 1937, King Features Syndicate, Inc., World rights reserved.
10-10

October 10th, 1937.

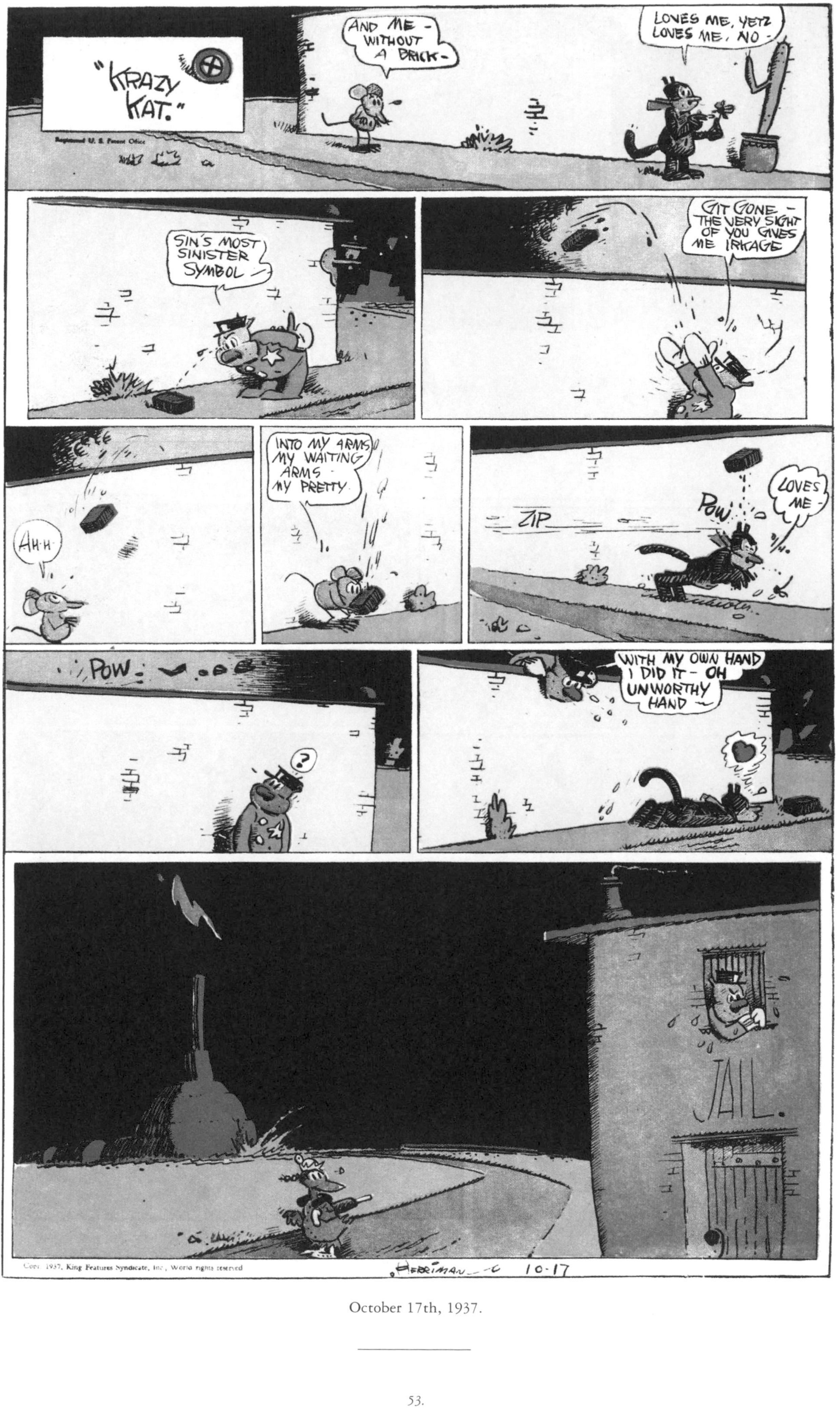
"KRAZY KAT."
Registered U. S. Patent Office
AND ME - WITHOUT A BRICK -
LOVES ME, YETZ LOVES ME, NO -
SIN'S MOST SINISTER SYMBOL
GIT GONE - THE VERY SIGHT OF YOU GIVES ME IRKAGE
AH-H
INTO MY ARMS, MY WAITING ARMS - MY PRETTY
ZIP
POW
LOVES ME -
POW
?
WITH MY OWN HAND I DID IT - OH UNWORTHY HAND
JAIL.
Copr. 1937, King Features Syndicate, Inc., World rights reserved
HERRIMAN 10-17

October 17th, 1937.

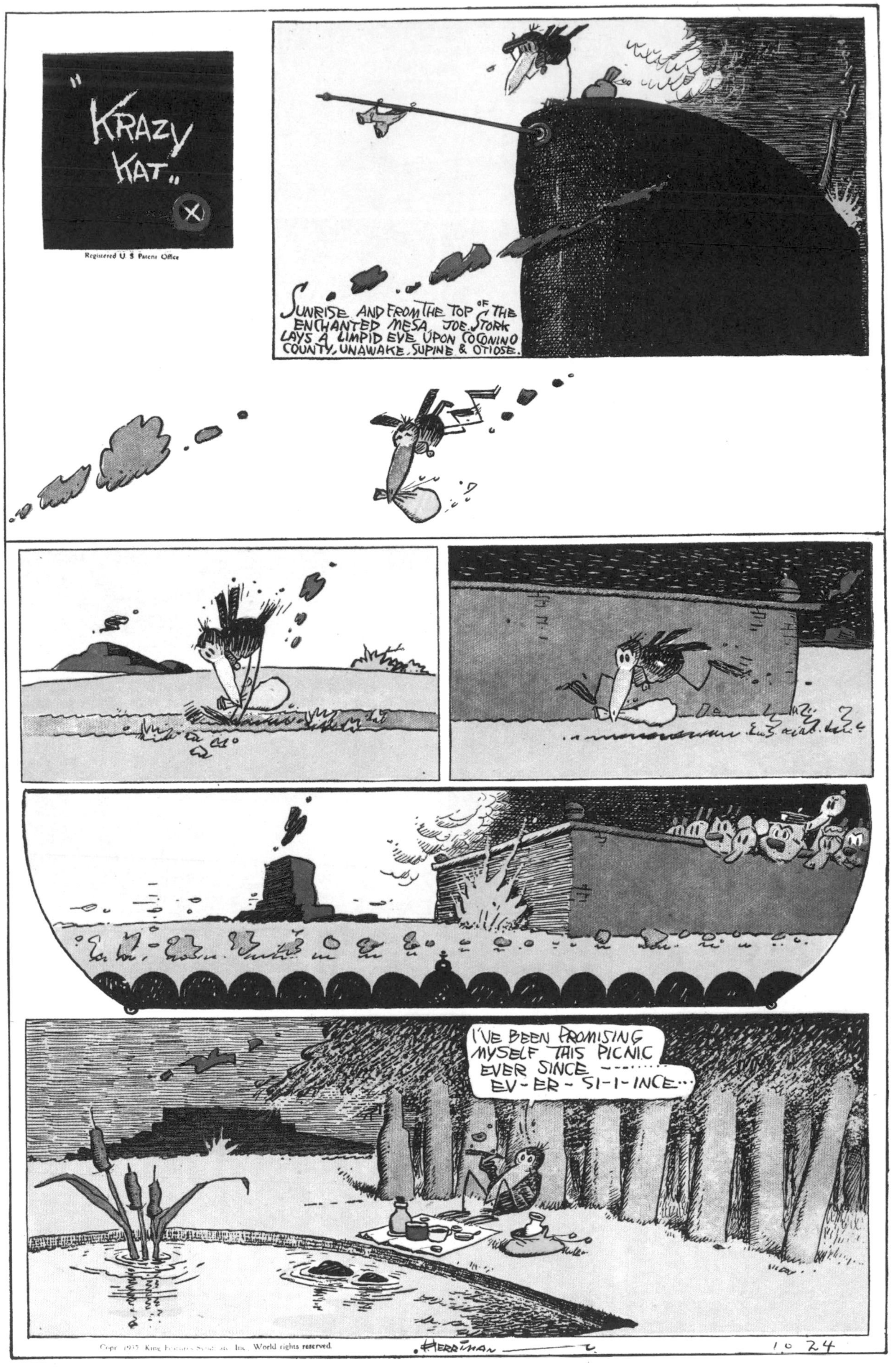
"KRAZY KAT."
Registered U. S. Patent Office
SUNRISE AND FROM THE TOP OF THE ENCHANTED MESA, JOE STORK LAYS A LIMPID EYE UPON COCONINO COUNTY, UNAWAKE, SUPINE & OTIOSE.
I'VE BEEN PROMISING MYSELF THIS PICNIC EVER SINCE ------- EV-ER - SI-I-INCE...
World rights reserved.
HERRIMAN
10 24

October 24th, 1937.

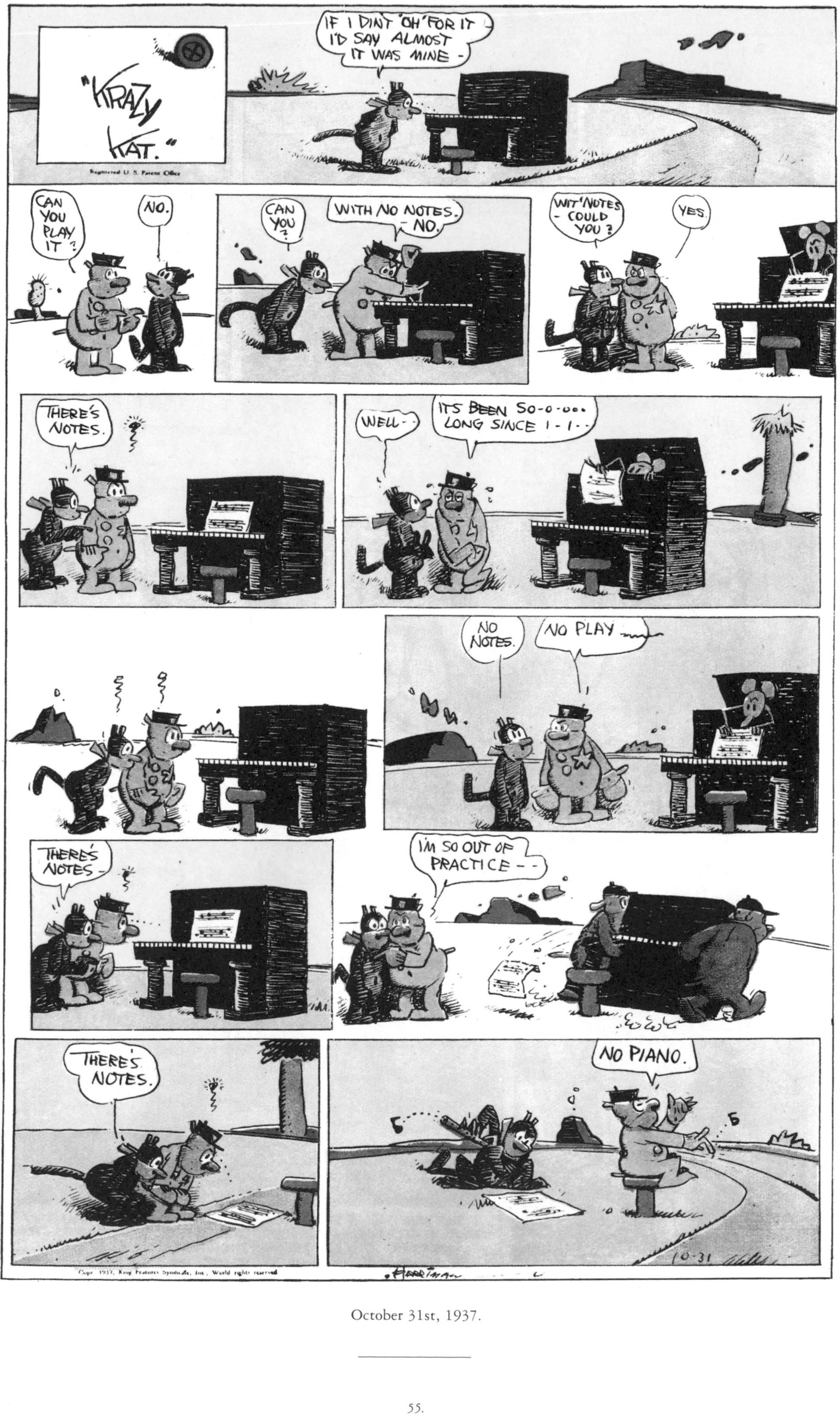
"KRAZY KAT."
Registered U. S. Patent Office
IF I DINT 'OH' FOR IT I'D SAY ALMOST IT WAS MINE -
CAN YOU PLAY IT ?
NO.
CAN YOU ?
WITH NO NOTES. - NO.
WIT' NOTES - COULD YOU ?
YES.
THERE'S NOTES.
WELL - -
ITS BEEN SO-O-OO. LONG SINCE I - I - -
NO NOTES.
NO PLAY
THERE'S NOTES -
I'M SO OUT OF PRACTICE - -
THERE'S NOTES.
NO PIANO.
Copr. 1937, King Features Syndicate, Inc., World rights reserved
HERRIMAN
10-31

October 31st, 1937.

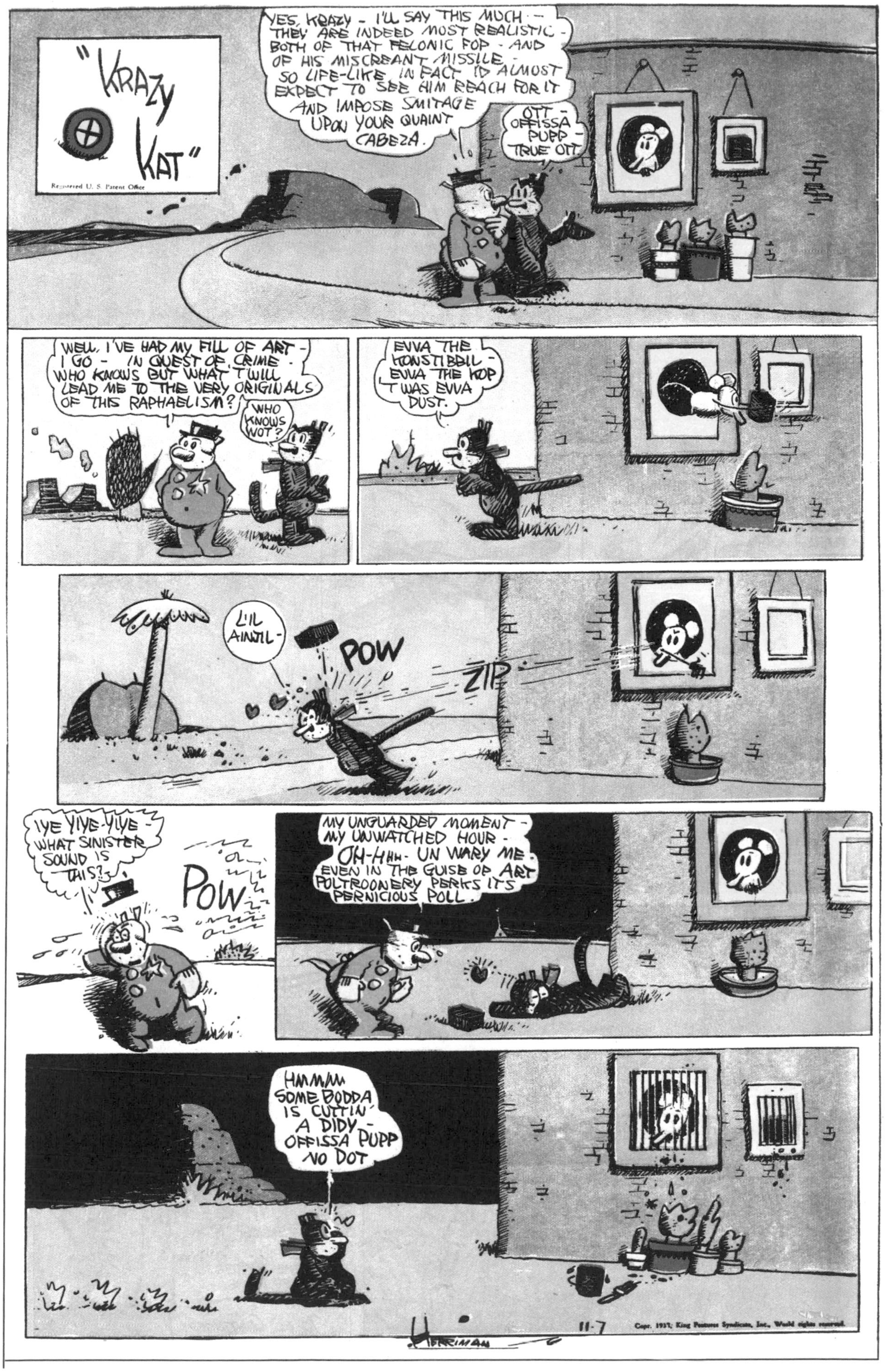
"KRAZY KAT"
Registered U. S. Patent Office
YES, KRAZY - I'LL SAY THIS MUCH - THEY ARE INDEED MOST REALISTIC - BOTH OF THAT FELONIC FOP - AND OF HIS MISCREANT MISSILE - SO LIFE-LIKE IN FACT I'D ALMOST EXPECT TO SEE HIM REACH FOR IT AND IMPOSE SMITAGE UPON YOUR QUAINT CABEZA.
OTT - OFFISSA PUPP - TRUE OTT
WELL, I'VE HAD MY FILL OF ART - I GO - IN QUEST OF CRIME - WHO KNOWS BUT WHAT 'T WILL LEAD ME TO THE VERY ORIGINALS OF THIS RAPHAELISM?
WHO KNOWS NOT?
EVVA THE KONSTIBBIL - EVVA THE KOP 'T WAS EVVA DUST.
L'IL AINJIL -
POW
ZIP
IYE YIYE-YIYE - WHAT SINISTER SOUND IS THIS?
POW
MY UNGUARDED MOMENT - MY UNWATCHED HOUR - OH-HHH- UN WARY ME. EVEN IN THE GUISE OF ART POLTROONERY PERKS ITS PERNICIOUS POLL.
HMMM SOME BODDA IS CUTTIN' A DIDY - OFFISSA PUPP NO DOT
11-7
Copr. 1937, King Features Syndicate, Inc., World rights reserved.
HERRIMAN

November 7th, 1937.

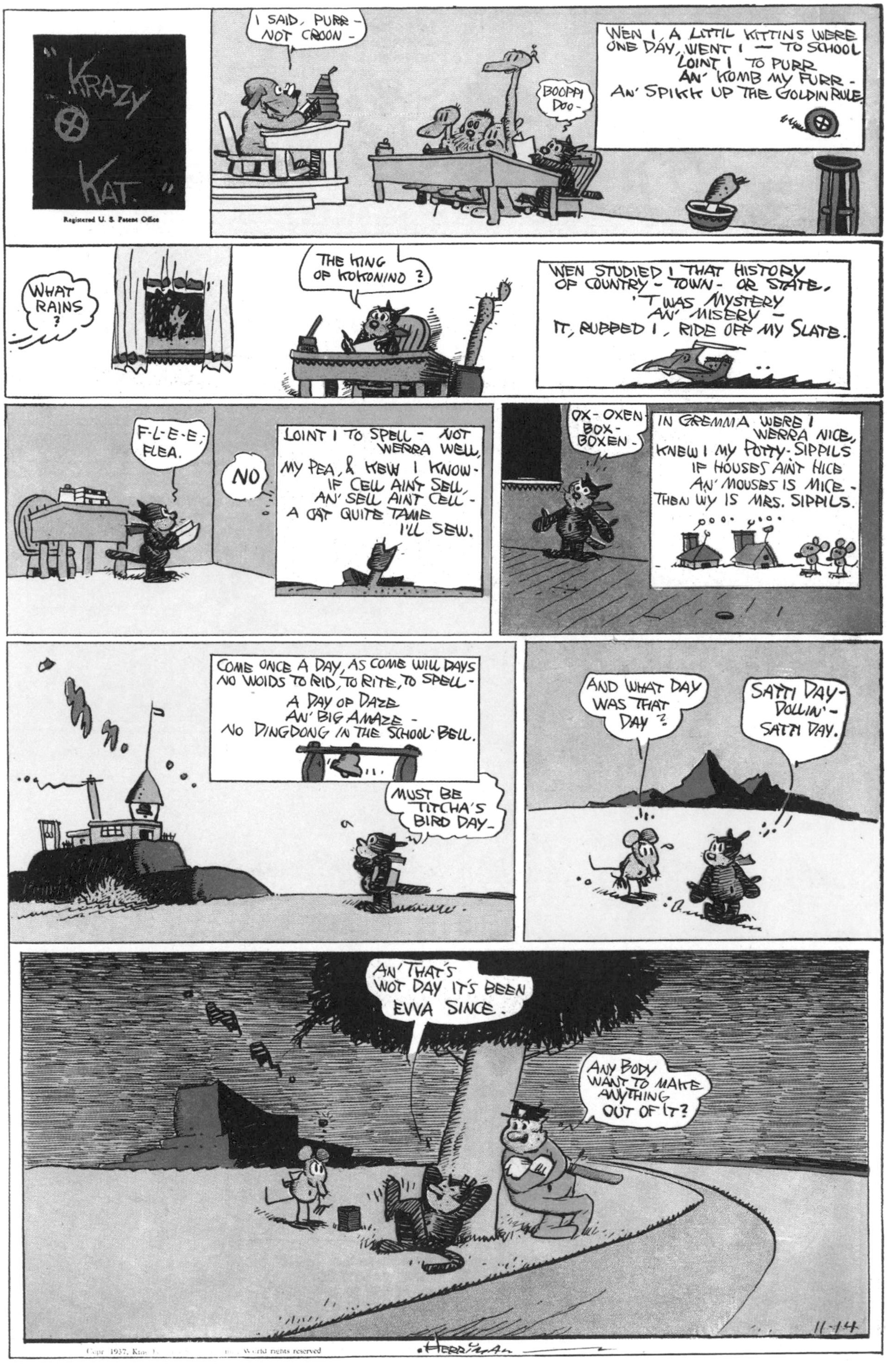
"KRAZY KAT."
Registered U. S. Patent Office
I SAID, PURR - NOT CROON -
BOOPPI DOO-
WEN I, A LITTIL KITTINS WERE ONE DAY, WENT I — TO SCHOOL LOINT I TO PURR AN' KOMB MY FURR - AN' SPIKH UP THE GOLDIN RULE.
WHAT RAINS ?
THE KING OF KOKONINO ?
WEN STUDIED I THAT HISTORY OF COUNTRY - TOWN - OR STATE, 'T WAS MYSTERY AN' MISERY - IT, RUBBED I, RIDE OFF MY SLATE.
F-L-E-E, FLEA.
NO
LOINT I TO SPELL - NOT WERRA WELL, MY PEA, & KEW I KNOW - IF CELL AIN'T SELL, AN' SELL AIN'T CELL - A CAT QUITE TAME I'LL SEW.
OX - OXEN BOX - BOXEN -
IN GREMMA WERE I WERRA NICE, KNEW I MY POTTY - SIPPILS IF HOUSES AIN'T HICE AN' MOUSES IS MICE - THEN WY IS MRS. SIPPILS.
COME ONCE A DAY, AS COME WILL DAYS NO WOIDS TO RID, TO RITE, TO SPELL - A DAY OF DAZE AN' BIG AMAZE - NO DINGDONG IN THE SCHOOL BELL.
MUST BE TITCHA'S BIRD DAY -
AND WHAT DAY WAS THAT DAY ?
SATTI DAY - DOLLIN' - SATTI DAY.
AN' THAT'S WOT DAY IT'S BEEN EVVA SINCE.
ANY BODY WANT TO MAKE ANYTHING OUT OF IT?
11-14
HERRIMAN

November 14th, 1937.

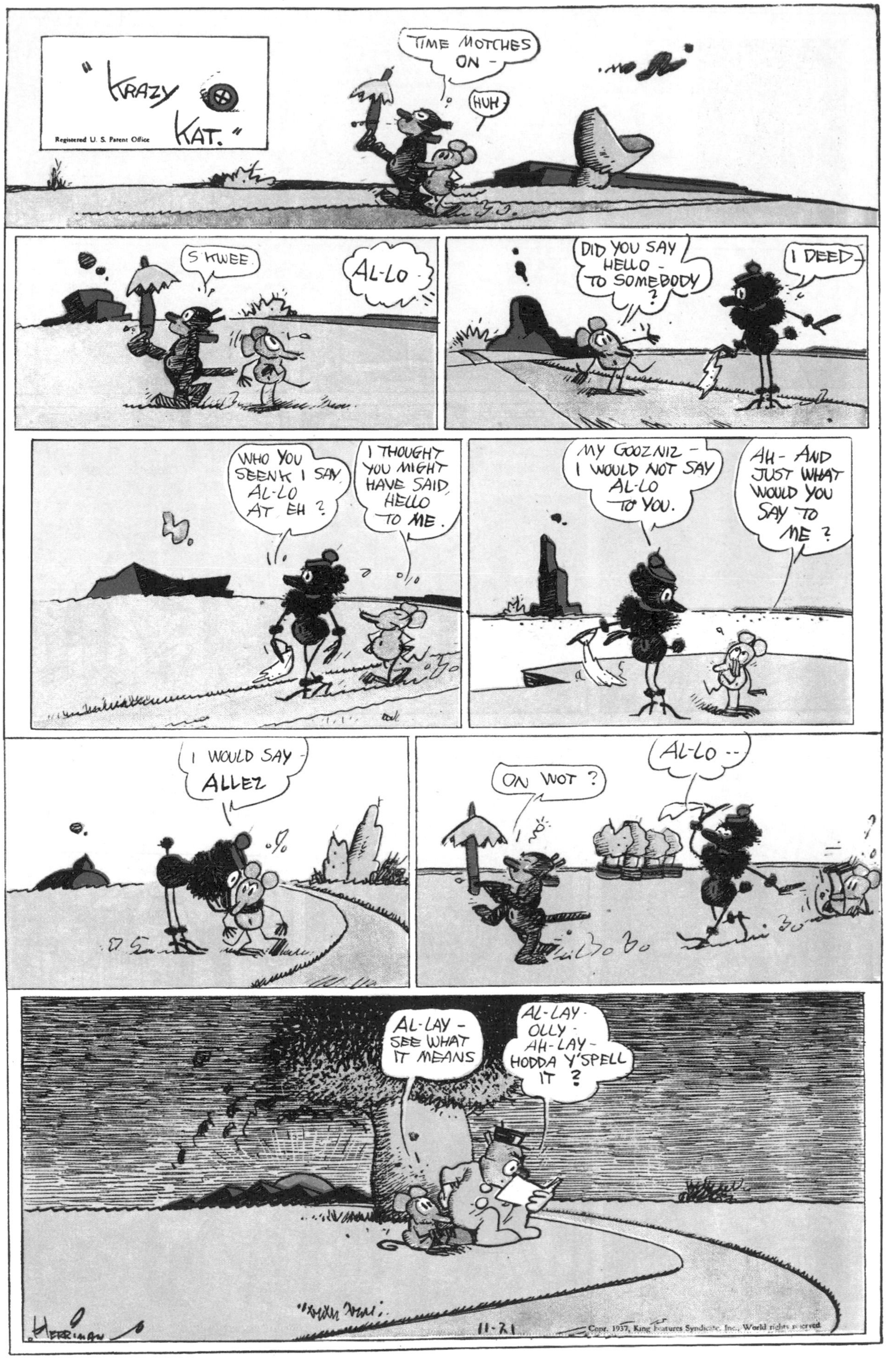
"Krazy Kat."
Registered U. S. Patent Office
TIME MOTCHES ON -
HUH
S'KWEE.
AL-LO
DID YOU SAY HELLO - TO SOMEBODY ?
I DEED
WHO YOU SEENK I SAY AL-LO AT EH ?
I THOUGHT YOU MIGHT HAVE SAID, HELLO TO ME.
MY GOOZNIZ - I WOULD NOT SAY AL-LO TO YOU.
AH - AND JUST WHAT WOULD YOU SAY TO ME ?
I WOULD SAY - ALLEZ
ON WOT ?
AL-LO --
AL-LAY - SEE WHAT IT MEANS
AL-LAY - OLLY - AH-LAY - HODDA Y'SPELL IT ?
Herriman
11-21
Copr. 1937, King Features Syndicate, Inc., World rights reserved

November 21st, 1937.

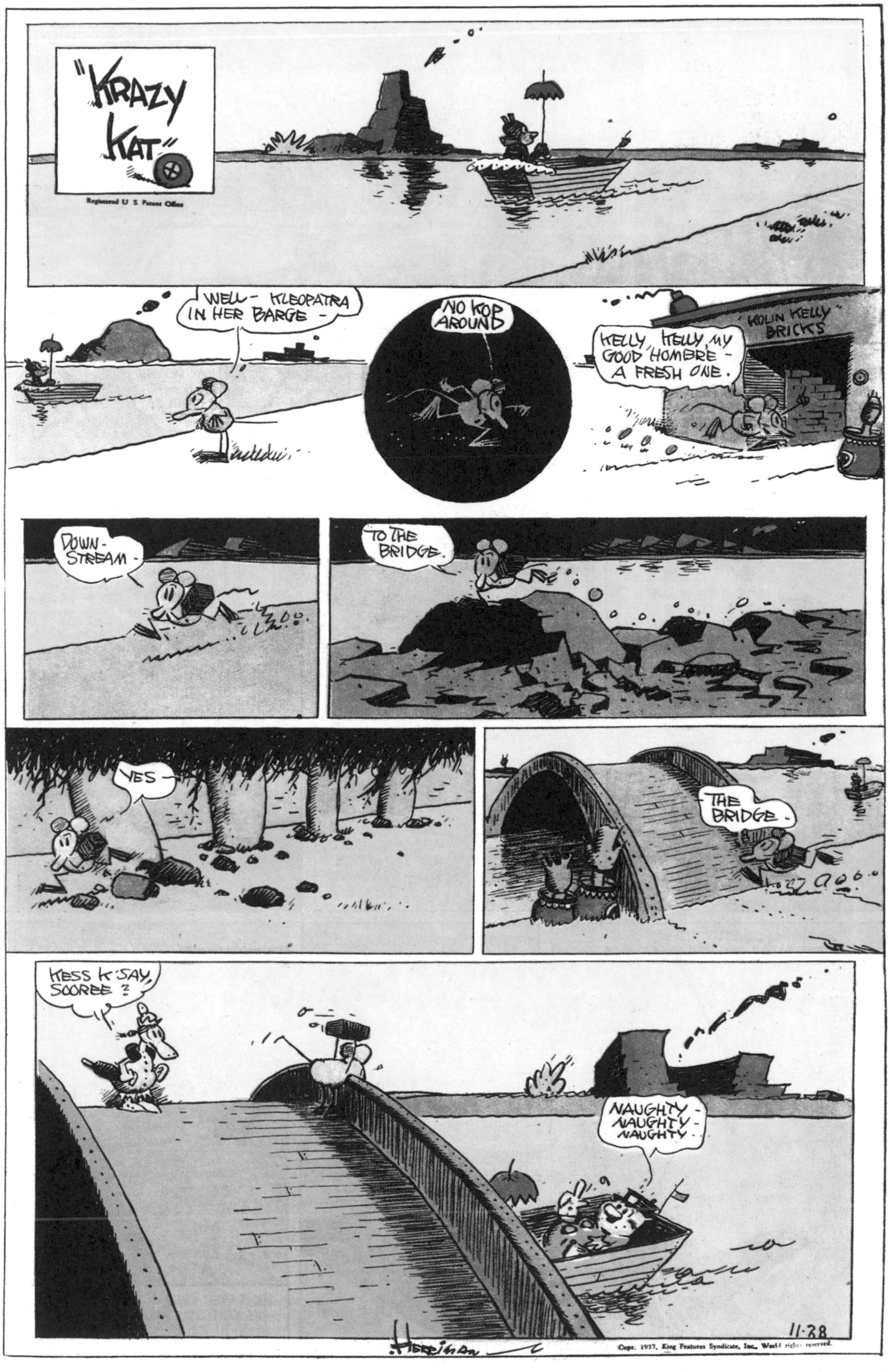
"KRAZY KAT"
Registered U. S. Patent Office
WELL - KLEOPATRA IN HER BARGE -
NO KOB AROUND
KOLIN KELLY BRICKS
KELLY, KELLY, MY GOOD HOMBRE - A FRESH ONE.
DOWN-STREAM -
TO THE BRIDGE.
YES -
THE BRIDGE.
KESS K'SAY, SOOREE ?
NAUGHTY - NAUGHTY - NAUGHTY -
Herriman
11·28
Copr. 1937, King Features Syndicate, Inc. World rights reserved.

November 28th, 1937.

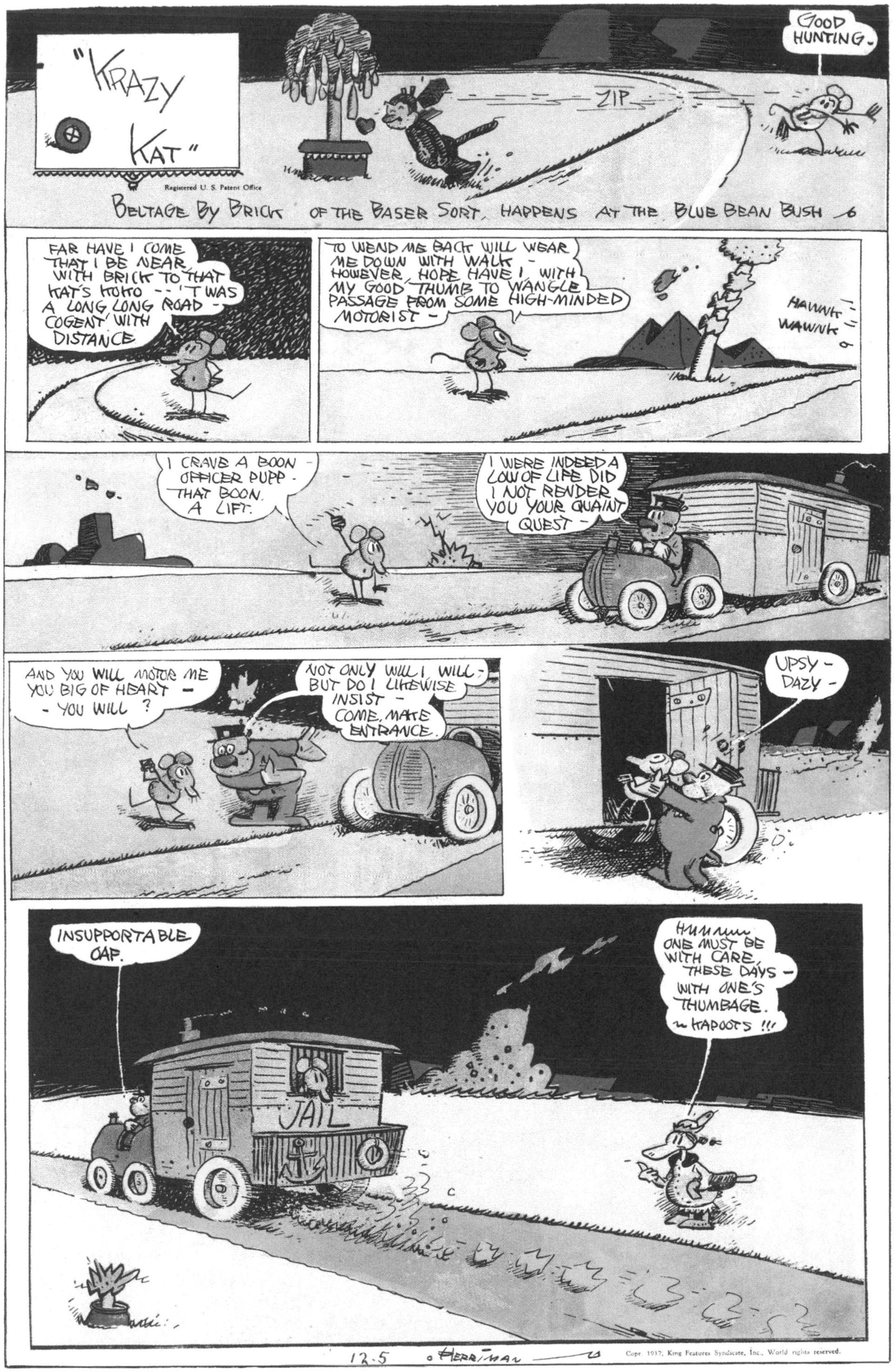
"KRAZY KAT"
Registered U. S. Patent Office
ZIP
GOOD HUNTING.
BELTAGE BY BRICK OF THE BASER SORT, HAPPENS AT THE BLUE BEAN BUSH
FAR HAVE I COME THAT I BE NEAR, WITH BRICK TO THAT KAT'S KOKO -- 'T WAS A LONG LONG ROAD - COGENT WITH DISTANCE
TO WEND ME BACK WILL WEAR ME DOWN WITH WALK - HOWEVER, HOPE HAVE I, WITH MY GOOD THUMB TO WANGLE PASSAGE FROM SOME HIGH-MINDED MOTORIST -
HAWNK - WAWNK -
I CRAVE A BOON OFFICER PUPP - THAT BOON, A LIFT.
I WERE INDEED A LOW OF LIFE DID I NOT RENDER YOU YOUR QUAINT QUEST -
AND YOU WILL MOTOR ME YOU BIG OF HEART - - YOU WILL ?
NOT ONLY WILL I WILL - BUT DO I LIKEWISE INSIST - COME, MAKE ENTRANCE.
UPSY - DAZY -
INSUPPORTABLE OAF.
JAIL
HUMMMM ONE MUST BE WITH CARE, THESE DAYS - WITH ONE'S THUMBAGE. - KAPOOTS !!!
12-5 HERRIMAN
Copr. 1937, King Features Syndicate, Inc., World rights reserved.

December 5th, 1937.

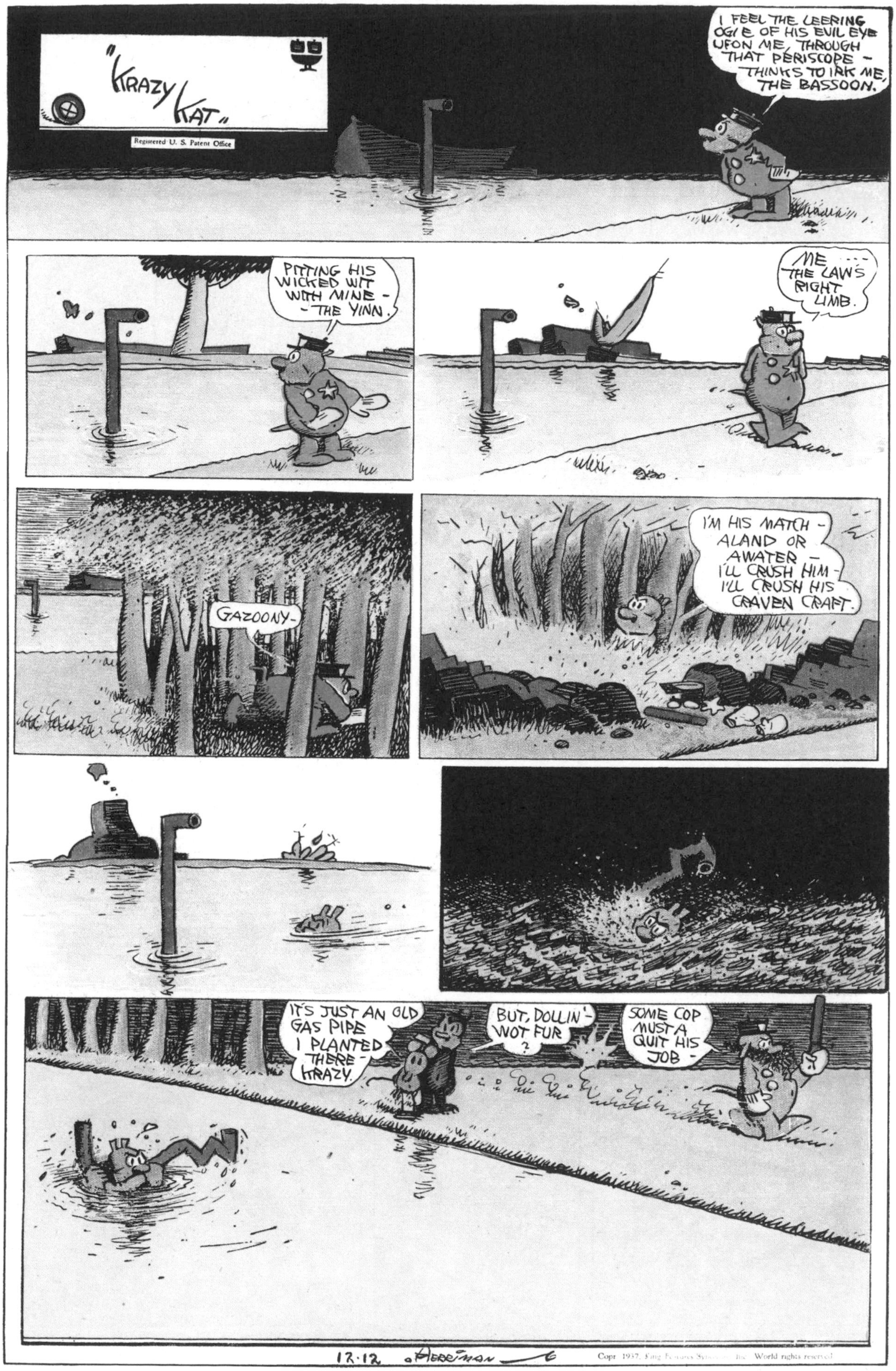
"Krazy Kat"
Registered U. S. Patent Office
I FEEL THE LEERING OGLE OF HIS EVIL EYE UPON ME, THROUGH THAT PERISCOPE - THINKS TO IRK ME, THE BASSOON.
PITTING HIS WICKED WIT WITH MINE - - THE YINN.
ME ... THE LAW'S RIGHT LIMB.
GAZOONY-
I'M HIS MATCH - ALAND OR AWATER - I'LL CRUSH HIM - I'LL CRUSH HIS CRAVEN CRAFT.
IT'S JUST AN OLD GAS PIPE I PLANTED THERE - KRAZY.
BUT, DOLLIN' - WOT FUR ?
SOME COP MUST A QUIT HIS JOB -
12.12
Herriman

December 12th, 1937.

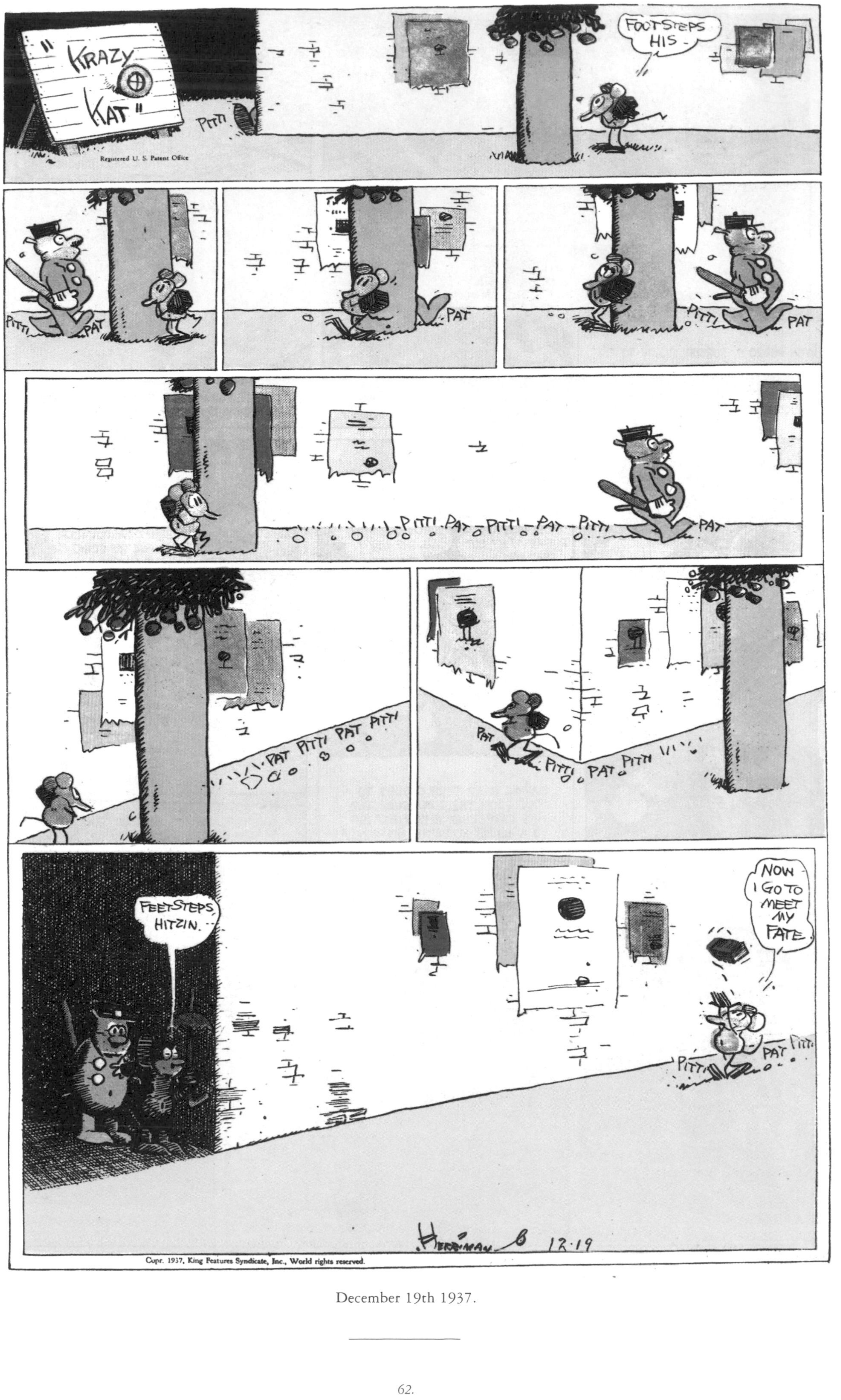

"KRAZY KAT"
Registered U. S. Patent Office
PITTI
FOOTSTEPS HIS
PITTI
PAT
PAT
PITTI
PAT
PITTI PAT PITTI PAT PITTI PAT
PAT PITTI PITTI PAT PITTI
PAT PITTI PAT PITTI
FEETSTEPS HITZIN.
NOW I GO TO MEET MY FATE.
PITTI PAT PITTI
HERRIMAN 12·19
Copr. 1937, King Features Syndicate, Inc., World rights reserved.

December 19th 1937.

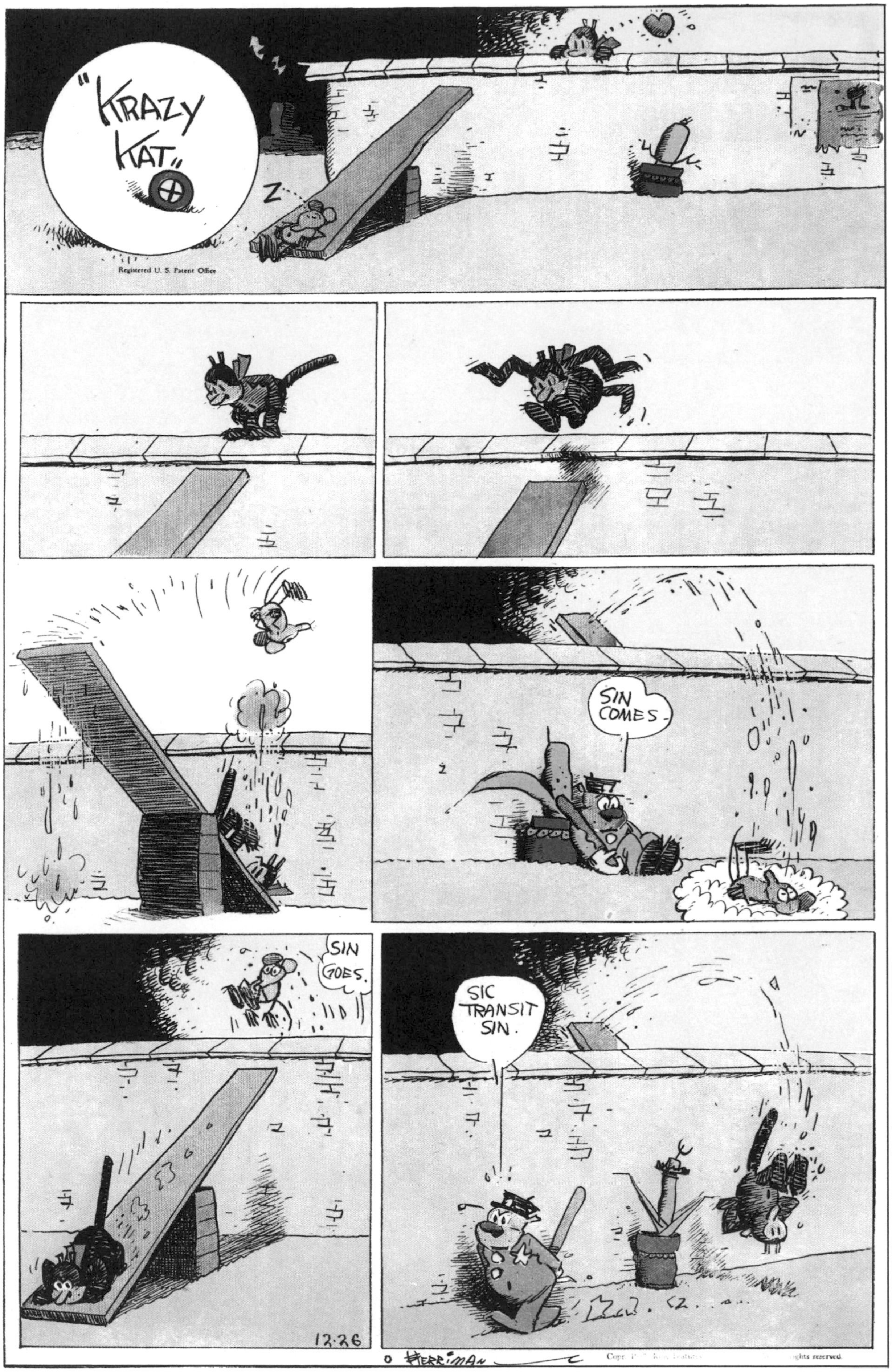
"KRAZY KAT"
Registered U. S. Patent Office
SIN COMES
SIN GOES.
SIC TRANSIT SIN.
12·26
HERRIMAN
rights reserved.

December 26th, 1937.

1938.

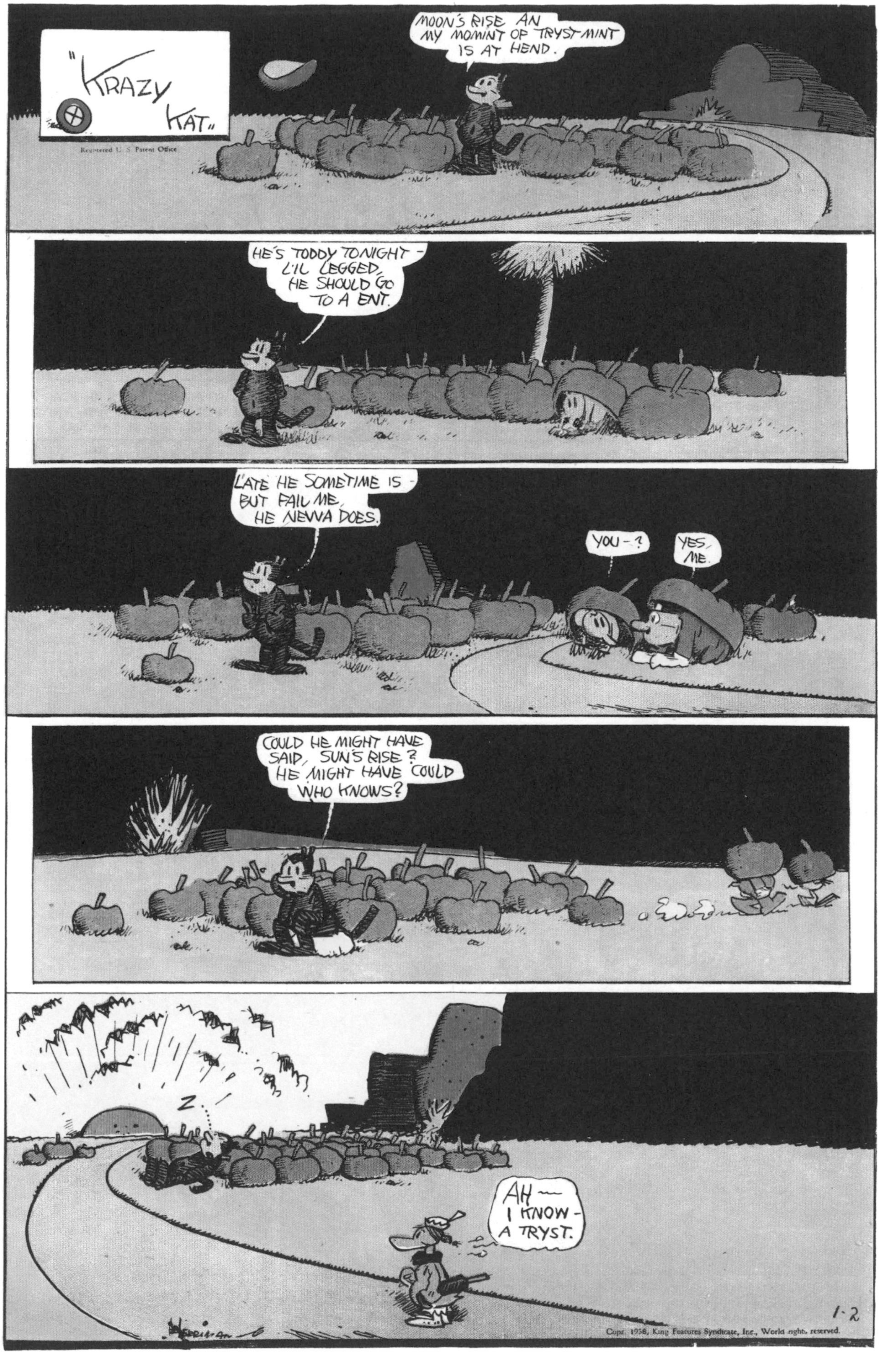
"Krazy Kat"
Registered U. S. Patent Office
MOON'S RISE AN MY MOMINT OF TRYST-MINT IS AT HEND.
HE'S TODDY TONIGHT - L'IL LEGGED, HE SHOULD GO TO A ENT.
LATE HE SOMETIME IS - BUT FAIL ME, HE NEVVA DOES.
YOU - ?
YES, ME.
COULD HE MIGHT HAVE SAID, SUN'S RISE? HE MIGHT HAVE COULD WHO KNOWS?
Z
AH — I KNOW - A TRYST.
1-2
Copr. 1938, King Features Syndicate, Inc., World rights reserved.

January 2nd, 1938.

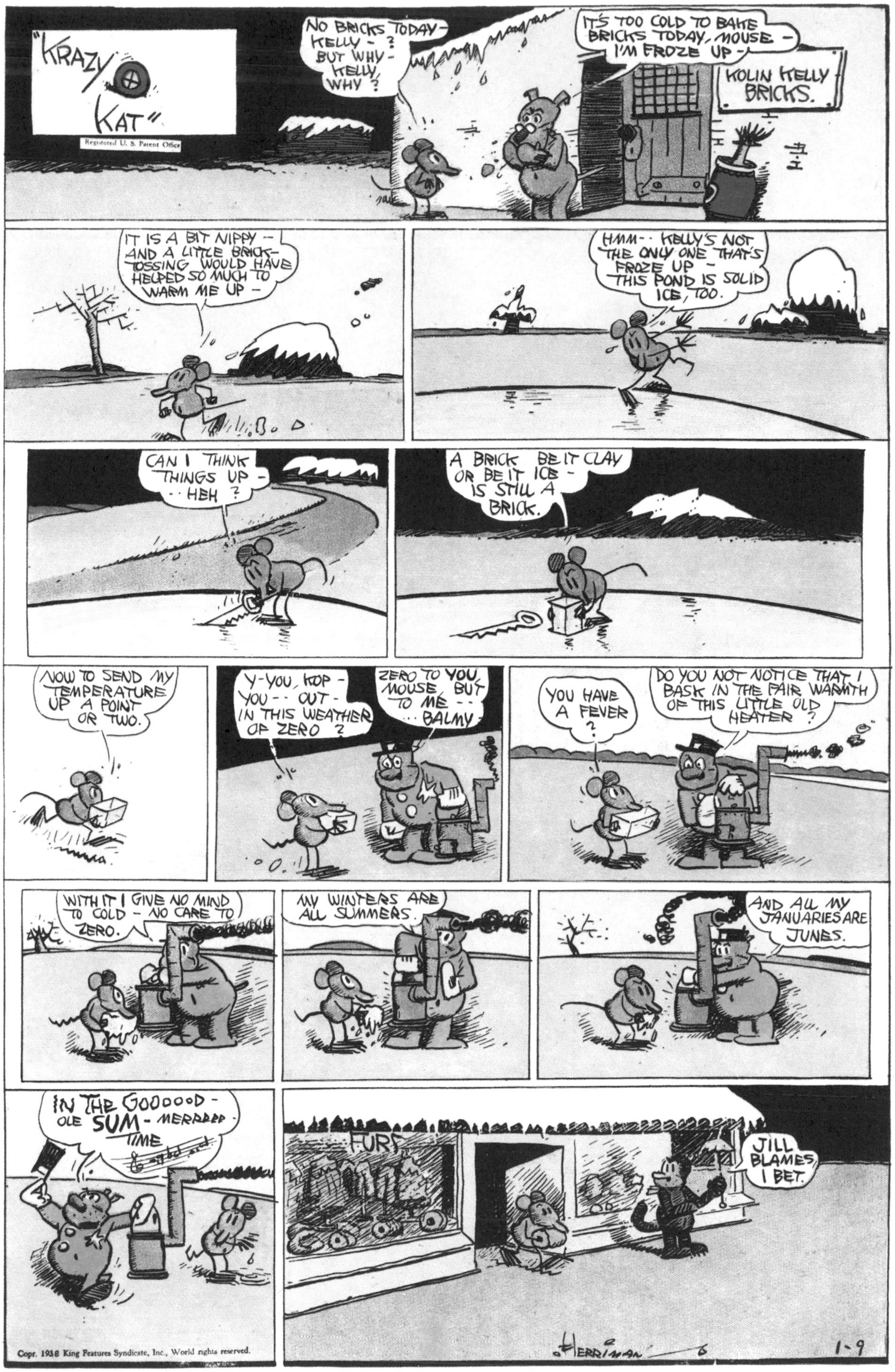
"KRAZY KAT"
Registered U. S. Patent Office
NO BRICKS TODAY - KELLY - ? BUT WHY - KELLY, WHY ?
IT'S TOO COLD TO BAKE BRICKS TODAY, MOUSE - I'M FROZE UP -
KOLIN KELLY BRICKS.
IT IS A BIT NIPPY -- AND A LITTLE BRICK-TOSSING WOULD HAVE HELPED SO MUCH TO WARM ME UP -
HMM -- KELLY'S NOT THE ONLY ONE THAT'S FROZE UP - THIS POND IS SOLID ICE, TOO.
CAN I THINK THINGS UP - -- HEH ?
A BRICK BE IT CLAY OR BE IT ICE - IS STILL A BRICK.
NOW TO SEND MY TEMPERATURE UP A POINT OR TWO.
Y-YOU, KOP - YOU -- OUT - IN THIS WEATHER OF ZERO ?
ZERO TO YOU, MOUSE, BUT TO ME -- ... BALMY.
YOU HAVE A FEVER ?
DO YOU NOT NOTICE THAT I BASK IN THE FAIR WARMTH OF THIS LITTLE OLD HEATER ?
WITH IT I GIVE NO MIND TO COLD - NO CARE TO ZERO.
MY WINTERS ARE ALL SUMMERS.
AND ALL MY JANUARIES ARE JUNES.
IN THE GOOOOOD - OLE SUM - MERRRR - TIME
FURS
JILL BLAMES, I BET.
Copr. 1938 King Features Syndicate, Inc., World rights reserved.
HERRIMAN
1-9

January 9th, 1938.

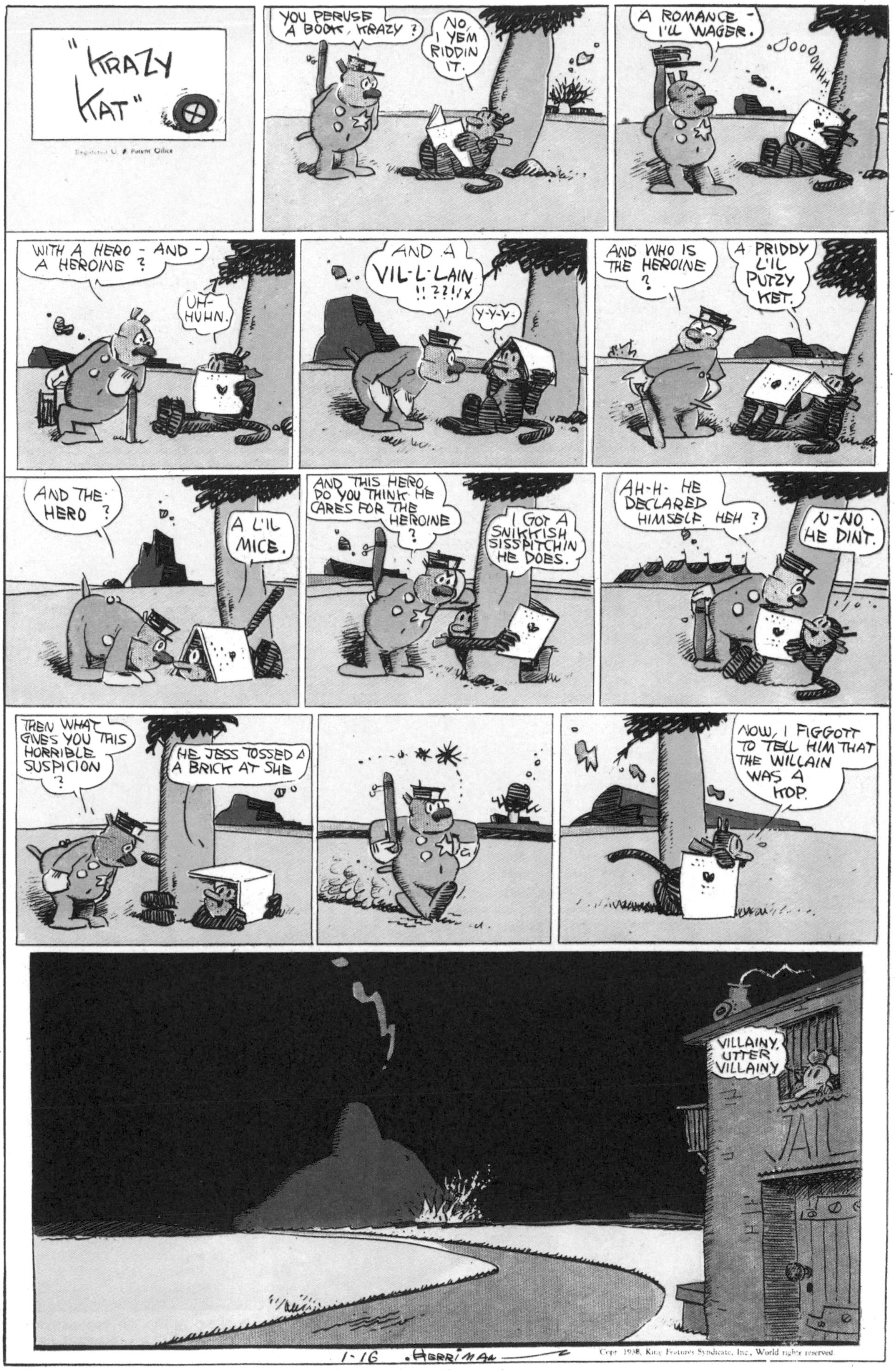
"KRAZY KAT"
YOU PERUSE A BOOK, KRAZY ?
NO, I YEM RIDDIN IT.
A ROMANCE - I'LL WAGER.
OOOOOHHH
WITH A HERO - AND - A HEROINE ?
UH-HUHN.
AND A VIL-L-LAIN !! ??!/X
Y-Y-Y-
AND WHO IS THE HEROINE ?
A PRIDDY L'IL PUTZY KET.
AND THE HERO ?
A L'IL MICE.
AND THIS HERO, DO YOU THINK HE CARES FOR THE HEROINE ?
I GOT A SNIKITISH SISSPITCHIN HE DOES.
AH-H- HE DECLARED HIMSELF, HEH ?
N-NO HE DINT.
THEN WHAT GIVES YOU THIS HORRIBLE SUSPICION ?
HE JESS TOSSED A A BRICK AT SHE
NOW, I FIGGOTT TO TELL HIM THAT THE WILLAIN WAS A KOP.
VILLAINY, UTTER VILLAINY
JAIL
1-16 HERRIMAN

January 16th, 1938.

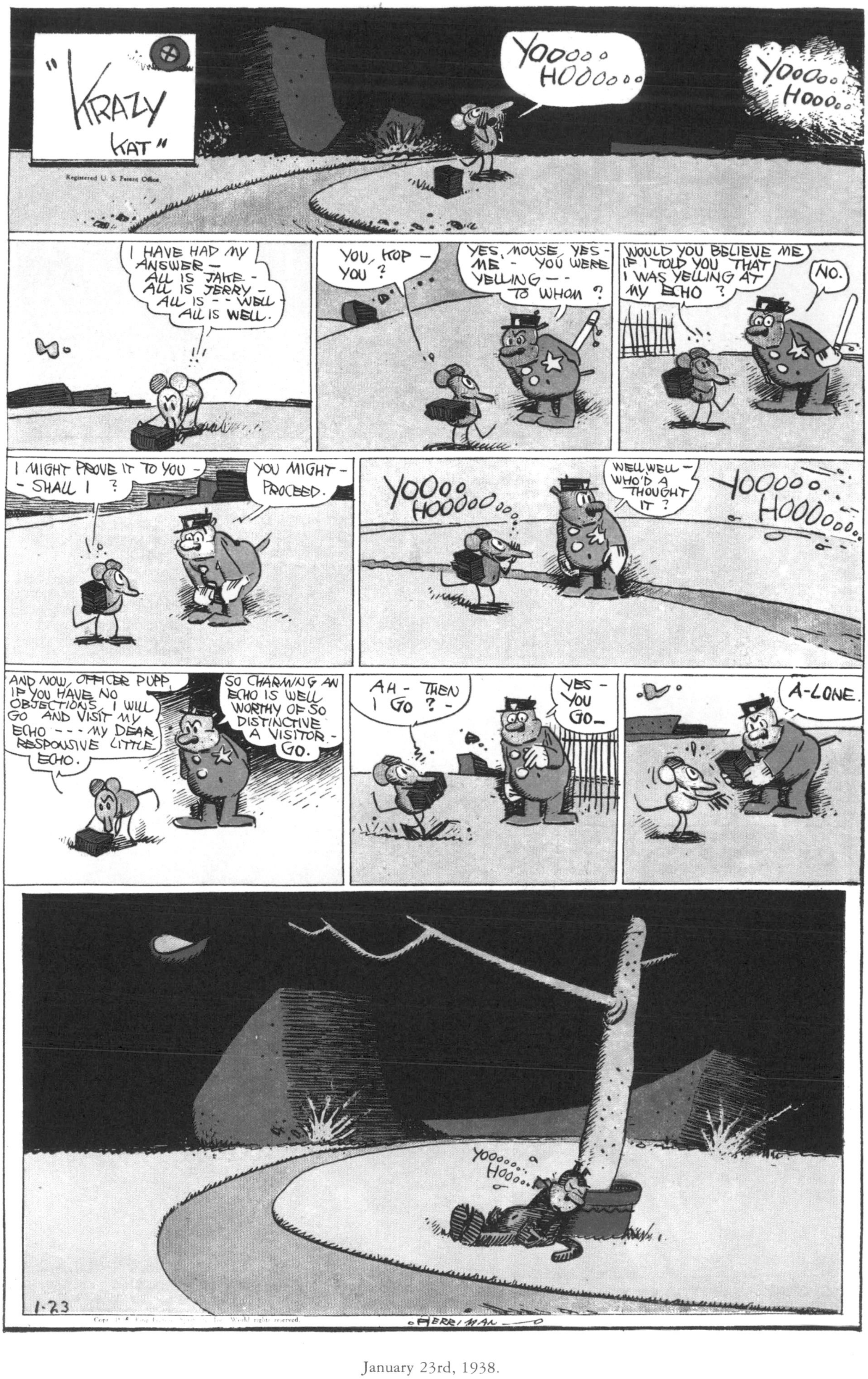
"KRAZY KAT"
Registered U. S. Patent Office.
YOOooo HOOoooo
YOOoo. HOOo..
I HAVE HAD MY ANSWER - ALL IS JAKE - ALL IS JERRY - ALL IS - - WELL ALL IS WELL.
YOU, KOP - YOU ?
YES, MOUSE, YES - ME - YOU WERE YELLING - - TO WHOM ?
WOULD YOU BELIEVE ME IF I TOLD YOU THAT I WAS YELLING AT MY ECHO ?
NO.
I MIGHT PROVE IT TO YOU - - SHALL I ?
YOU MIGHT - PROCEED.
YOOoo HOOOOOooo
WELL, WELL - WHO'D A THOUGHT IT ?
YOOOOO... HOOOooo..
AND NOW, OFFICER PUPP, IF YOU HAVE NO OBJECTIONS, I WILL GO AND VISIT MY ECHO - - - MY DEAR RESPONSIVE LITTLE ECHO.
SO CHARMING AN ECHO IS WELL WORTHY OF SO DISTINCTIVE A VISITOR - GO.
AH - THEN I GO ? -
YES - YOU GO_
A-LONE.
YOOooo.. HOOo..
1-23
HERRIMAN

January 23rd, 1938.

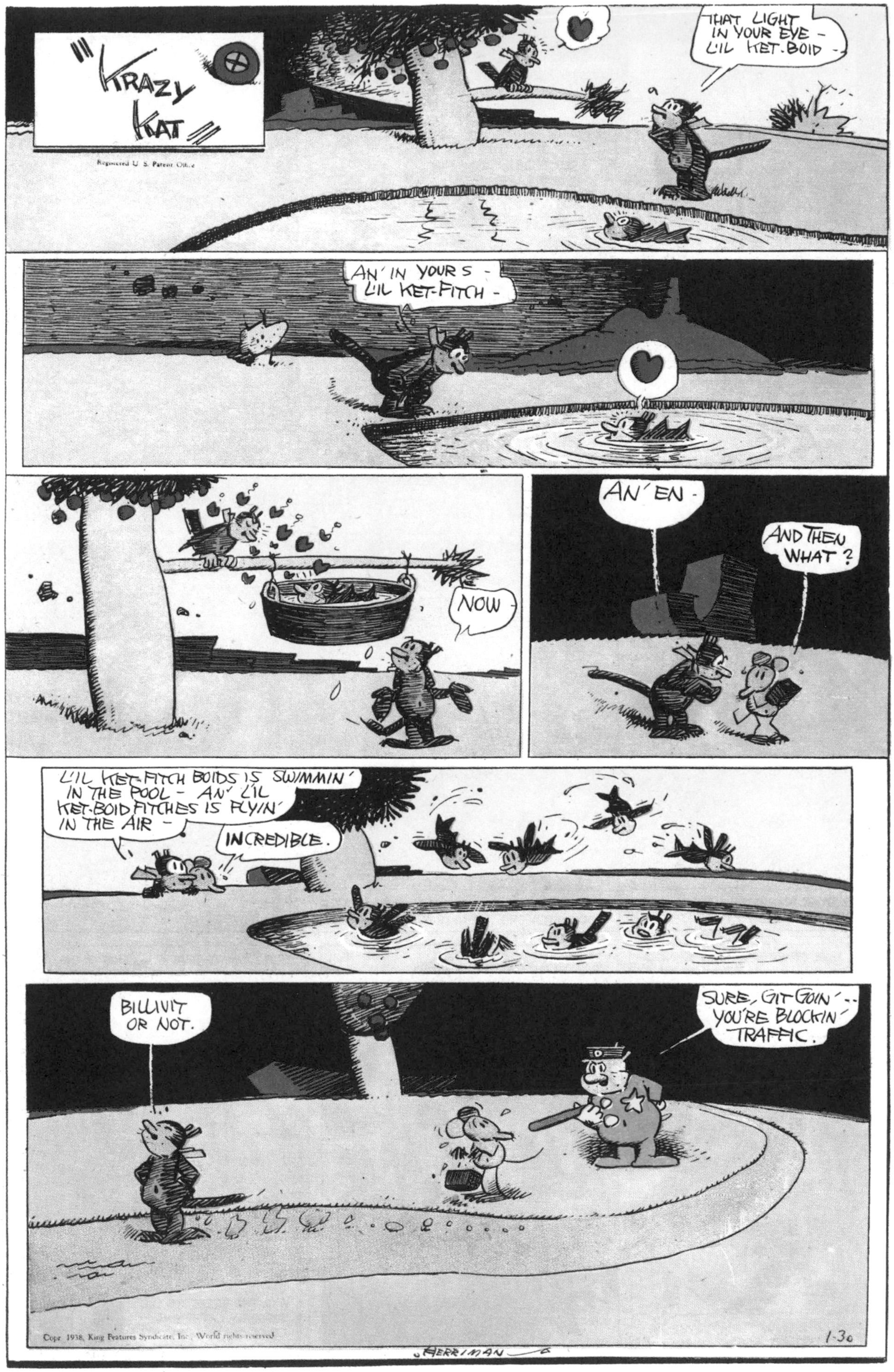
Krazy Kat
Registered U. S. Patent Office
THAT LIGHT IN YOUR EYE - L'IL KET-BOID -
AN' IN YOUR S - L'IL KET-FITCH -
NOW -
AN' EN -
AND THEN WHAT ?
L'IL KET-FITCH BOIDS IS SWIMMIN' IN THE POOL - AN' L'IL KET-BOID FITCHES IS FLYIN' IN THE AIR -
INCREDIBLE.
BILLIVIT OR NOT.
SURE, GIT GOIN' - YOU'RE BLOCKIN' TRAFFIC.
Copr. 1938, King Features Syndicate, Inc., World rights reserved
HERRIMAN
1-30

January 30th, 1938.

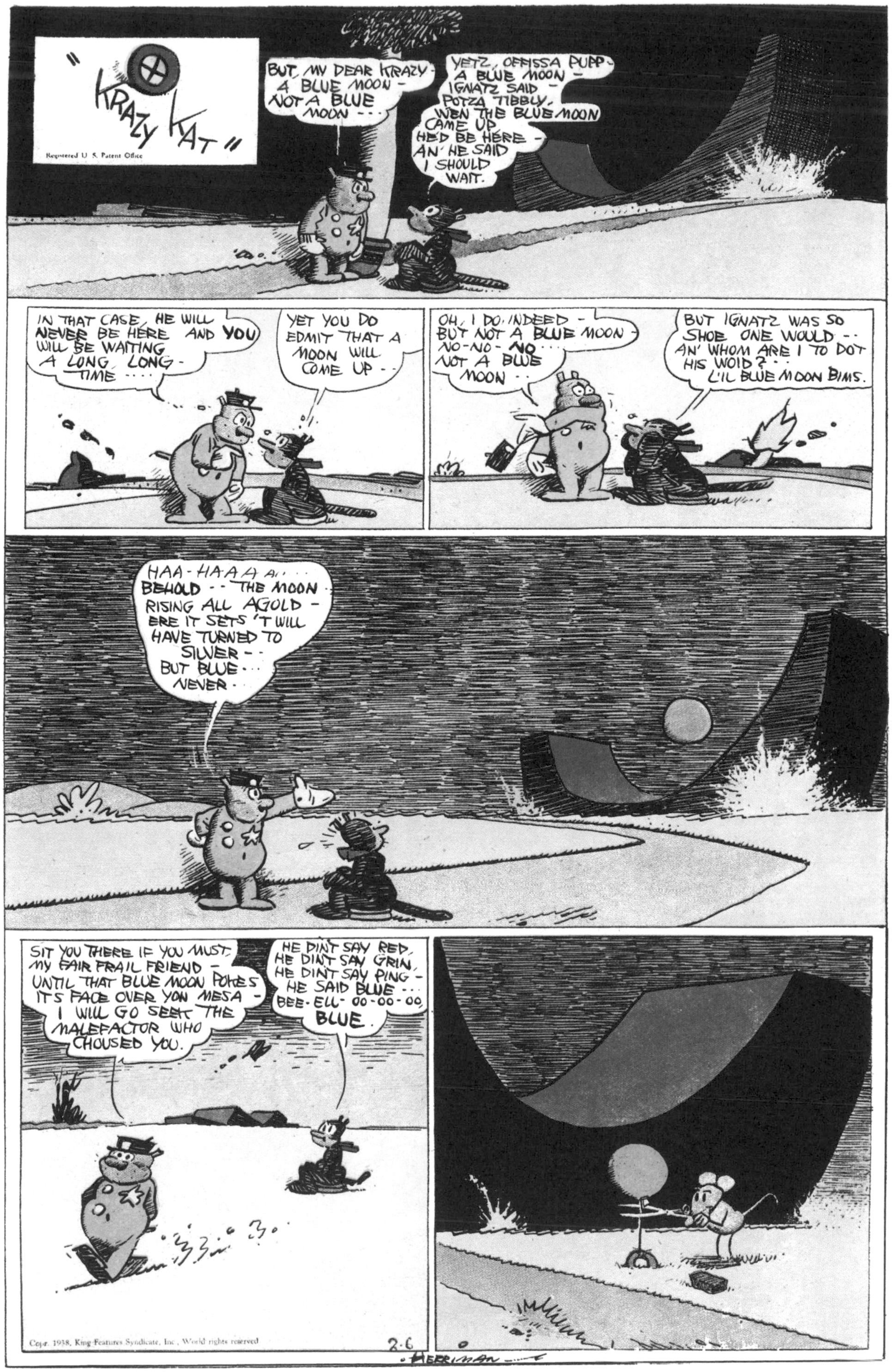
"KRAZY KAT"
Registered U. S. Patent Office
BUT, MY DEAR KRAZY - A BLUE MOON - NOT A BLUE MOON - - -
YETZ, OFFISSA PUPP - A BLUE MOON - IGNATZ SAID - POTZA TIBBLY, WEN THE BLUE MOON CAME UP HE'D BE HERE - AN' HE SAID I SHOULD WAIT.
IN THAT CASE, HE WILL NEVER BE HERE AND YOU WILL BE WAITING A LONG, LONG - TIME - - - -
YET YOU DO EDMIT THAT A MOON WILL COME UP - -
OH, I DO INDEED - BUT NOT A BLUE MOON - NO-NO - NO - - - NOT A BLUE MOON - -
BUT IGNATZ WAS SO SHOE ONE WOULD - - AN' WHOM ARE I TO DOT HIS WOID? - - L'IL BLUE MOON BIMS.
HAA-HAAAA A - - - BEHOLD - - THE MOON RISING ALL AGOLD - ERE IT SETS 'T WILL HAVE TURNED TO SILVER - - BUT BLUE - - - NEVER - -
SIT YOU THERE IF YOU MUST, MY FAIR FRAIL FRIEND - UNTIL THAT BLUE MOON POKES ITS FACE OVER YON MESA - I WILL GO SEEK THE MALEFACTOR WHO CHOUSED YOU.
HE DIN'T SAY RED, HE DIN'T SAY GRIN, HE DIN'T SAY PING - HE SAID BLUE - - - BEE - ELL - OO-OO-OO, BLUE.
Copr. 1938, King Features Syndicate, Inc., World rights reserved
2-6
HERRIMAN

February 6th, 1938.

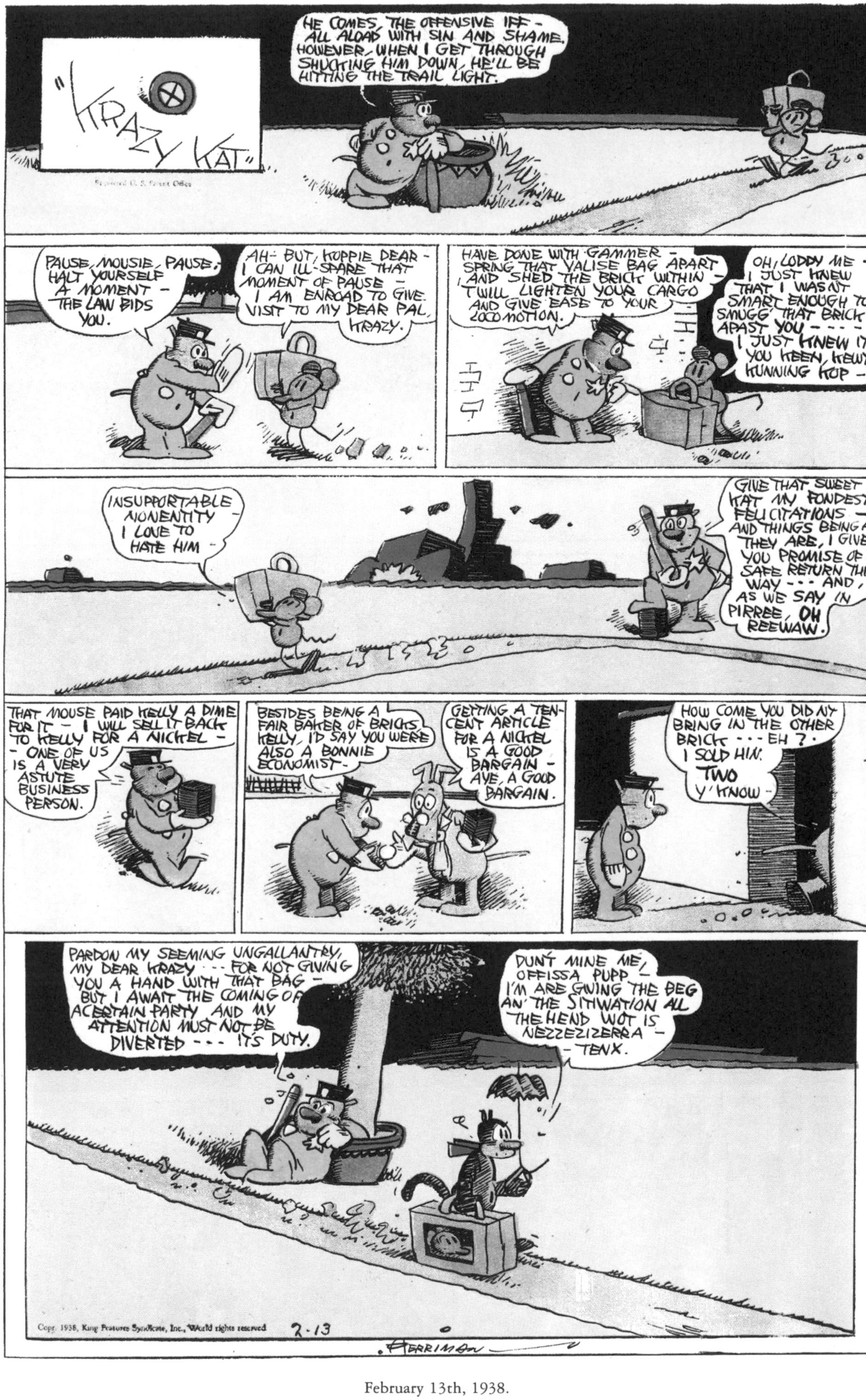
"KRAZY KAT"
Registered U. S. Patent Office
HE COMES, THE OFFENSIVE IFF - ALL ALOAD WITH SIN AND SHAME. HOWEVER, WHEN I GET THROUGH SHUCKING HIM DOWN, HE'LL BE HITTING THE TRAIL LIGHT.
PAUSE, MOUSIE, PAUSE, HALT YOURSELF A MOMENT - THE LAW BIDS YOU.
AH- BUT, KOPPIE DEAR - I CAN ILL-SPARE THAT MOMENT OF PAUSE - I AM ENROAD TO GIVE VISIT TO MY DEAR PAL KRAZY.
HAVE DONE WITH GAMMER - SPRING THAT VALISE BAG APART AND SHED THE BRICK WITHIN - T'WILL LIGHTEN YOUR CARGO AND GIVE EASE TO YOUR LOCOMOTION.
OH, LODDY ME - I JUST KNEW THAT I WASN'T SMART ENOUGH TO SMUGG' THAT BRICK APAST YOU - - - I JUST KNEW IT, YOU KEEN, KEWT, KUNNING KOP -
INSUPPORTABLE NONENTITY - I LOVE TO HATE HIM -
GIVE THAT SWEET KAT MY FONDEST FELICITATIONS - AND THINGS BEING AS THEY ARE, I GIVE YOU PROMISE OF A SAFE RETURN THIS WAY - - - AND, AS WE SAY IN PIRREE, OH REEWAW.
THAT MOUSE PAID KELLY A DIME FOR IT - I WILL SELL IT BACK TO KELLY FOR A NICKEL - - ONE OF US IS A VERY ASTUTE BUSINESS PERSON.
BESIDES BEING A FAIR BAKER OF BRICKS, KELLY, I'D SAY YOU WERE ALSO A BONNIE ECONOMIST -
GETTING A TEN-CENT ARTICLE FOR A NICKEL IS A GOOD BARGAIN - AYE, A GOOD BARGAIN.
HOW COME YOU DID NT BRING IN THE OTHER BRICK - - - EH ? - I SOLD HIM TWO Y'KNOW -
PARDON MY SEEMING UNGALLANTRY, MY DEAR KRAZY - - - FOR NOT GIVING YOU A HAND WITH THAT BAG - BUT I AWAIT THE COMING OF A CERTAIN PARTY AND MY ATTENTION MUST NOT BE DIVERTED - - - IT'S DUTY.
DUN'T MINE ME, OFFISSA PUPP - I'M ARE GIVING THE BEG AN' THE SITIWATION ALL THE HEND WOT IS NEZZEZIZERRA - - TENX.
Copr. 1938, King Features Syndicate, Inc., World rights reserved
2-13
HERRIMAN

February 13th, 1938.

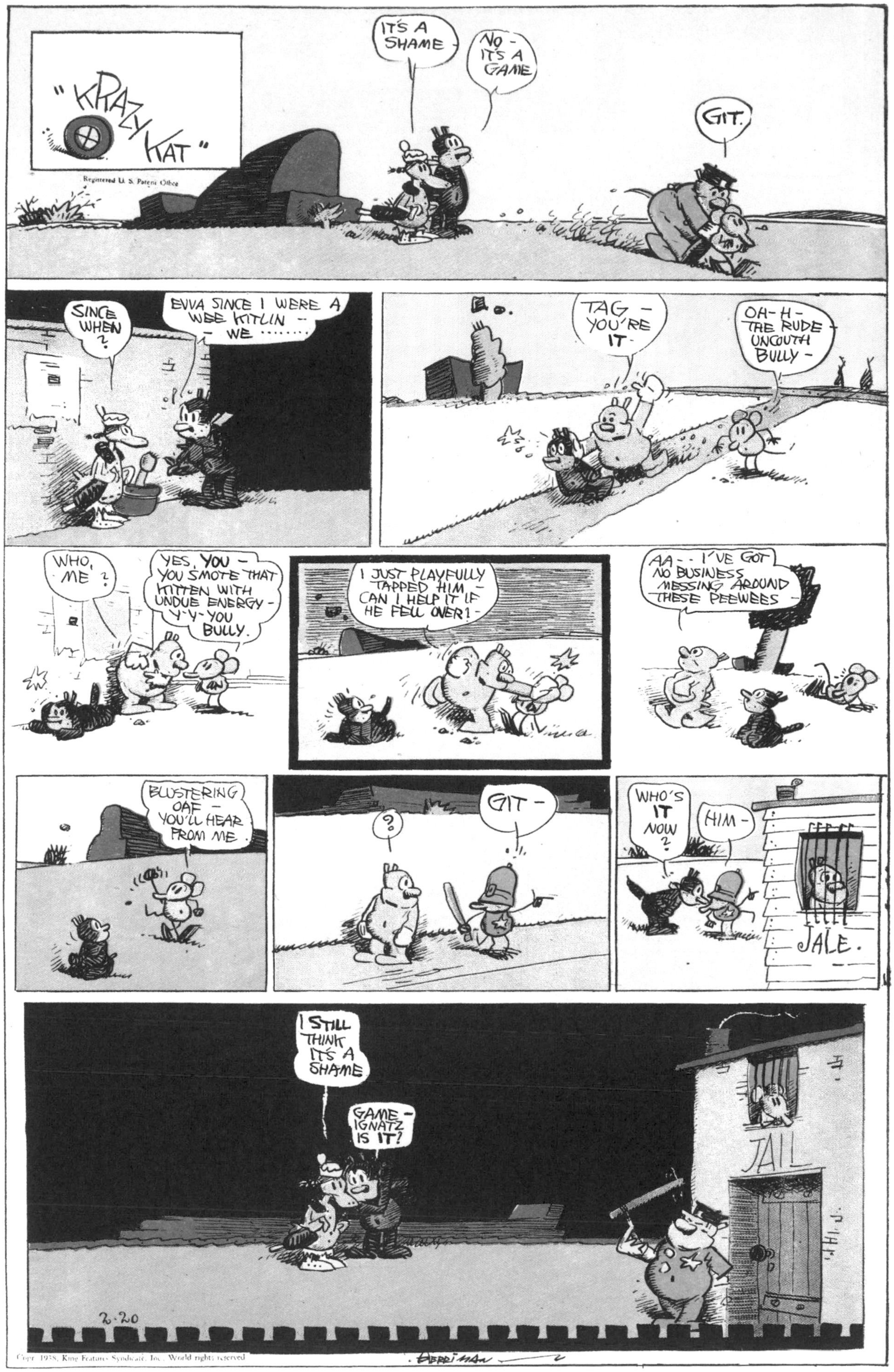
"KRAZY KAT"
Registered U. S. Patent Office
IT'S A SHAME
NO - IT'S A GAME
GIT.
SINCE WHEN ?
EVVA SINCE I WERE A WEE KITLIN - - WE ....
TAG - YOU'RE IT -
OH-H- THE RUDE UNCOUTH BULLY -
WHO, ME ?
YES, YOU - YOU SMOTE THAT KITTEN WITH UNDUE ENERGY - Y-Y-YOU BULLY.
I JUST PLAYFULLY TAPPED HIM - CAN I HELP IT IF HE FELL OVER ? -
AA - - I'VE GOT NO BUSINESS MESSING AROUND THESE PEEWEES -
BLUSTERING OAF - YOU'LL HEAR FROM ME.
?
GIT -
WHO'S IT NOW ?
HIM -
JALE.
I STILL THINK IT'S A SHAME
GAME - IGNATZ IS IT?
JAIL
2·20
Copr. 1938, King Features Syndicate, Inc., World rights reserved
HERRIMAN

February 20th, 1938.

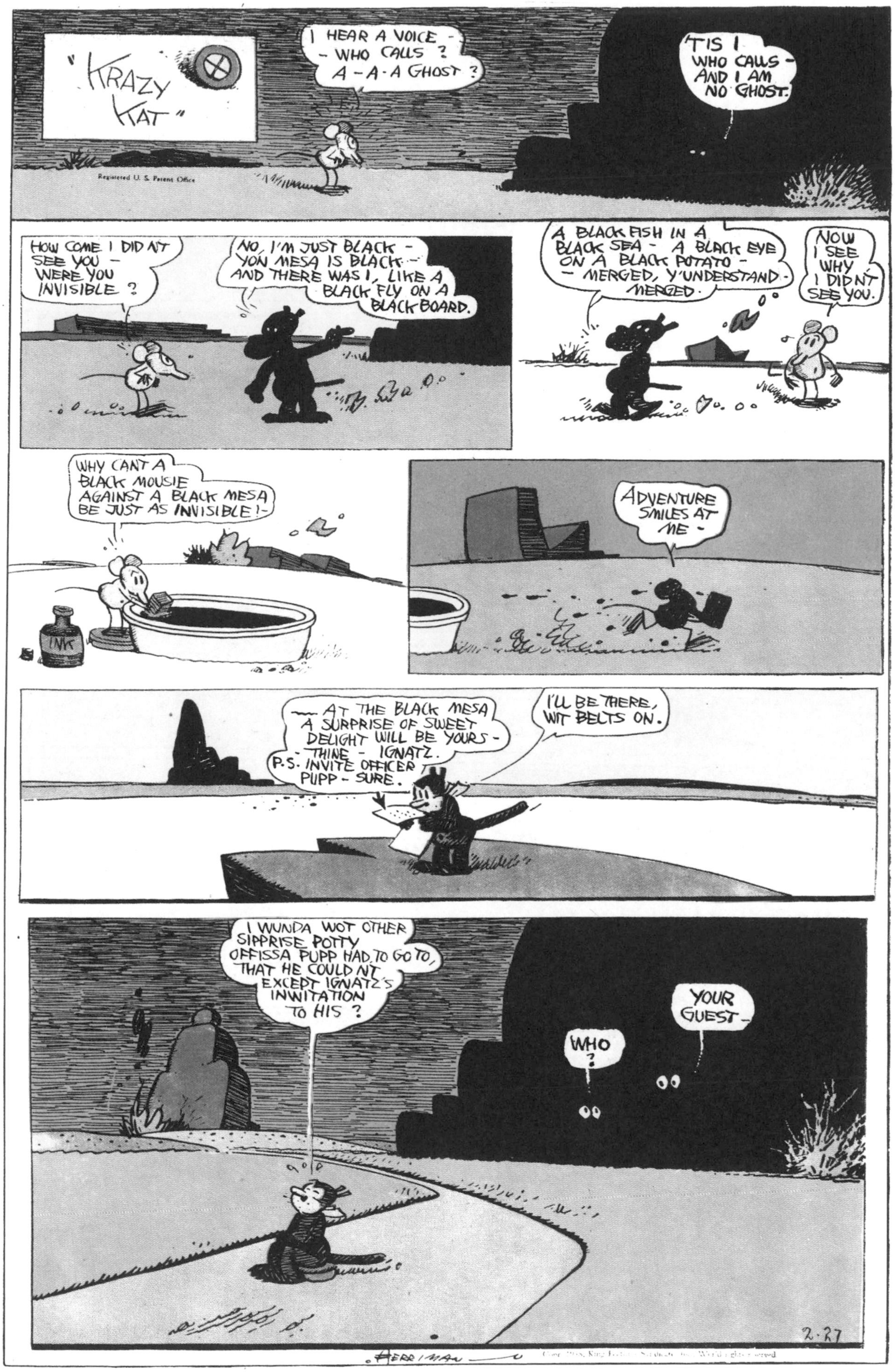
"KRAZY KAT"
Registered U. S. Patent Office
I HEAR A VOICE - - WHO CALLS ? A - A - A GHOST ?
'TIS I WHO CALLS - AND I AM NO GHOST.
HOW COME I DID N'T SEE YOU - WERE YOU INVISIBLE ?
NO, I'M JUST BLACK - YON MESA IS BLACK - AND THERE WAS I, LIKE A BLACK FLY ON A BLACK BOARD.
A BLACK FISH IN A BLACK SEA - A BLACK EYE ON A BLACK POTATO - - MERGED, Y'UNDERSTAND - MERGED.
NOW I SEE WHY I DIDN'T SEE YOU.
WHY CANT A BLACK MOUSIE AGAINST A BLACK MESA BE JUST AS INVISIBLE ! -
INK
ADVENTURE SMILES AT ME -
— AT THE BLACK MESA A SURPRISE OF SWEET DELIGHT WILL BE YOURS - THINE - IGNATZ. P.S. INVITE OFFICER PUPP - SURE.
I'LL BE THERE, WIT BELTS ON.
I WUNDA WOT OTHER SIPPRISE POTTY OFFISSA PUPP HAD TO GO TO, THAT HE COULD N'T EXCEPT IGNATZ'S INWITATION TO HIS ?
YOUR GUEST -
WHO ?
2-27
HERRIMAN

February 27th, 1938.

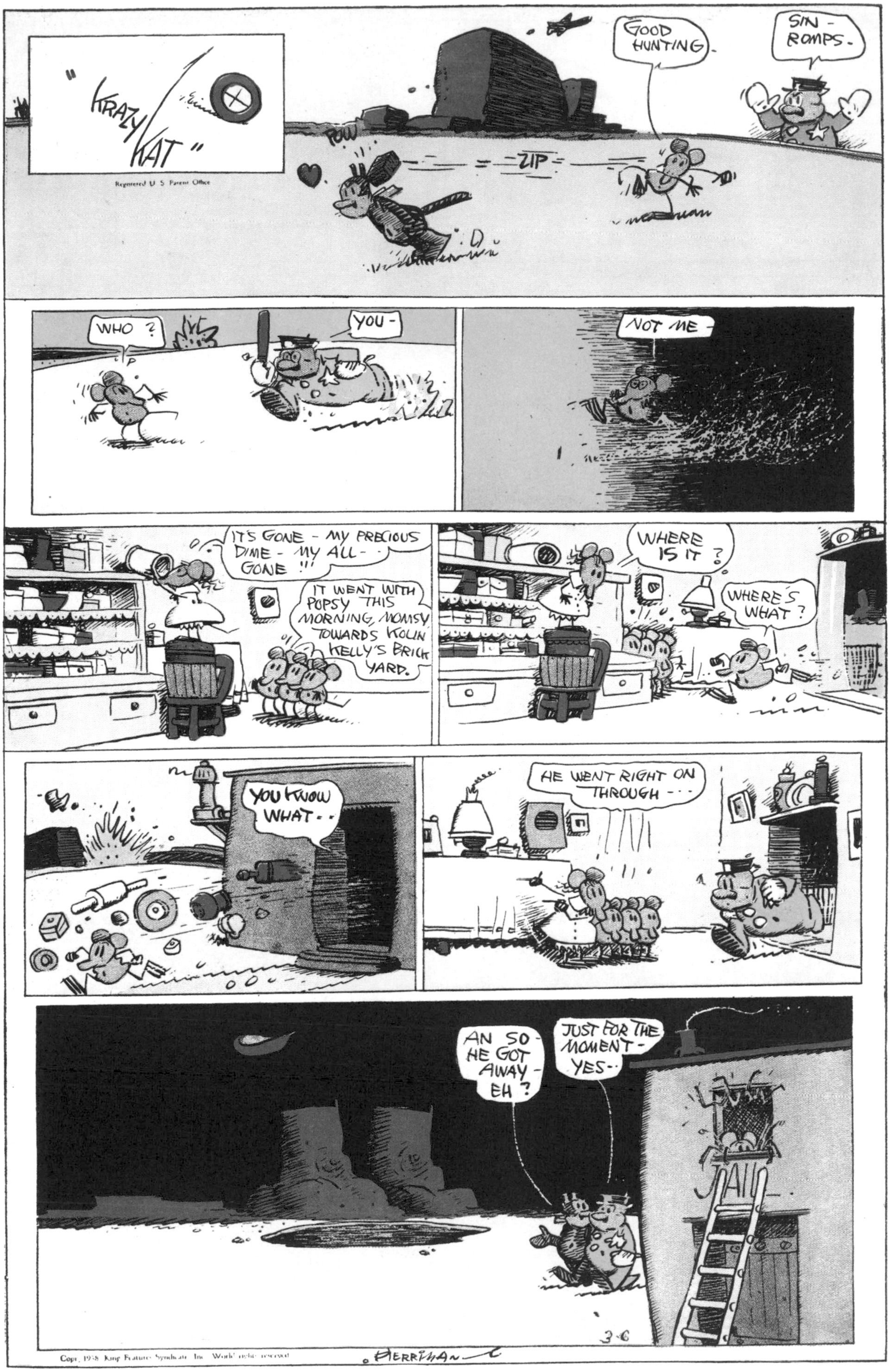
"KRAZY KAT"
Registered U. S. Patent Office
POW
ZIP
GOOD HUNTING
SIN-ROMPS-
WHO ?
YOU-
NOT ME-
IT'S GONE - MY PRECIOUS DIME - MY ALL - GONE !!!
IT WENT WITH POPSY THIS MORNING, MOMSY TOWARDS KOLIN KELLY'S BRICK YARD.
WHERE IS IT ?
WHERE'S WHAT ?
YOU KNOW WHAT - -
HE WENT RIGHT ON THROUGH - - -
AN SO HE GOT AWAY - EH ?
JUST FOR THE MOMENT - YES - -
JAIL
3-6
Copr. 1938 King Features Syndicate, Inc. World rights reserved
HERRIMAN

March 6th, 1938.

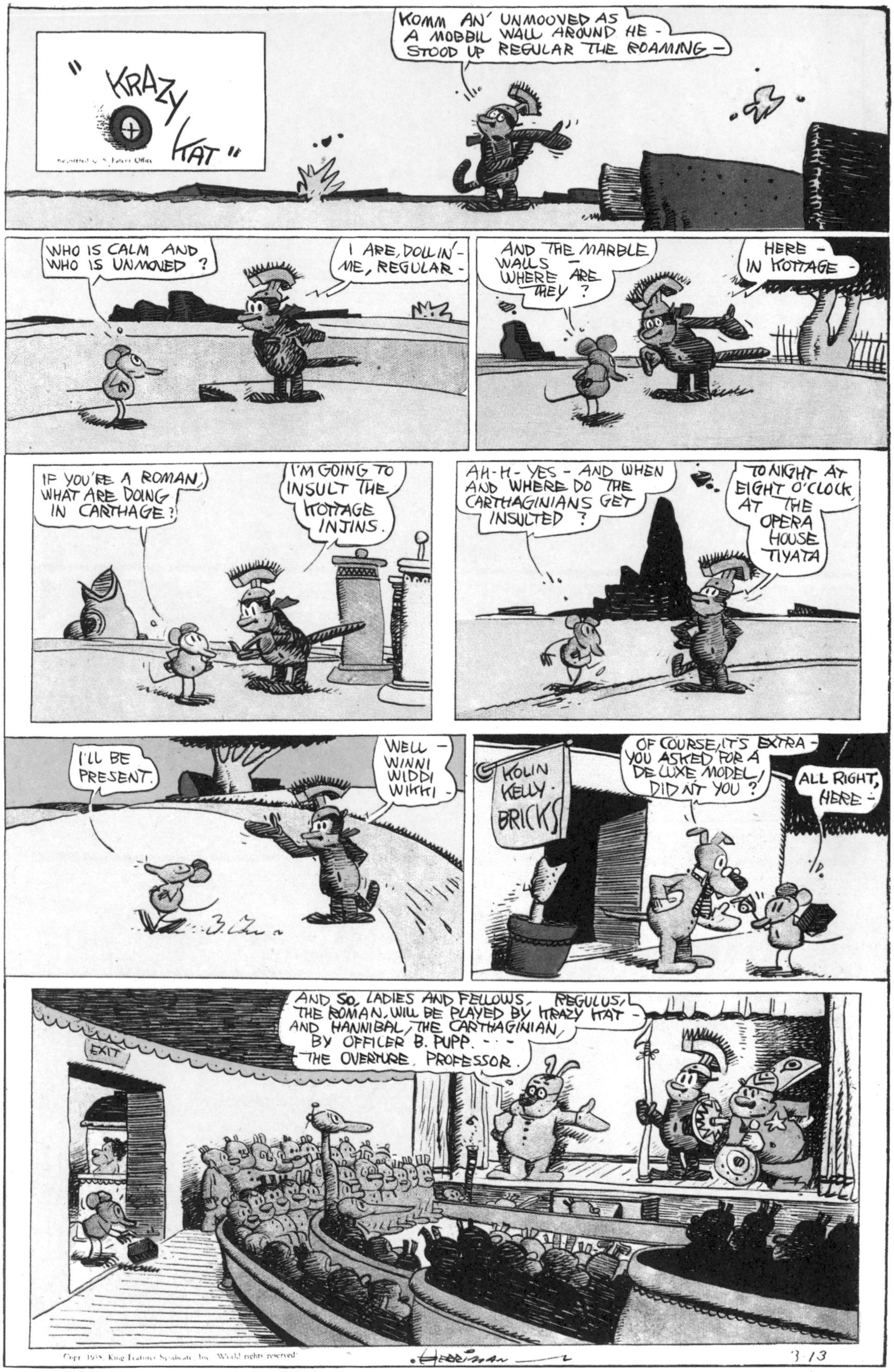
"KRAZY KAT"
KOMM AN' UNMOOVED AS A MOBBIL WALL AROUND HE - STOOD UP REGULAR THE ROAMING -
WHO IS CALM AND WHO IS UNMOVED ?
I ARE, DOLLIN' ME, REGULAR -
AND THE MARBLE WALLS - WHERE ARE THEY ?
HERE - IN KOTTAGE -
IF YOU'RE A ROMAN, WHAT ARE DOING IN CARTHAGE ?
I'M GOING TO INSULT THE KOTTAGE INJINS.
AH-H - YES - AND WHEN AND WHERE DO THE CARTHAGINIANS GET INSULTED ?
TONIGHT AT EIGHT O'CLOCK AT THE OPERA HOUSE TIYATA
I'LL BE PRESENT.
WELL - WINNI WIDDI WIKKI
KOLIN KELLY BRICKS
OF COURSE, IT'S EXTRA - YOU ASKED FOR A DE LUXE MODEL, DIDN'T YOU ?
ALL RIGHT, HERE -
AND SO, LADIES AND FELLOWS, REGULUS, THE ROMAN, WILL BE PLAYED BY KRAZY KAT - AND HANNIBAL, THE CARTHAGINIAN, BY OFFICER B. PUPP. - - THE OVERTURE, PROFESSOR.
EXIT
Copr. 1938, King Features Syndicate, Inc., World rights reserved.
HERRIMAN
3-13

March 13th, 1938.

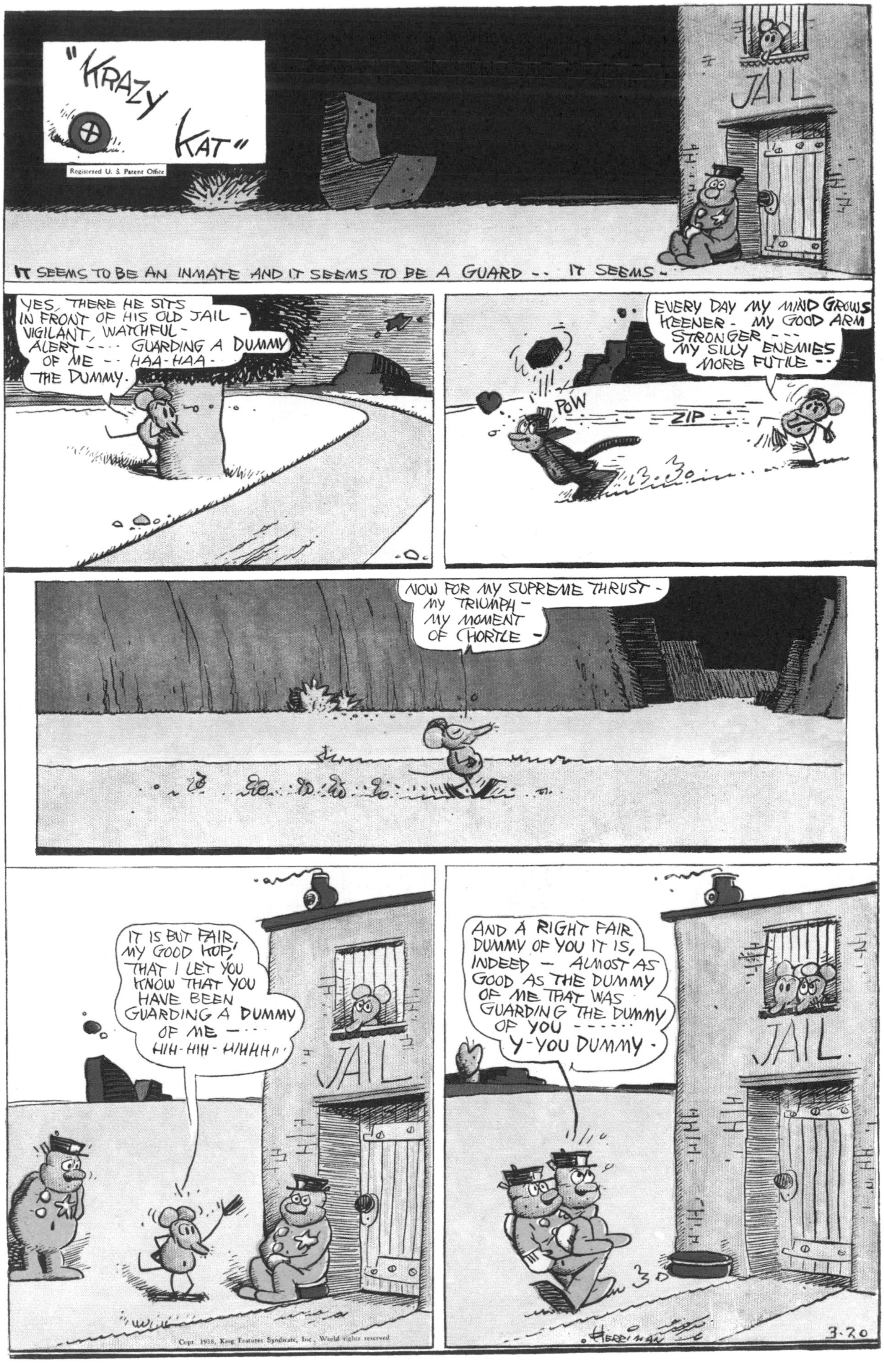
"KRAZY KAT"
Registered U. S. Patent Office
JAIL
IT SEEMS TO BE AN INMATE AND IT SEEMS TO BE A GUARD -- IT SEEMS -
YES, THERE HE SITS IN FRONT OF HIS OLD JAIL - VIGILANT, WATCHFUL - ALERT --- GUARDING A DUMMY OF ME -- HAA-HAA - THE DUMMY.
EVERY DAY MY MIND GROWS KEENER - MY GOOD ARM STRONGER --- MY SILLY ENEMIES MORE FUTILE --
POW
ZIP
NOW FOR MY SUPREME THRUST - MY TRIUMPH - MY MOMENT OF CHORTLE -
IT IS BUT FAIR, MY GOOD KOP, THAT I LET YOU KNOW THAT YOU HAVE BEEN GUARDING A DUMMY OF ME ---- HIH-HIH- HIHHH
JAIL
AND A RIGHT FAIR DUMMY OF YOU IT IS, INDEED - ALMOST AS GOOD AS THE DUMMY OF ME THAT WAS GUARDING THE DUMMY OF YOU ------ Y-YOU DUMMY -
JAIL
Copr. 1938, King Features Syndicate, Inc., World rights reserved
HERRIMAN
3-20

March 20th, 1938.

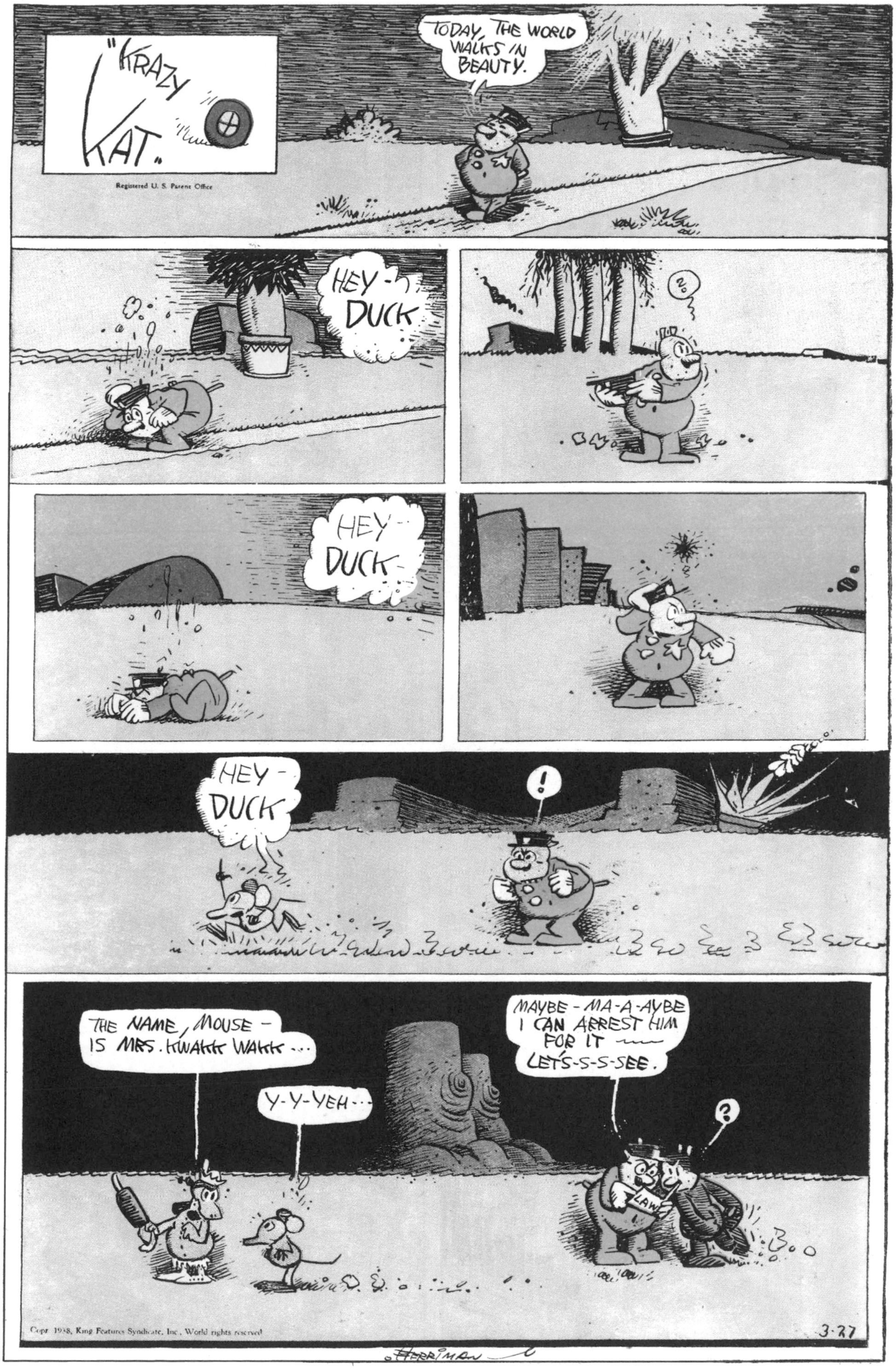
"KRAZY KAT."
Registered U. S. Patent Office
TODAY, THE WORLD WALKS IN BEAUTY.
HEY - DUCK
HEY - DUCK
HEY - DUCK
THE NAME, MOUSE - IS MRS. KWAKK WAKK ...
Y-Y-YEH ...
MAYBE - MA-A-AYBE I CAN ARREST HIM FOR IT ~~ LET'S-S-S-SEE.
LAW
Copr. 1938, King Features Syndicate, Inc., World rights reserved
3-27
HERRIMAN

March 27th, 1938.

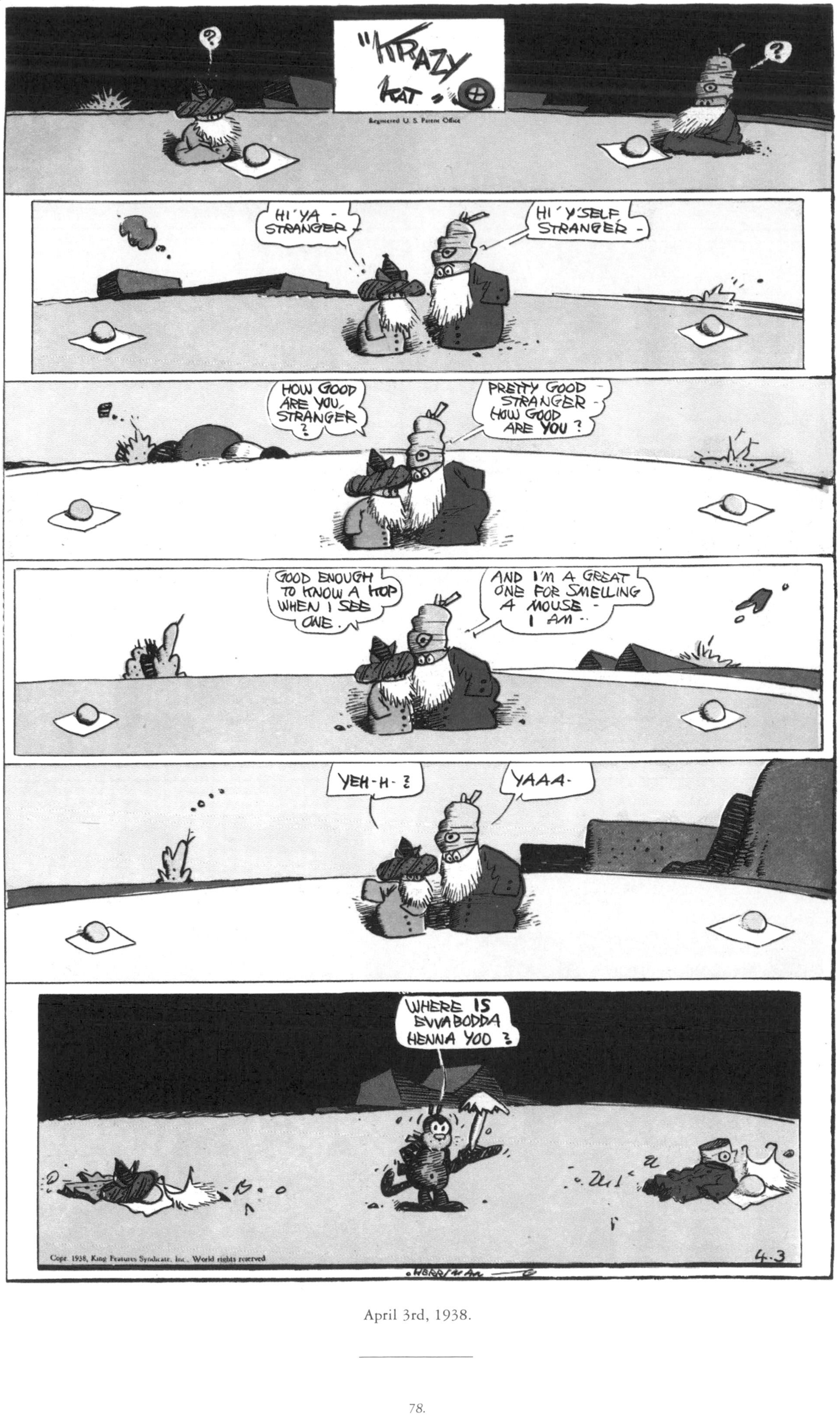
"Krazy Kat"
Registered U. S. Patent Office
?
?
HI 'YA - STRANGER -
HI 'Y'SELF STRANGER -
HOW GOOD ARE YOU, STRANGER ?
PRETTY GOOD - STRANGER - HOW GOOD ARE YOU ?
GOOD ENOUGH TO KNOW A KOP WHEN I SEE ONE.
AND I'M A GREAT ONE FOR SMELLING A MOUSE - I AM -
YEH-H- ?
YAAA-
WHERE IS EVVABODDA HENNA YOO ?
Copr. 1938, King Features Syndicate, Inc., World rights reserved
4.3
HERRIMAN

April 3rd, 1938.

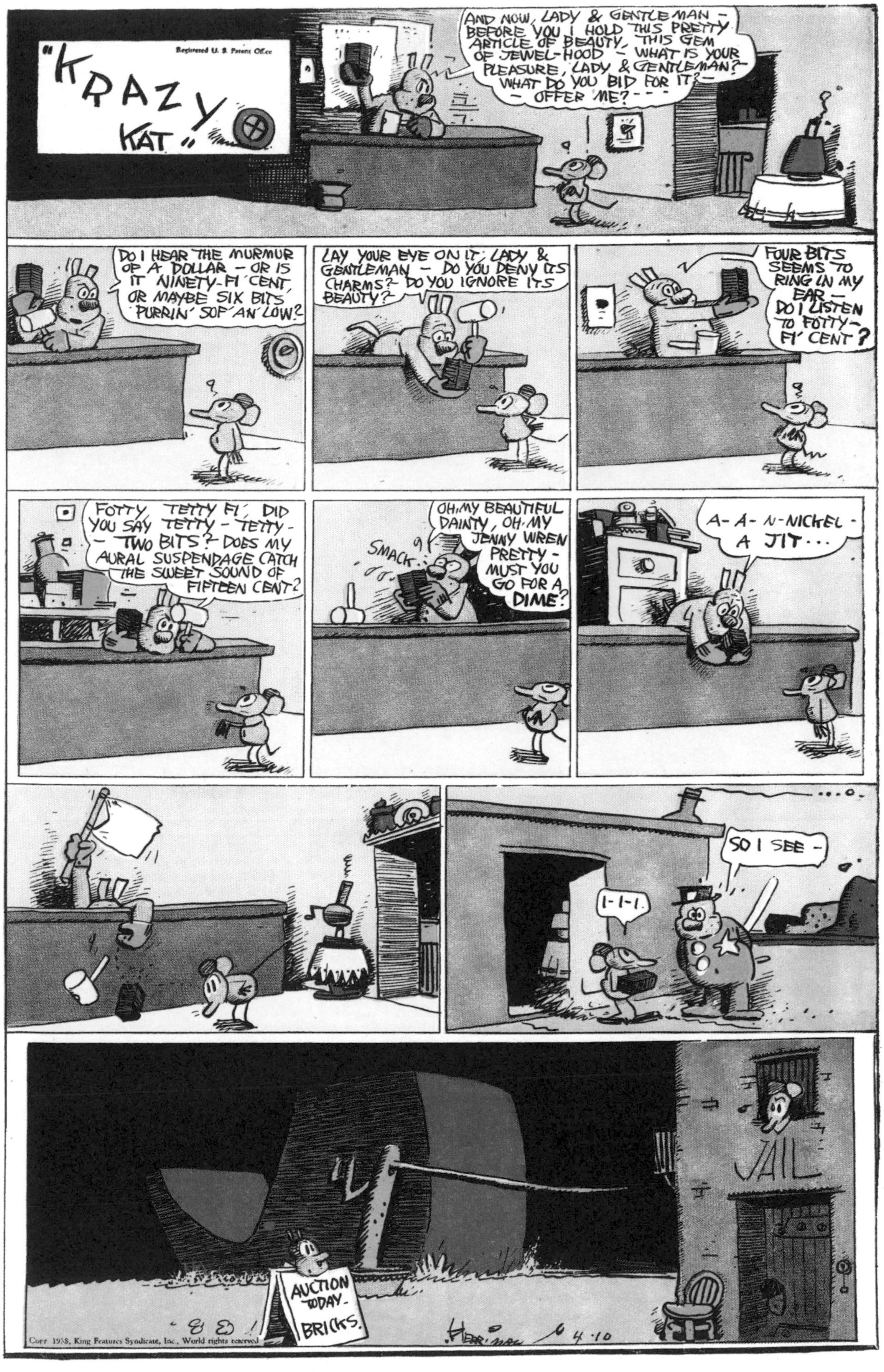
Registered U. S. Patent Office
"KRAZY KAT"
AND NOW, LADY & GENTLEMAN - BEFORE YOU I HOLD THIS PRETTY ARTICLE OF BEAUTY, THIS GEM OF JEWEL-HOOD - WHAT IS YOUR PLEASURE, LADY & GENTLEMAN? - WHAT DO YOU BID FOR IT? - OFFER ME? - - -
DO I HEAR THE MURMUR OF A DOLLAR - OR IS IT NINETY-FI' CENT, OR MAYBE SIX BITS 'PURRIN' SOF' AN' LOW?
LAY YOUR EYE ON IT, LADY & GENTLEMAN - DO YOU DENY ITS CHARMS? - DO YOU IGNORE ITS BEAUTY?
FOUR BITS SEEMS TO RING IN MY EAR - DO I LISTEN TO FOTTY-FI' CENT?
FOTTY, TETTY FI', DID YOU SAY TETTY - TETTY - TWO BITS? - DOES MY AURAL SUSPENDAGE CATCH THE SWEET SOUND OF FIFTEEN CENT?
SMACK
OH, MY BEAUTIFUL DAINTY, OH, MY JENNY WREN PRETTY - MUST YOU GO FOR A DIME?
A-A-N-NICKEL - A JIT...
SO I SEE -
I-I-I.
JAIL
AUCTION TODAY - BRICKS.
Copr. 1938, King Features Syndicate, Inc., World rights reserved
Herriman 4-10

April 10th, 1938.

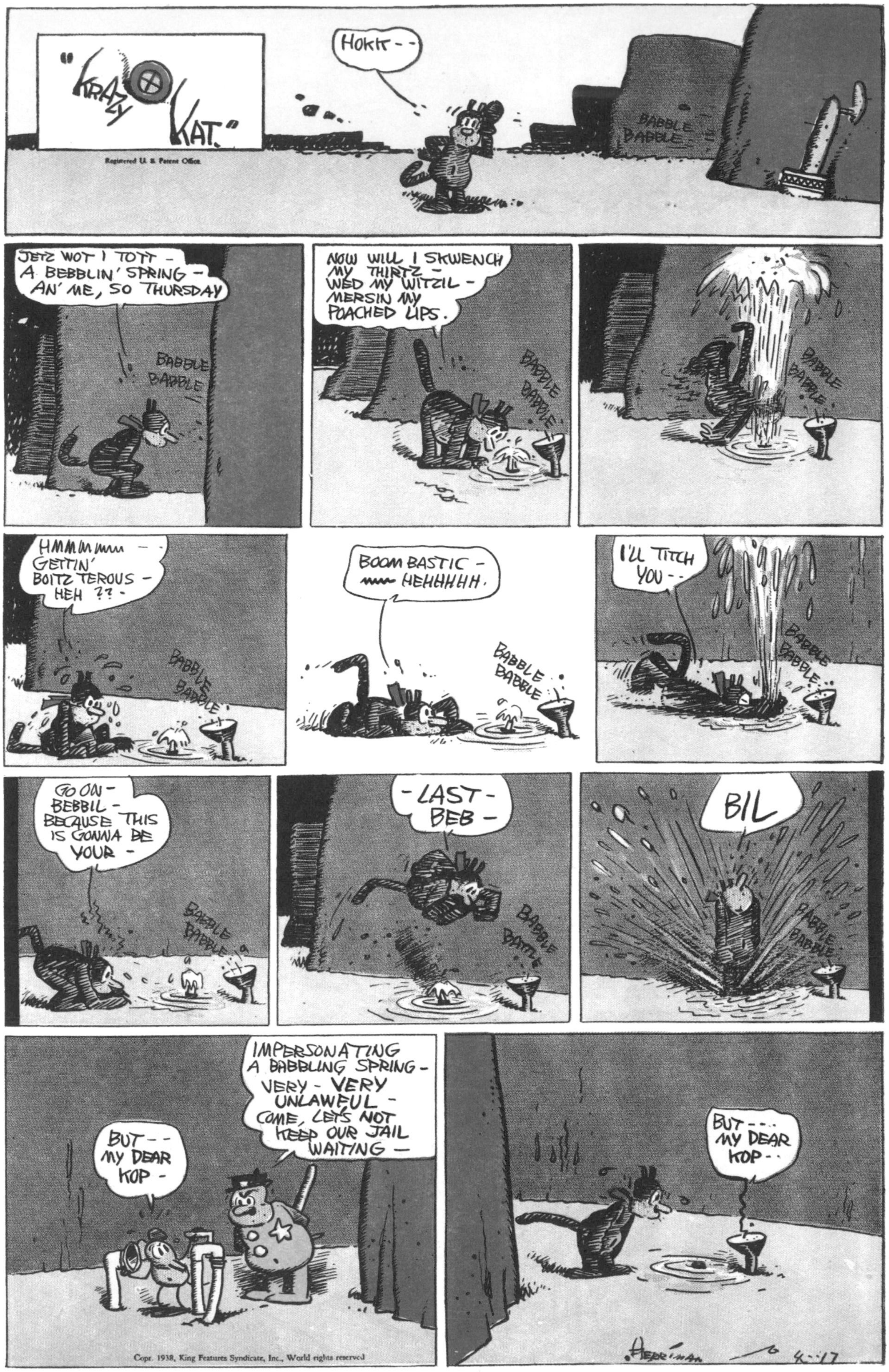
"KRAZY KAT."
Registered U. S. Patent Office
HOKK--
BABBLE BABBLE
JETZ WOT I TOTT - A BEBBLIN' SPRING - AN' ME, SO THURSDAY
BABBLE BABBLE
NOW WILL I SKWENCH MY THIRTZ - WED MY WITZIL - MERSIN MY POACHED LIPS.
BABBLE BABBLE
BABBLE BABBLE
HMMMMMM - GETTIN' BOITZ TEROUS - HEH ??
BABBLE BABBLE
BOOM BASTIC - HEHHHHH.
BABBLE BABBLE
I'LL TITCH YOU--
BABBLE BABBLE
GO ON - BEBBIL - BECAUSE THIS IS GONNA BE YOUR -
BABBLE BABBLE
-LAST- BEB -
BIL
BABBLE BABBLE
BUT-- MY DEAR KOP -
IMPERSONATING A BABBLING SPRING - VERY - VERY UNLAWFUL - COME, LET'S NOT KEEP OUR JAIL WAITING -
Copr. 1938, King Features Syndicate, Inc., World rights reserved
BUT--- MY DEAR KOP--
HERRIMAN 4-17

April 17th, 1938.

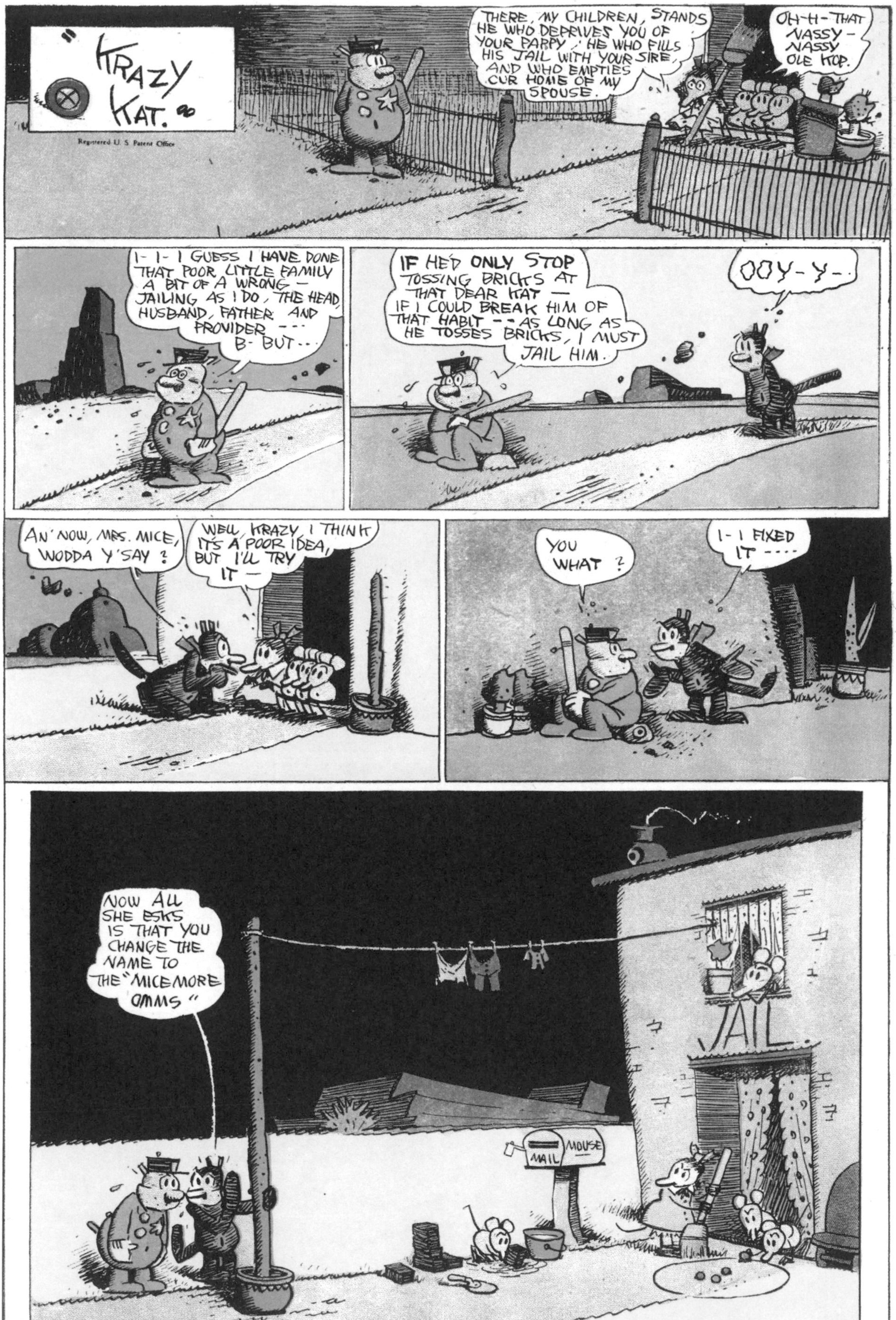
"KRAZY KAT."
Registered U. S. Patent Office
THERE, MY CHILDREN, STANDS HE WHO DEPRIVES YOU OF YOUR PAPPY, HE WHO FILLS HIS JAIL WITH YOUR SIRE, AND WHO EMPTIES OUR HOME OF MY SPOUSE.
OH-H-THAT NASSY-NASSY OLE KOP.
I- I- I GUESS I HAVE DONE THAT POOR, LITTLE FAMILY A BIT OF A WRONG - JAILING AS I DO, THE HEAD, HUSBAND, FATHER AND PROVIDER --- B- BUT--
IF HE'D ONLY STOP TOSSING BRICKS AT THAT DEAR KAT - IF I COULD BREAK HIM OF THAT HABIT -- AS LONG AS HE TOSSES BRICKS, I MUST JAIL HIM.
OOY-Y-.
AN' NOW, MRS. MICE, WODDA Y'SAY ?
WELL, KRAZY, I THINK IT'S A POOR IDEA, BUT I'LL TRY IT -
YOU WHAT ?
I- I FIXED IT ----
NOW ALL SHE ESKS IS THAT YOU CHANGE THE NAME TO THE "MICEMORE OMMS"
JAIL
MAIL
MOUSE
4·24
HERRIMAN

April 24th, 1938.

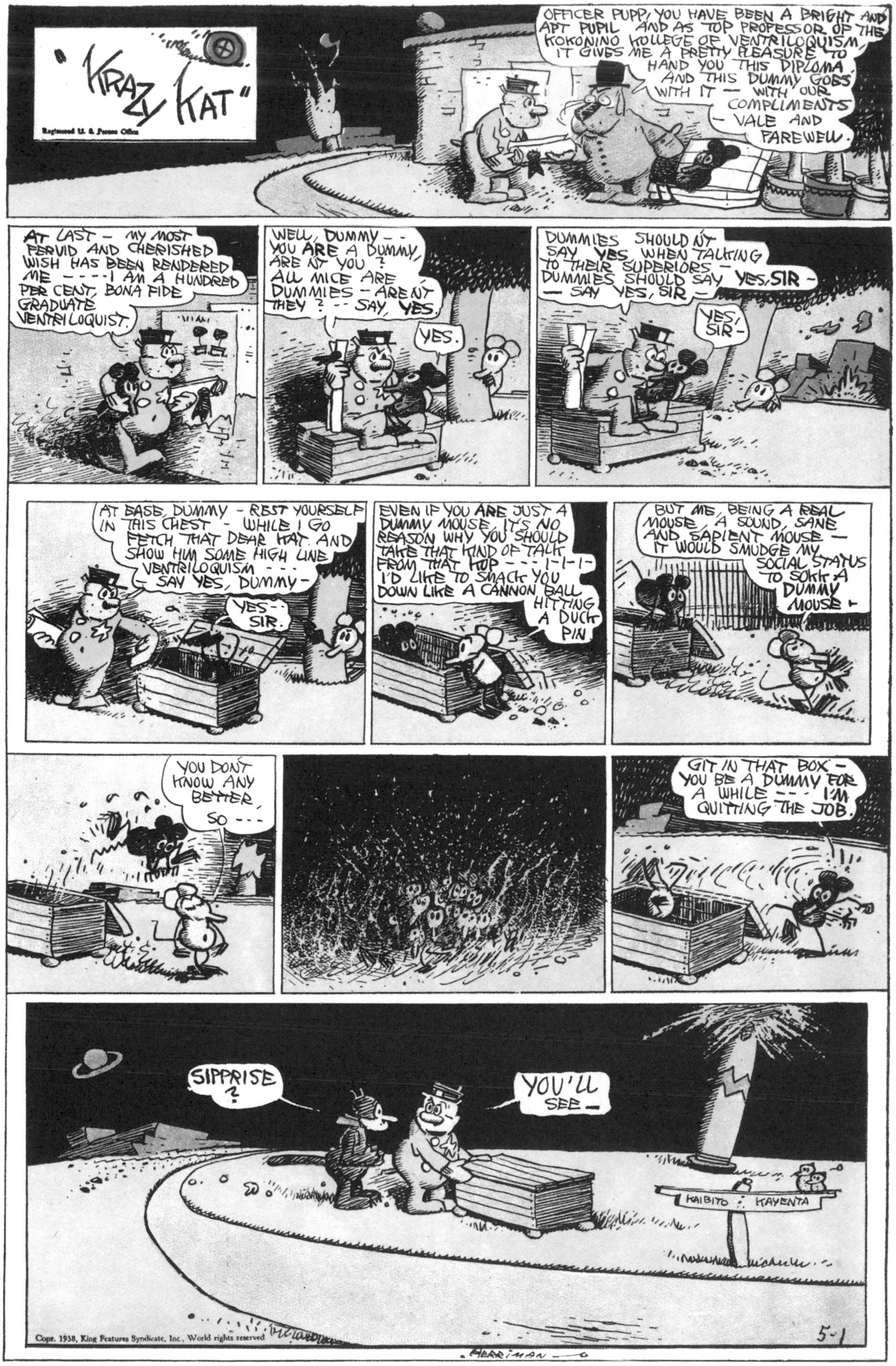
"KRAZY KAT"
Registered U.S. Patent Office
OFFICER PUPP, YOU HAVE BEEN A BRIGHT AND APT PUPIL AND AS TOP PROFESSOR OF THE KOKONINO KOLLEGE OF VENTRILOQUISM, IT GIVES ME A PRETTY PLEASURE TO HAND YOU THIS DIPLOMA AND THIS DUMMY GOES WITH IT -- WITH OUR COMPLIMENTS - VALE AND FAREWELL.
AT LAST - MY MOST FERVID AND CHERISHED WISH HAS BEEN RENDERED ME ----I AM A HUNDRED PER CENT, BONA FIDE GRADUATE VENTRILOQUIST.
WELL, DUMMY -- YOU ARE A DUMMY, ARE N'T YOU? ALL MICE ARE DUMMIES - AREN'T THEY? -- SAY, YES.
YES.
DUMMIES SHOULD N'T SAY YES WHEN TALKING TO THEIR SUPERIORS - DUMMIES SHOULD SAY YES, SIR - - SAY YES, SIR -
YES, SIR-
AT EASE, DUMMY - REST YOURSELF IN THIS CHEST - WHILE I GO FETCH THAT DEAR KAT AND SHOW HIM SOME HIGH LINE VENTRILOQUISM --- - SAY YES, DUMMY-
YES- SIR.
EVEN IF YOU ARE JUST A DUMMY MOUSE, IT'S NO REASON WHY YOU SHOULD TAKE THAT KIND OF TALK FROM THAT KOP --- I-I-I- I'D LIKE TO SMACK YOU DOWN LIKE A CANNON BALL HITTING A DUCK PIN
BUT ME, BEING A REAL MOUSE, A SOUND, SANE AND SAPIENT MOUSE - IT WOULD SMUDGE MY SOCIAL STATUS TO SOKK A DUMMY MOUSE -
YOU DON'T KNOW ANY BETTER SO ---
GIT IN THAT BOX - YOU BE A DUMMY FOR A WHILE --- I'M QUITTING THE JOB.
SIPPRISE ?
YOU'LL SEE -
KAIBITO KAYENTA
Copr. 1938, King Features Syndicate, Inc., World rights reserved.
5-1
HERRIMAN

May 1st, 1938.

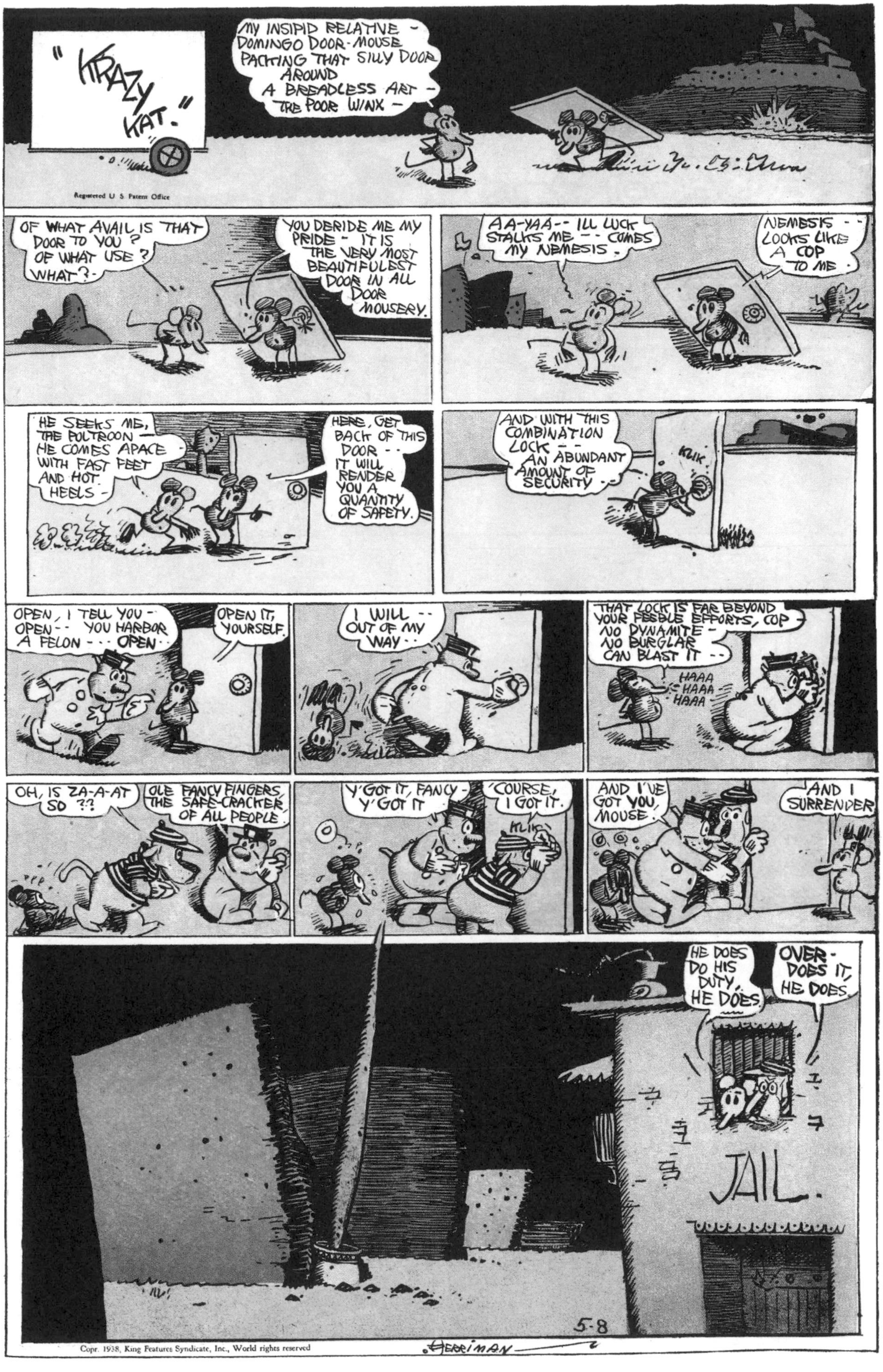
"KRAZY KAT."
Registered U. S. Patent Office
MY INSIPID RELATIVE - DOMINGO DOOR-MOUSE PACKING THAT SILLY DOOR AROUND A BREADLESS ART - THE POOR WINX -
OF WHAT AVAIL IS THAT DOOR TO YOU ? OF WHAT USE ? WHAT ?-
YOU DERIDE ME MY PRIDE - IT IS THE VERY MOST BEAUTIFULEST DOOR IN ALL DOOR MOUSERY.
AA-YAA-- ILL LUCK STALKS ME -- COMES MY NEMESIS.
NEMESIS -- LOOKS LIKE A COP TO ME.
HE SEEKS ME, THE POLTROON - HE COMES APACE WITH FAST FEET AND HOT HEELS -
HERE, GET BACK OF THIS DOOR -- IT WILL RENDER YOU A QUANTITY OF SAFETY.
AND WITH THIS COMBINATION LOCK -- AN ABUNDANT AMOUNT OF SECURITY --
KLIK
OPEN, I TELL YOU - OPEN -- YOU HARBOR A FELON --- OPEN
OPEN IT, YOURSELF.
I WILL -- OUT OF MY WAY --
THAT LOCK IS FAR BEYOND YOUR FEEBLE EFFORTS, COP - NO DYNAMITE - NO BURGLAR CAN BLAST IT --
HAAA HAAA HAAA
OH, IS ZA-A-AT SO ??
OLE FANCY FINGERS, THE SAFE-CRACKER OF ALL PEOPLE.
Y'GOT IT, FANCY - Y'GOT IT
'COURSE, I GOT IT.
KLIK
AND I'VE GOT YOU, MOUSE.
AND I SURRENDER
HE DOES DO HIS DUTY, HE DOES.
OVER-DOES IT, HE DOES.
JAIL.
5-8
Copr. 1938, King Features Syndicate, Inc., World rights reserved
HERRIMAN

May 8th, 1938.

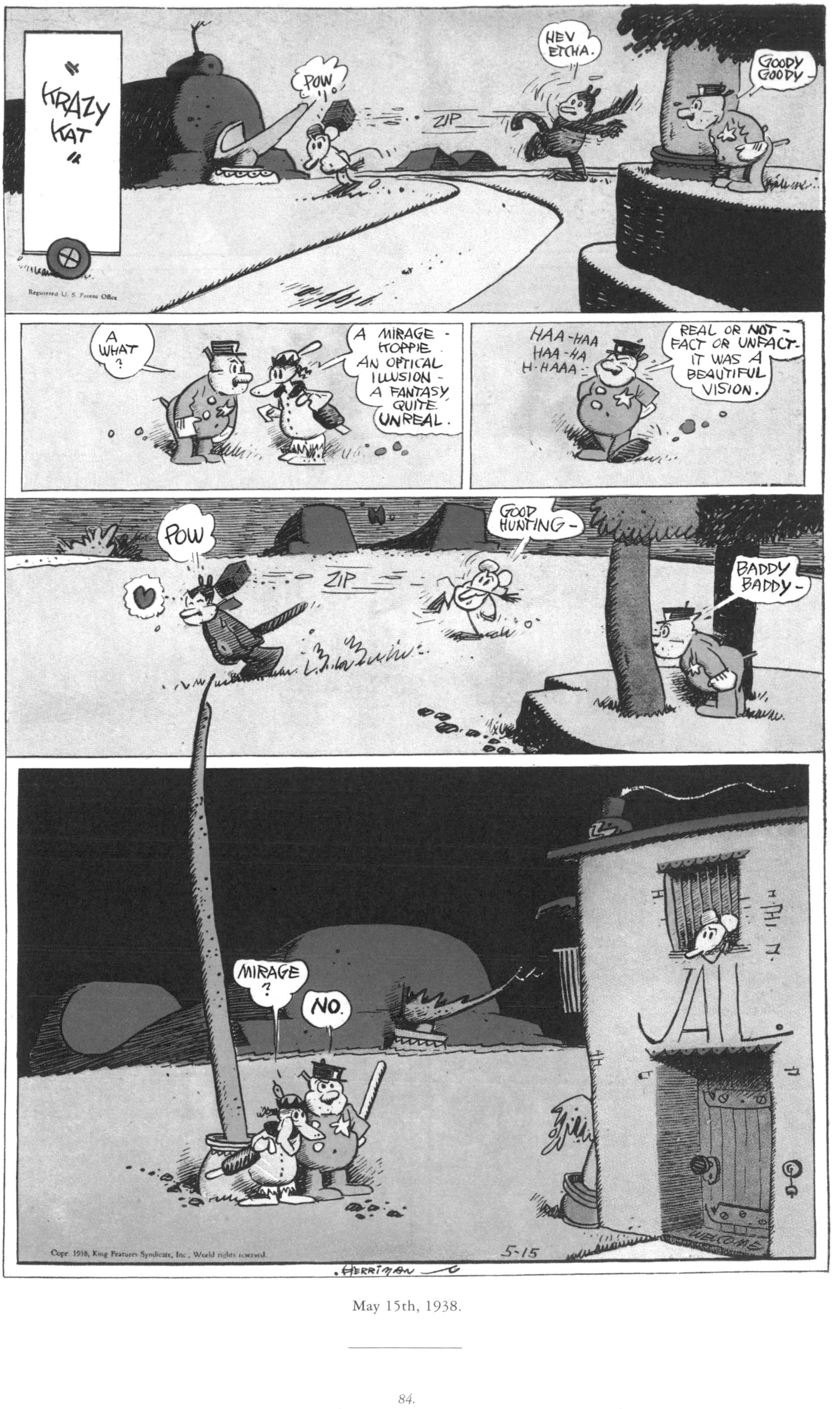
"KRAZY KAT"
Registered U. S. Patent Office
POW
ZIP
HEV ETCHA.
GOODY GOODY -
A WHAT ?
A MIRAGE - KOPPIE - AN OPTICAL ILLUSION - A FANTASY, QUITE UNREAL.
HAA-HAA HAA-HA H-HAAA
REAL OR NOT - FACT OR UNFACT - IT WAS A BEAUTIFUL VISION.
POW
ZIP
GOOD HUNTING -
BADDY BADDY -
MIRAGE ?
NO.
JAIL.
WELCOME
Copr. 1938, King Features Syndicate, Inc., World rights reserved.
5-15
HERRIMAN

May 15th, 1938.

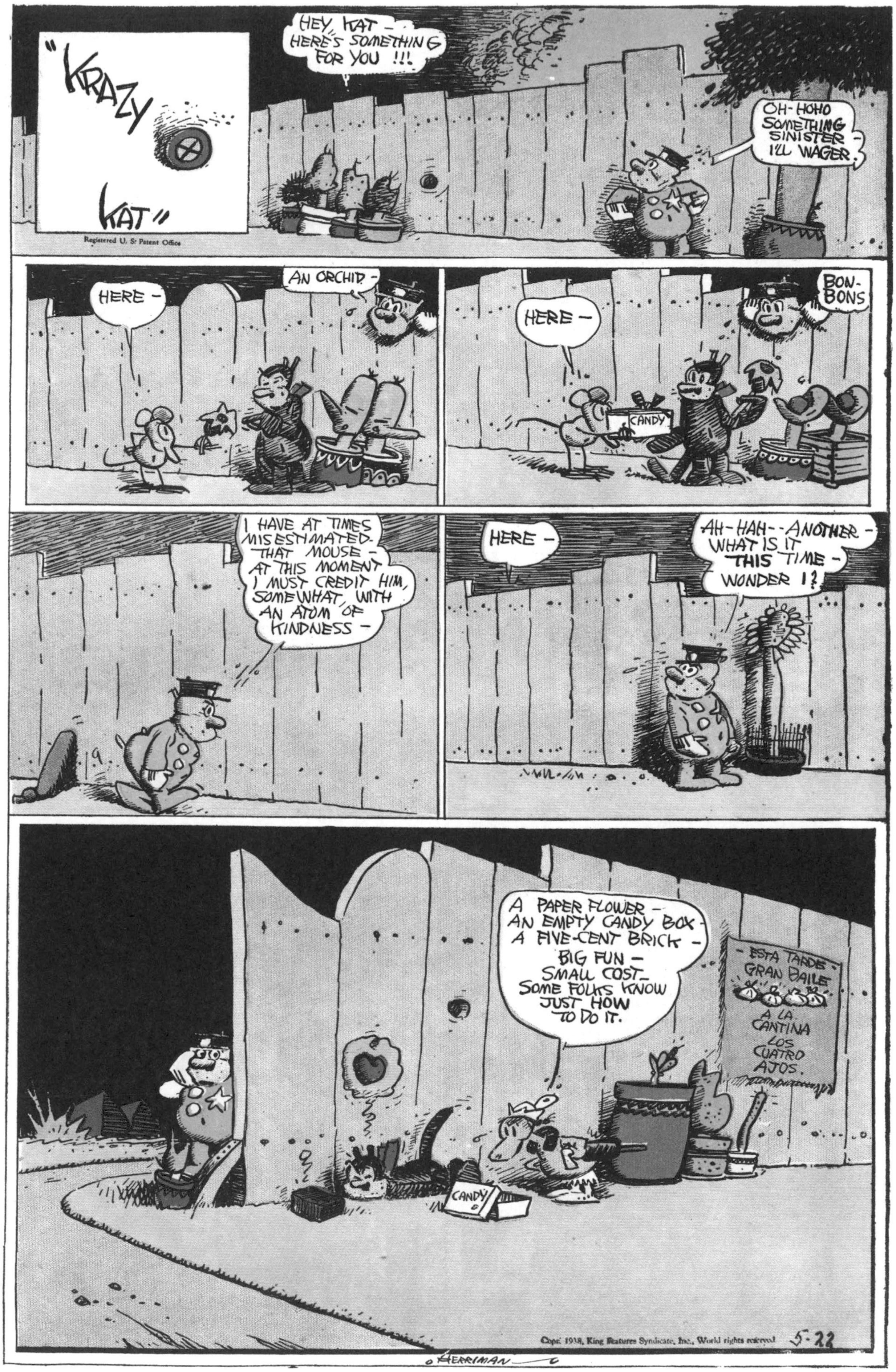
"KRAZY KAT"
Registered U. S. Patent Office
HEY, KAT - HERE'S SOMETHING FOR YOU !!!
OH-HOHO SOMETHING SINISTER - I'LL WAGER.
HERE -
AN ORCHID -
HERE -
BON-BONS
CANDY
I HAVE AT TIMES MISESTIMATED THAT MOUSE - AT THIS MOMENT I MUST CREDIT HIM, SOMEWHAT, WITH AN ATOM OF KINDNESS -
HERE -
AH-HAH - - ANOTHER - WHAT IS IT THIS TIME - WONDER I?
A PAPER FLOWER - AN EMPTY CANDY BOX - A FIVE-CENT BRICK - BIG FUN - SMALL COST - SOME FOLKS KNOW JUST HOW TO DO IT.
ESTA TARDE GRAN BAILE A LA CANTINA LOS CUATRO AJOS.
CANDY
Copr. 1938, King Features Syndicate, Inc., World rights reserved. 5-22
HERRIMAN

May 22nd, 1938.

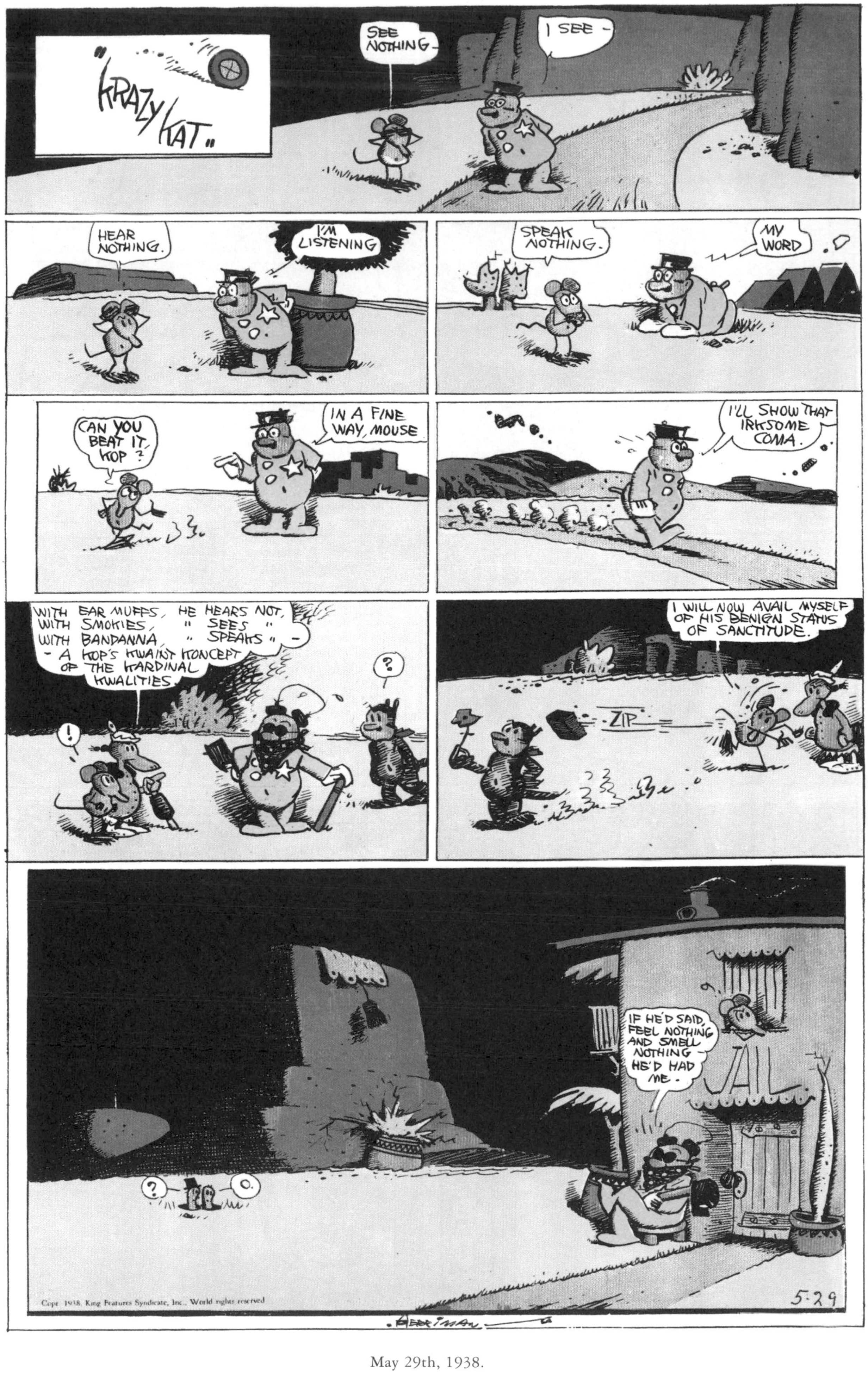
"KRAZY KAT"
SEE NOTHING -
I SEE -
HEAR NOTHING.
I'M LISTENING
SPEAK NOTHING.
MY WORD
CAN YOU BEAT IT, KOP ?
IN A FINE WAY, MOUSE
I'LL SHOW THAT IRKSOME COMA.
WITH EAR MUFFS, HE HEARS NOT, WITH SMOKIES, " SEES " WITH BANDANNA, " SPEAKS " - A KOP'S KWAINT KONCEPT OF THE KARDINAL KWALITIES.
?
!
I WILL NOW AVAIL MYSELF OF HIS BENIGN STATUS OF SANCTITUDE.
ZIP
IF HE'D SAID, FEEL NOTHING AND SMELL NOTHING HE'D HAD ME.
? O.
Copr. 1938, King Features Syndicate, Inc., World rights reserved
5-29

May 29th, 1938.

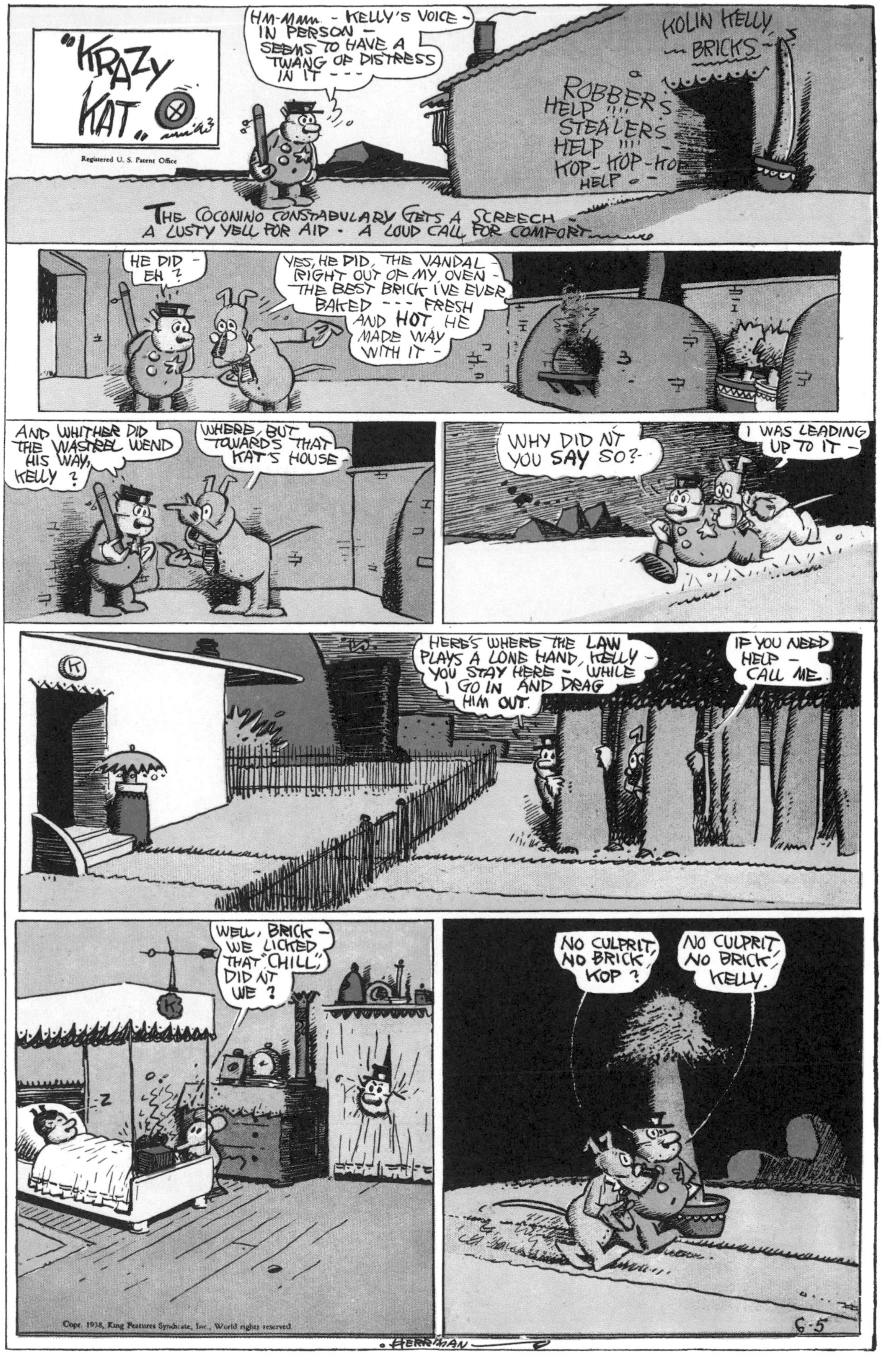

"KRAZY KAT."
Registered U. S. Patent Office
HM-MAM - KELLY'S VOICE - IN PERSON - SEEMS TO HAVE A TWANG OF DISTRESS IN IT - - -
KOLIN KELLY - BRICKS
ROBBERS HELP !!!! STEALERS HELP !!!! - HOP-HOP-HOP HELP - -
THE COCONINO CONSTABULARY GETS A SCREECH - A LUSTY YELL FOR AID - A LOUD CALL FOR COMFORT
HE DID - EH ? -
YES, HE DID, THE VANDAL - RIGHT OUT OF MY OVEN - THE BEST BRICK I'VE EVER BAKED - - - FRESH AND HOT HE MADE WAY WITH IT -
AND WHITHER DID THE WASTREL WEND HIS WAY, KELLY ?
WHERE, BUT TOWARD'S THAT KAT'S HOUSE -
WHY DID N'T YOU SAY SO? -
I WAS LEADING UP TO IT -
HERE'S WHERE THE LAW PLAYS A LONE HAND, KELLY - YOU STAY HERE - WHILE I GO IN AND DRAG HIM OUT.
IF YOU NEED HELP - CALL ME.
WELL, BRICK - WE LICKED THAT "CHILL", DID N'T WE ?
NO CULPRIT, NO BRICK, KOP ?
NO CULPRIT, NO BRICK, KELLY.
Copr. 1938, King Features Syndicate, Inc., World rights reserved.
6-5
HERRIMAN

June 5th, 1938.

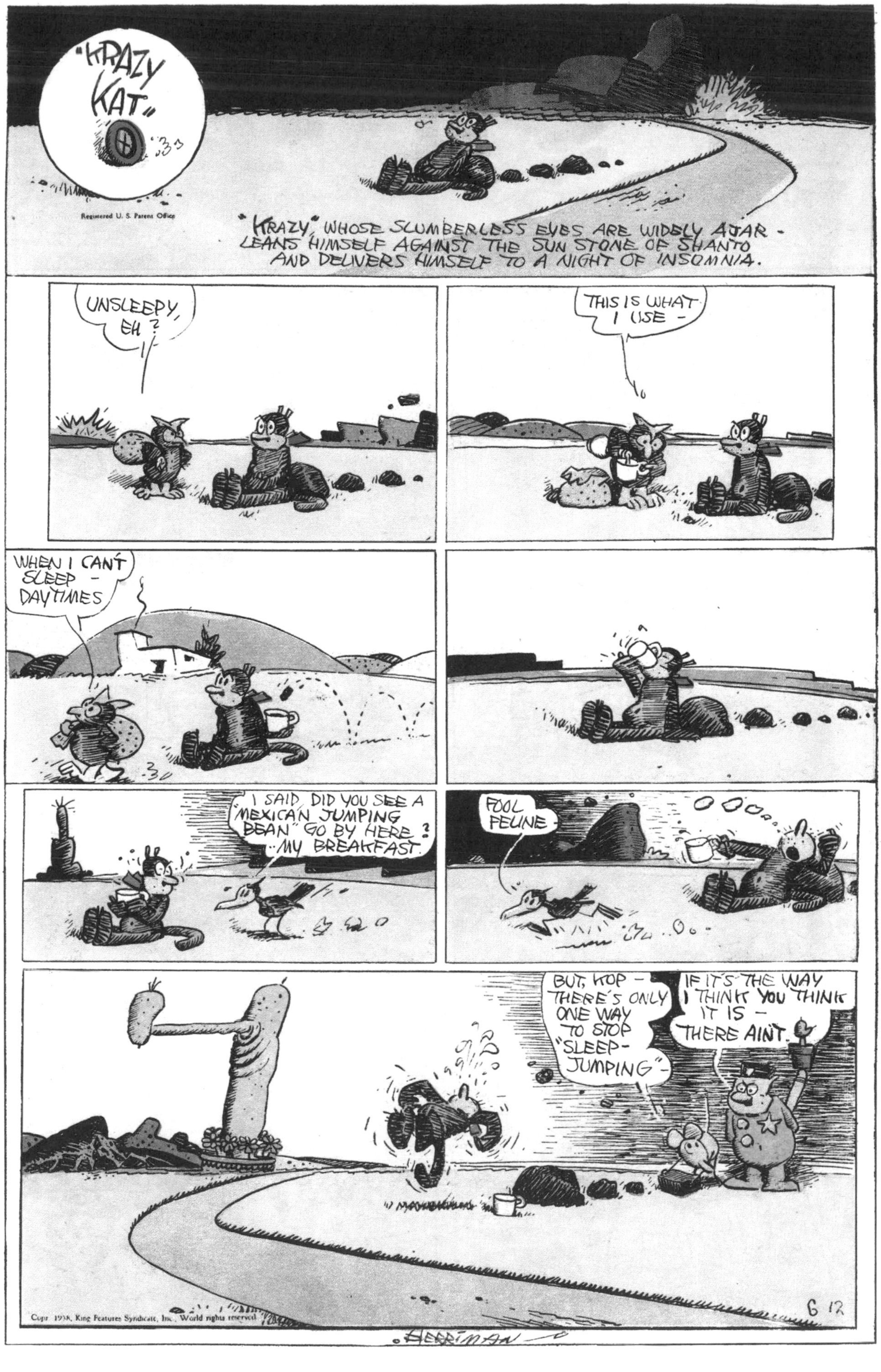
"KRAZY KAT"
Registered U. S. Patent Office
"KRAZY," WHOSE SLUMBERLESS EYES ARE WIDELY AJAR - LEANS HIMSELF AGAINST THE SUN STONE OF SHANTO AND DELIVERS HIMSELF TO A NIGHT OF INSOMNIA.
UNSLEEPY, EH ?
THIS IS WHAT I USE -
WHEN I CAN'T SLEEP - DAYTIMES
I SAID, DID YOU SEE A "MEXICAN JUMPING BEAN" GO BY HERE ? - MY BREAKFAST
FOOL FELINE
BUT, KOP - THERE'S ONLY ONE WAY TO STOP "SLEEP-JUMPING" -
IF IT'S THE WAY I THINK YOU THINK IT IS - THERE AIN'T.
Copr. 1938, King Features Syndicate, Inc., World rights reserved.
6 12
HERRIMAN

June 12th, 1938.

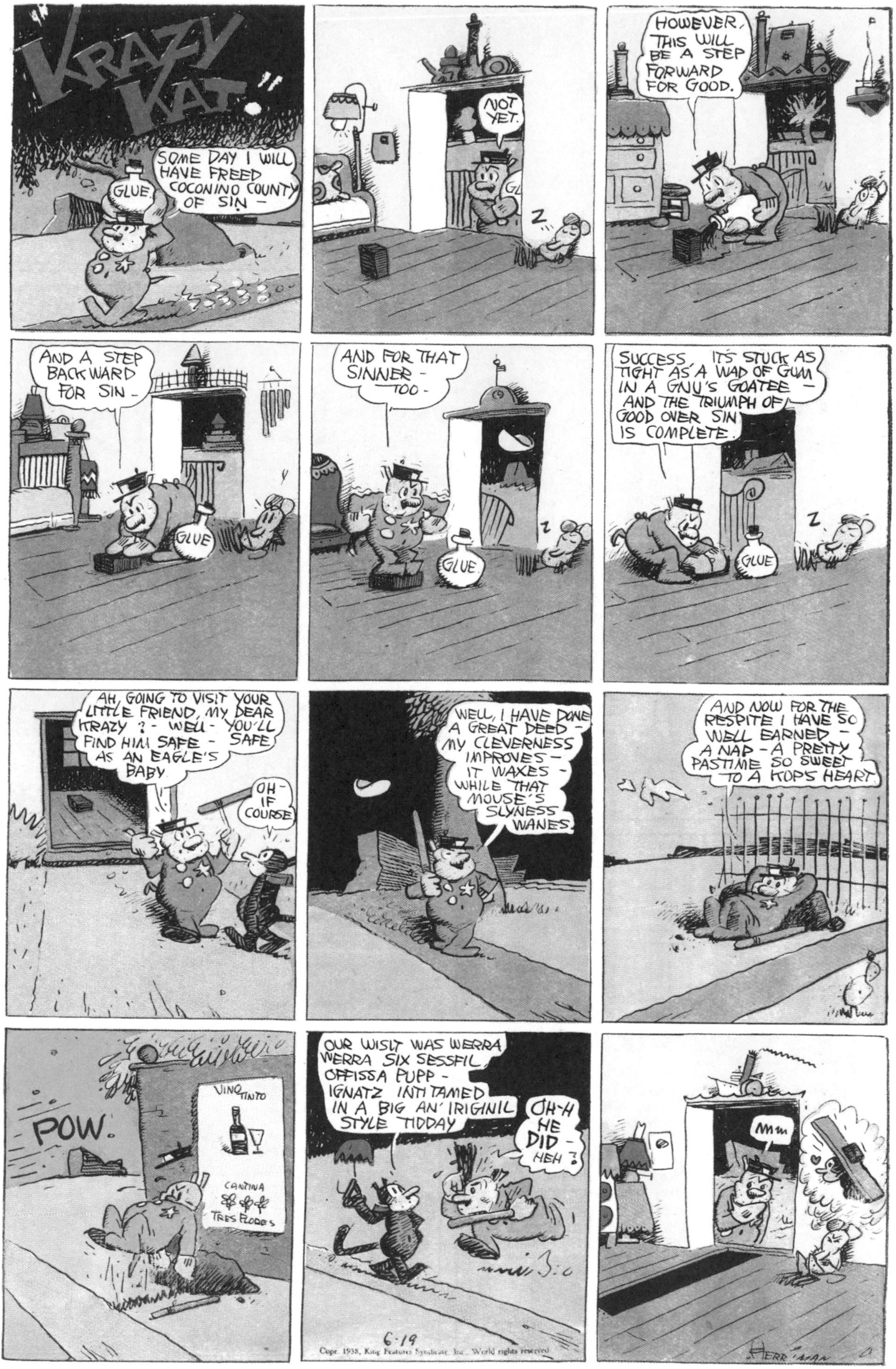
"KRAZY KAT."
SOME DAY I WILL HAVE FREED COCONINO COUNTY OF SIN -
GLUE
NOT YET.
Z
HOWEVER, THIS WILL BE A STEP FORWARD FOR GOOD.
AND A STEP BACKWARD FOR SIN -
GLUE
AND FOR THAT SINNER - TOO -
GLUE
Z
SUCCESS. IT'S STUCK AS TIGHT AS A WAD OF GUM IN A GNU'S GOATEE - AND THE TRIUMPH OF GOOD OVER SIN IS COMPLETE.
GLUE
Z
AH, GOING TO VISIT YOUR LITTLE FRIEND, MY DEAR KRAZY ? - WELL - YOU'LL FIND HIM SAFE - SAFE AS AN EAGLE'S BABY
OH - IF COURSE
WELL, I HAVE DONE A GREAT DEED - MY CLEVERNESS IMPROVES - IT WAXES - WHILE THAT MOUSE'S SLYNESS WANES.
AND NOW FOR THE RESPITE I HAVE SO WELL EARNED - A NAP - A PRETTY PASTIME SO SWEET TO A KOP'S HEART.
POW.
VINO TINTO
CANTINA
TRES FLORES
OUR WISIT WAS WERRA WERRA SIX SESSFIL, OFFISSA PUPP - IGNATZ INTITAMED IN A BIG AN' IRIGINIL STYLE TIDDAY
OH-H HE DID - HEH ?
MM
6-19
Copr. 1938, King Features Syndicate, Inc., World rights reserved
HERRIMAN

June 19th, 1938.

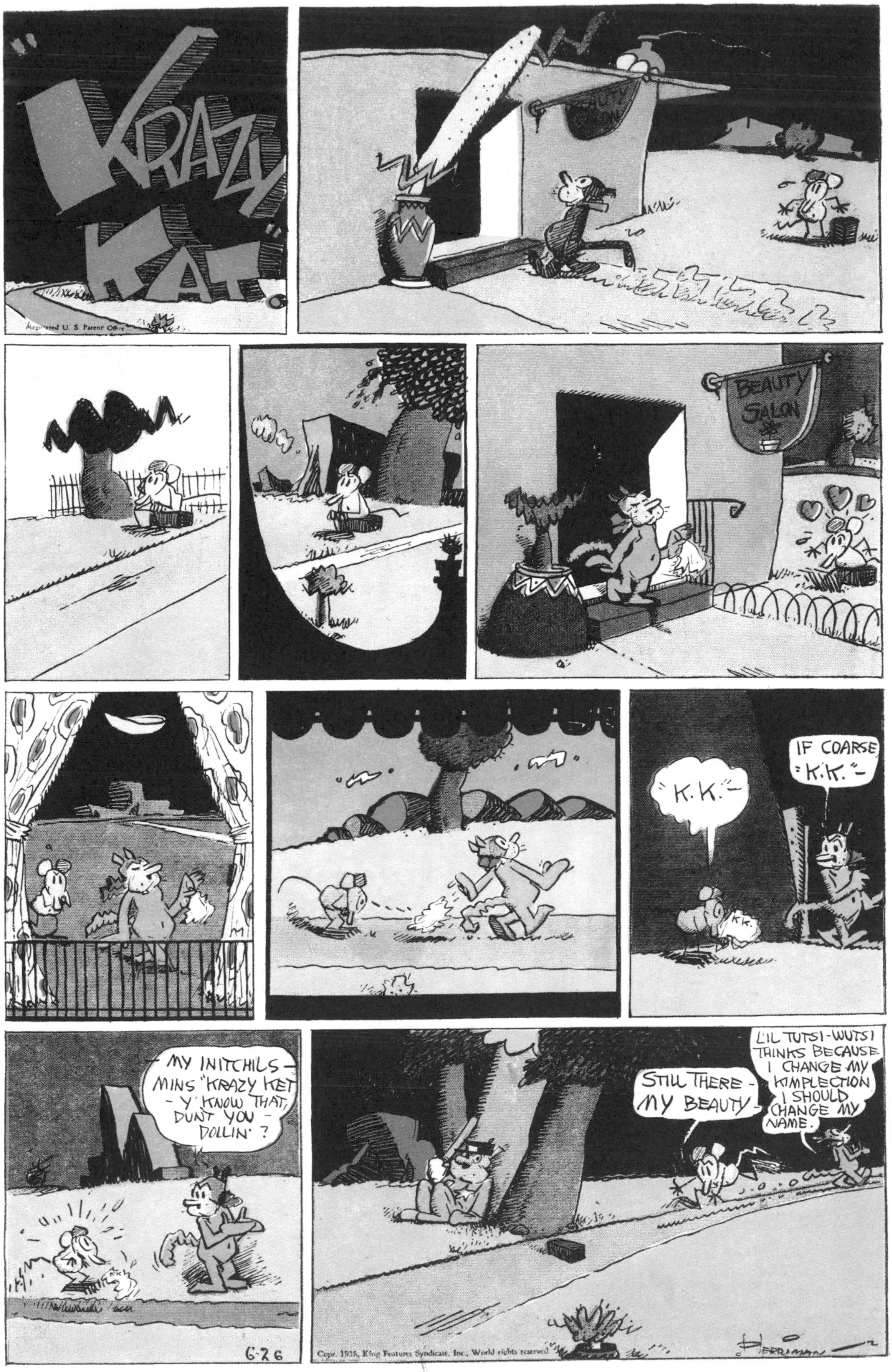
"KRAZY KAT"
Registered U. S. Patent Office
BEAUTY SALON
BEAUTY SALON
IF COARSE "K.K."
"K.K."
K.K.
MY INITCHILS MINS "KRAZY KET" - Y' KNOW THAT, DUN'T YOU DOLLIN' ?
STILL THERE - MY BEAUTY -
L'IL TUTSI-WUTSI THINKS BECAUSE I CHANGE MY KIMPLECTION I SHOULD CHANGE MY NAME.
6-26
Copr. 1938, King Features Syndicate, Inc., World rights reserved
HERRIMAN

June 26th, 1938.

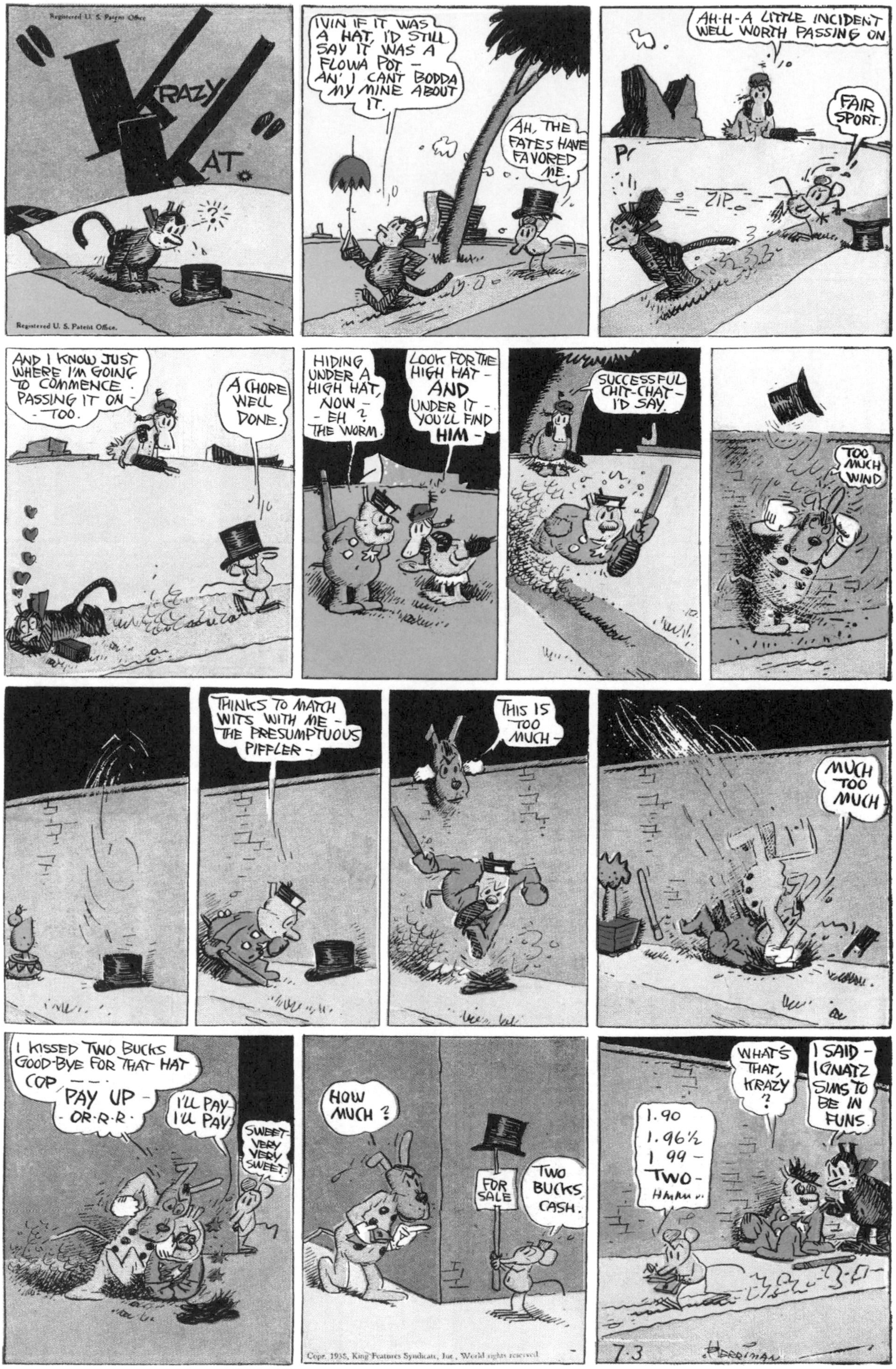
Registered U. S. Patent Office
"Krazy Kat."
Registered U. S. Patent Office.
IVIN IF IT WAS A HAT, I'D STILL SAY IT WAS A FLOWA POT — AN' I CANT BODDA MY MINE ABOUT IT.
AH, THE FATES HAVE FAVORED ME.
AH-H-A LITTLE INCIDENT WELL WORTH PASSING ON.
FAIR SPORT.
ZIP
AND I KNOW JUST WHERE I'M GOING TO COMMENCE PASSING IT ON - TOO.
A CHORE WELL DONE.
HIDING UNDER A HIGH HAT, NOW - - EH ? THE WORM.
LOOK FOR THE HIGH HAT - AND UNDER IT - YOU'LL FIND HIM -
SUCCESSFUL CHIT-CHAT - I'D SAY.
TOO MUCH WIND
THINKS TO MATCH WITS WITH ME - THE PRESUMPTUOUS PIFFLER -
THIS IS TOO MUCH -
MUCH TOO MUCH
I KISSED TWO BUCKS GOOD-BYE FOR THAT HAT COP — —
PAY UP - OR-R-R -
I'LL PAY I'LL PAY
SWEET - VERY VERY SWEET.
HOW MUCH ?
FOR SALE
TWO BUCKS CASH.
WHAT'S THAT, KRAZY ?
I SAID - IGNATZ SIMS TO BE IN FUNS.
1.90
1.96½
1.99 -
TWO -
7-3
HERRIMAN

July 3rd, 1938.

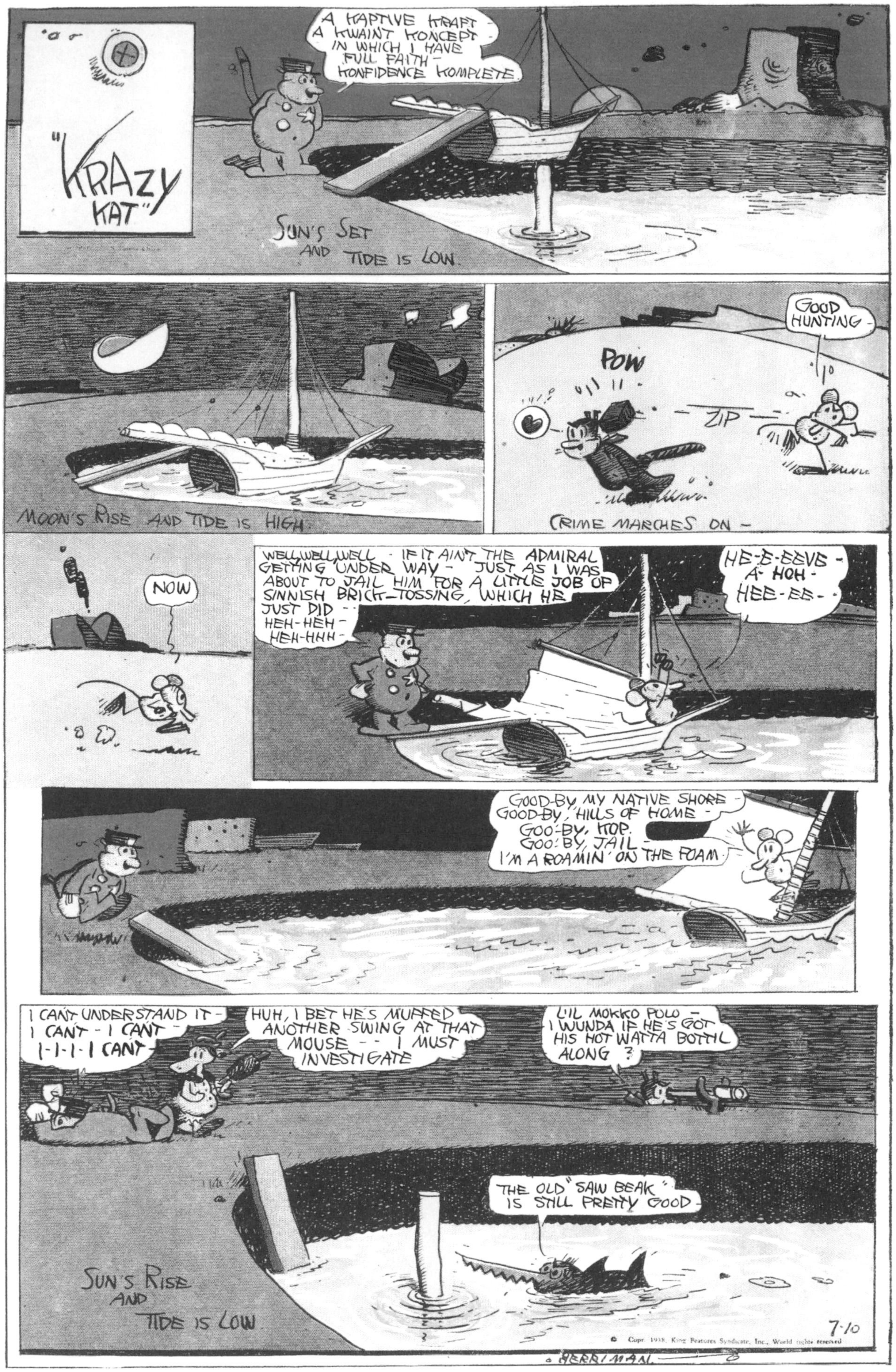
"KRAZY KAT"
A KAPTIVE KRAFT - A KWAINT KONCEPT - IN WHICH I HAVE FULL FAITH - KONFIDENCE KOMPLETE
SUN'S SET AND TIDE IS LOW.
MOON'S RISE AND TIDE IS HIGH.
GOOD HUNTING -
POW
ZIP
CRIME MARCHES ON -
NOW
WELL, WELL, WELL - IF IT AIN'T THE ADMIRAL GETTING UNDER WAY - JUST AS I WAS ABOUT TO JAIL HIM FOR A LITTLE JOB OF SINNISH BRICK-TOSSING, WHICH HE JUST DID - HEH-HEH HEH-HHH -
HE-E-EEVE - A HOH - HEE-EE -
GOOD-BY, MY NATIVE SHORE - GOOD-BY, HILLS OF HOME - GOO-BY, KOP. GOO-BY, JAIL - I'M A ROAMIN' ON THE FOAM -
I CAN'T UNDERSTAND IT - I CAN'T - I CAN'T I-I-I-I CAN'T -
HUH, I BET HE'S MUFFED ANOTHER SWING AT THAT MOUSE - - I MUST INVESTIGATE
L'IL MOKKO POLO - I WUNDA IF HE'S GOT HIS HOT WATTA BOTTIL ALONG ?
THE OLD "SAW BEAK" IS STILL PRETTY GOOD -
SUN'S RISE AND TIDE IS LOW.
7-10
HERRIMAN

July 10th, 1938.

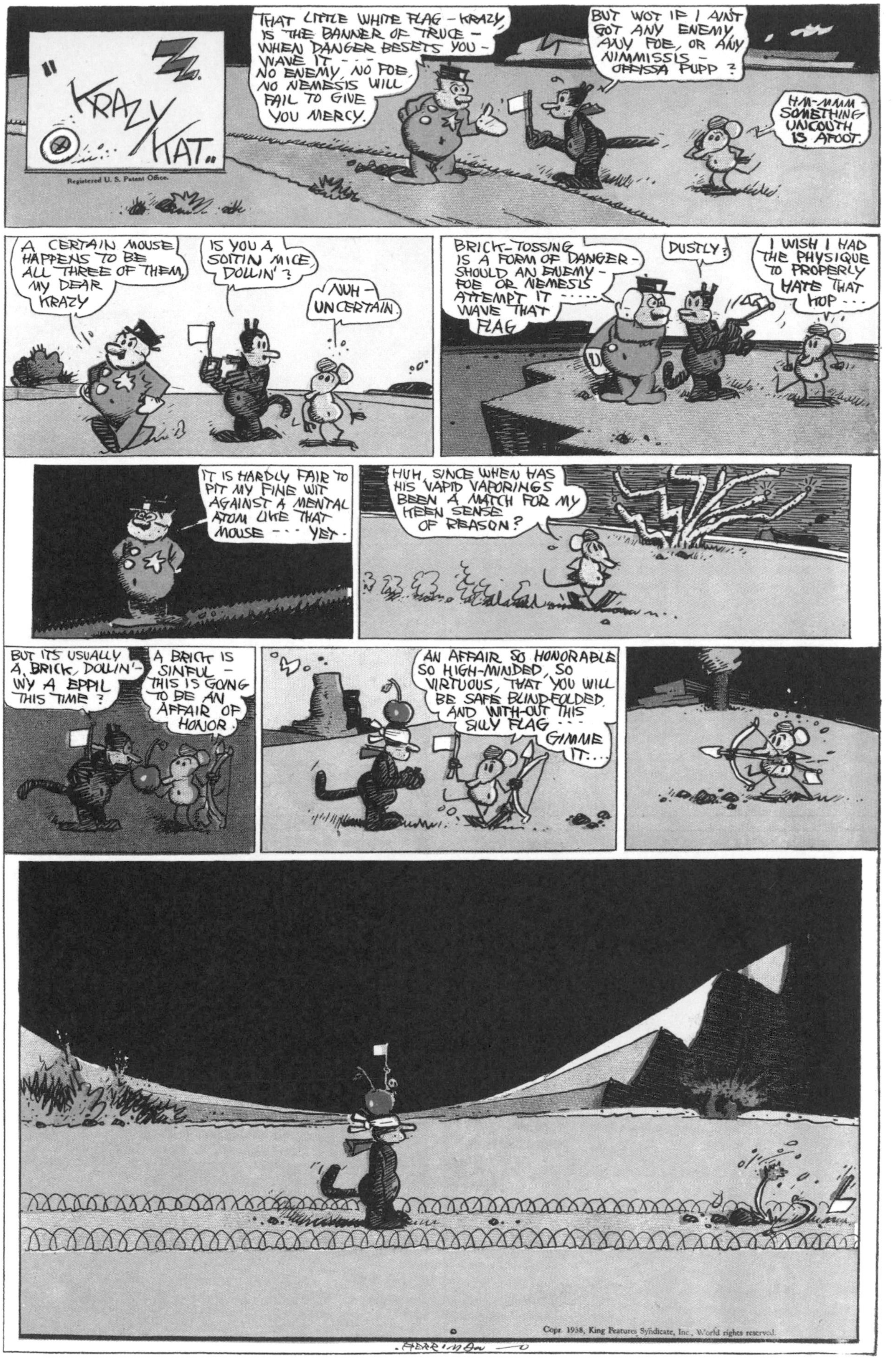
"KRAZY KAT."
Registered U. S. Patent Office.
THAT LITTLE WHITE FLAG - KRAZY IS THE BANNER OF TRUCE - WHEN DANGER BESETS YOU - WAVE IT - - - NO ENEMY, NO FOE, NO NEMESIS WILL FAIL TO GIVE YOU MERCY.
BUT WOT IF I AIN'T GOT ANY ENEMY, ANY FOE, OR ANY NIMMISSIS - OFFISSA PUPP ?
H-M-MMM - SOMETHING UNCOUTH IS AFOOT.
A CERTAIN MOUSE HAPPENS TO BE ALL THREE OF THEM, MY DEAR KRAZY
IS YOU A SOITIN MICE, DOLLIN' ?
NUH - UNCERTAIN.
BRICK-TOSSING IS A FORM OF DANGER - SHOULD AN ENEMY - FOE OR NEMESIS ATTEMPT IT - - - - - WAVE THAT FLAG
DUSTLY ?
I WISH I HAD THE PHYSIQUE TO PROPERLY HATE THAT HOP - - -
IT IS HARDLY FAIR TO PIT MY FINE WIT AGAINST A MENTAL ATOM LIKE THAT MOUSE - - - YET -
HUH, SINCE WHEN HAS HIS VAPID VAPORINGS BEEN A MATCH FOR MY KEEN SENSE OF REASON ?
BUT ITS USUALLY A BRICK, DOLLIN' - WY A EPPIL THIS TIME ?
A BRICK IS SINFUL - THIS IS GOING TO BE AN AFFAIR OF HONOR.
AN AFFAIR SO HONORABLE SO HIGH-MINDED, SO VIRTUOUS, THAT YOU WILL BE SAFE BLIND-FOLDED AND WITH-OUT THIS SILLY FLAG - - -
GIMME IT - - -
Copr. 1938, King Features Syndicate, Inc., World rights reserved.
HERRIMAN

July 17th, 1938.

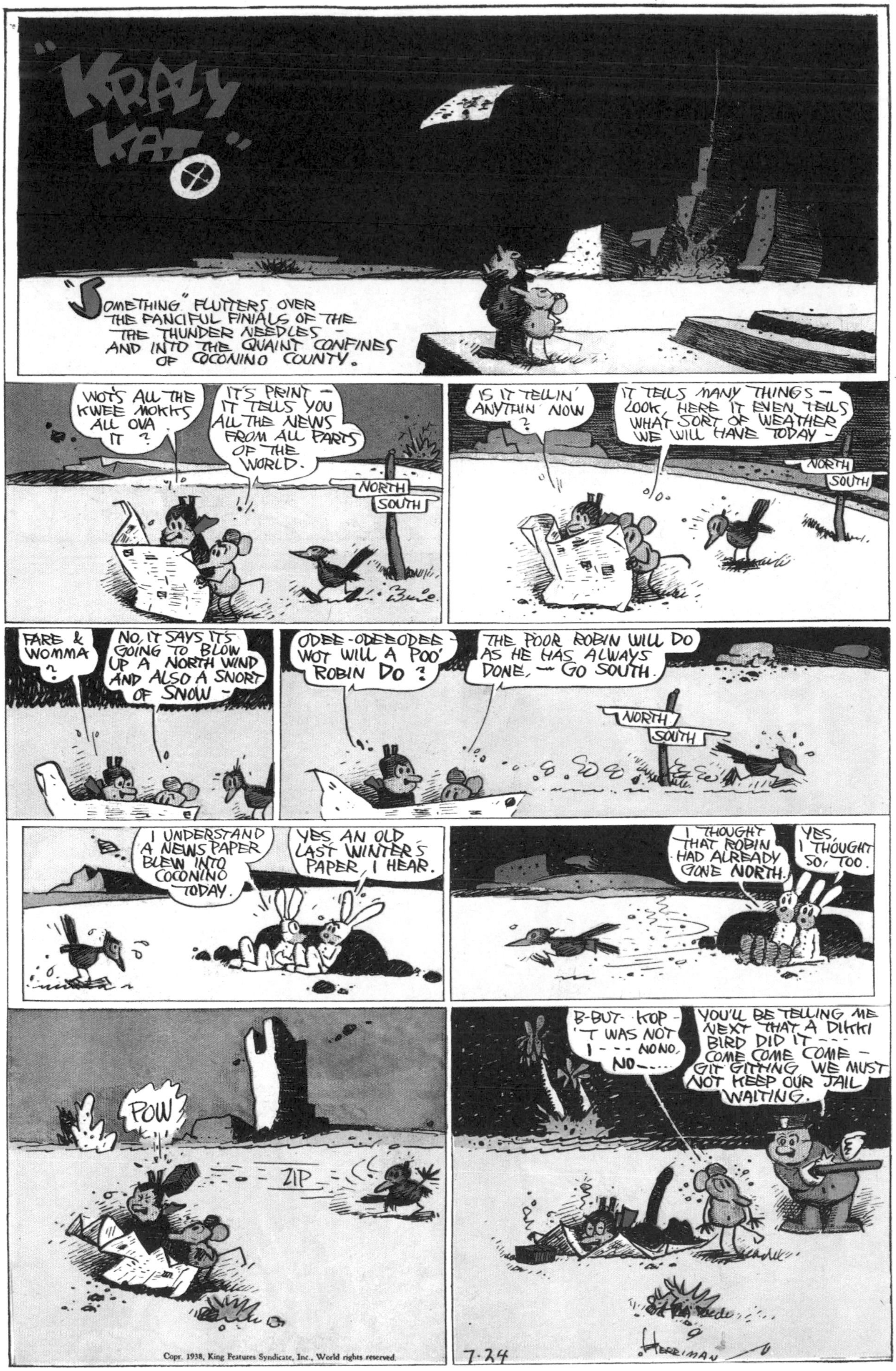
"KRAZY KAT."
"SOMETHING" FLUTTERS OVER THE FANCIFUL FINIALS OF THE THE THUNDER NEEDLES – AND INTO THE QUAINT CONFINES OF COCONINO COUNTY.
WOT'S ALL THE KWEE MOKITS ALL OVA IT ?
IT'S PRINT – IT TELLS YOU ALL THE NEWS FROM ALL PARTS OF THE WORLD.
NORTH
SOUTH
IS IT TELLIN' ANYTHIN NOW ?
IT TELLS MANY THINGS – LOOK, HERE IT EVEN TELLS WHAT SORT OF WEATHER WE WILL HAVE TODAY –
NORTH
SOUTH
FARE & WOMMA ?
NO, IT SAYS IT'S GOING TO BLOW UP A NORTH WIND AND ALSO A SNORT OF SNOW –
ODEE-ODEEODEE WOT WILL A POO' ROBIN DO ?
THE POOR ROBIN WILL DO AS HE HAS ALWAYS DONE, – GO SOUTH.
NORTH
SOUTH
I UNDERSTAND A NEWSPAPER BLEW INTO COCONINO TODAY.
YES, AN OLD LAST WINTER'S PAPER, I HEAR.
I THOUGHT THAT ROBIN HAD ALREADY GONE NORTH.
YES, I THOUGHT SO, TOO.
POW
ZIP
B-BUT KOP 'T WAS NOT I --- NO NO, NO-----
YOU'LL BE TELLING ME NEXT THAT A DIKKI BIRD DID IT --- COME COME COME – GIT GITTING WE MUST NOT KEEP OUR JAIL WAITING.
Copr. 1938, King Features Syndicate, Inc., World rights reserved.
7·24
HERRIMAN

July 24th, 1938.

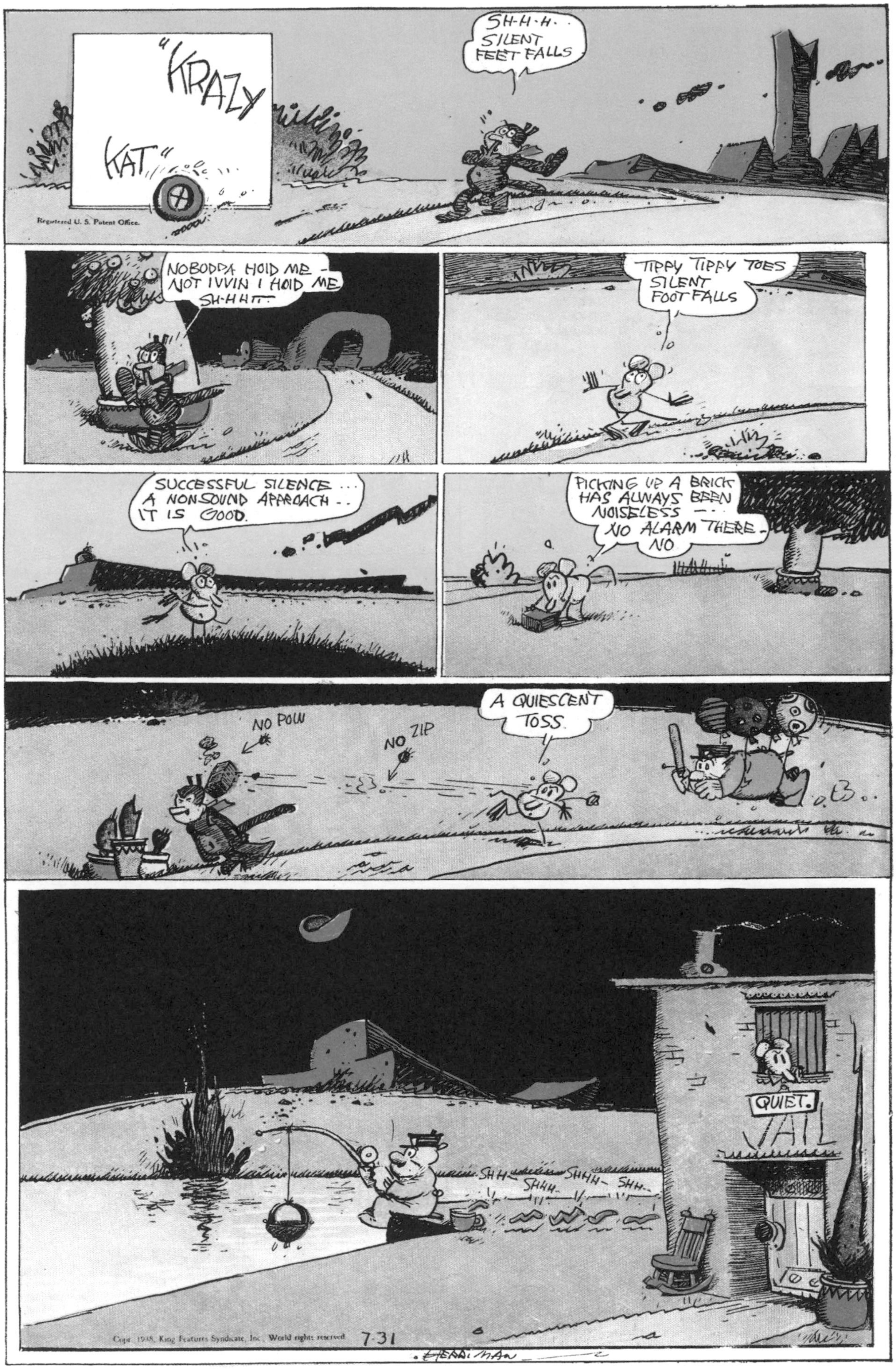
"KRAZY KAT"
Registered U. S. Patent Office.
SH-H-H. SILENT FEET FALLS
NOBODDA HOID ME - NOT IVVIN I HOID ME SH-HHH
TIPPY TIPPY TOES SILENT FOOT FALLS
SUCCESSFUL SILENCE... A NONSOUND APPROACH - - IT IS GOOD.
PICKING UP A BRICK HAS ALWAYS BEEN NOISELESS - - NO ALARM THERE NO
NO POW
NO ZIP
A QUIESCENT TOSS.
SHH SHHH SHHH SHH
QUIET.
JAIL
Copr. 1938, King Features Syndicate, Inc., World rights reserved.
7-31
HERRIMAN

July 31st, 1938.

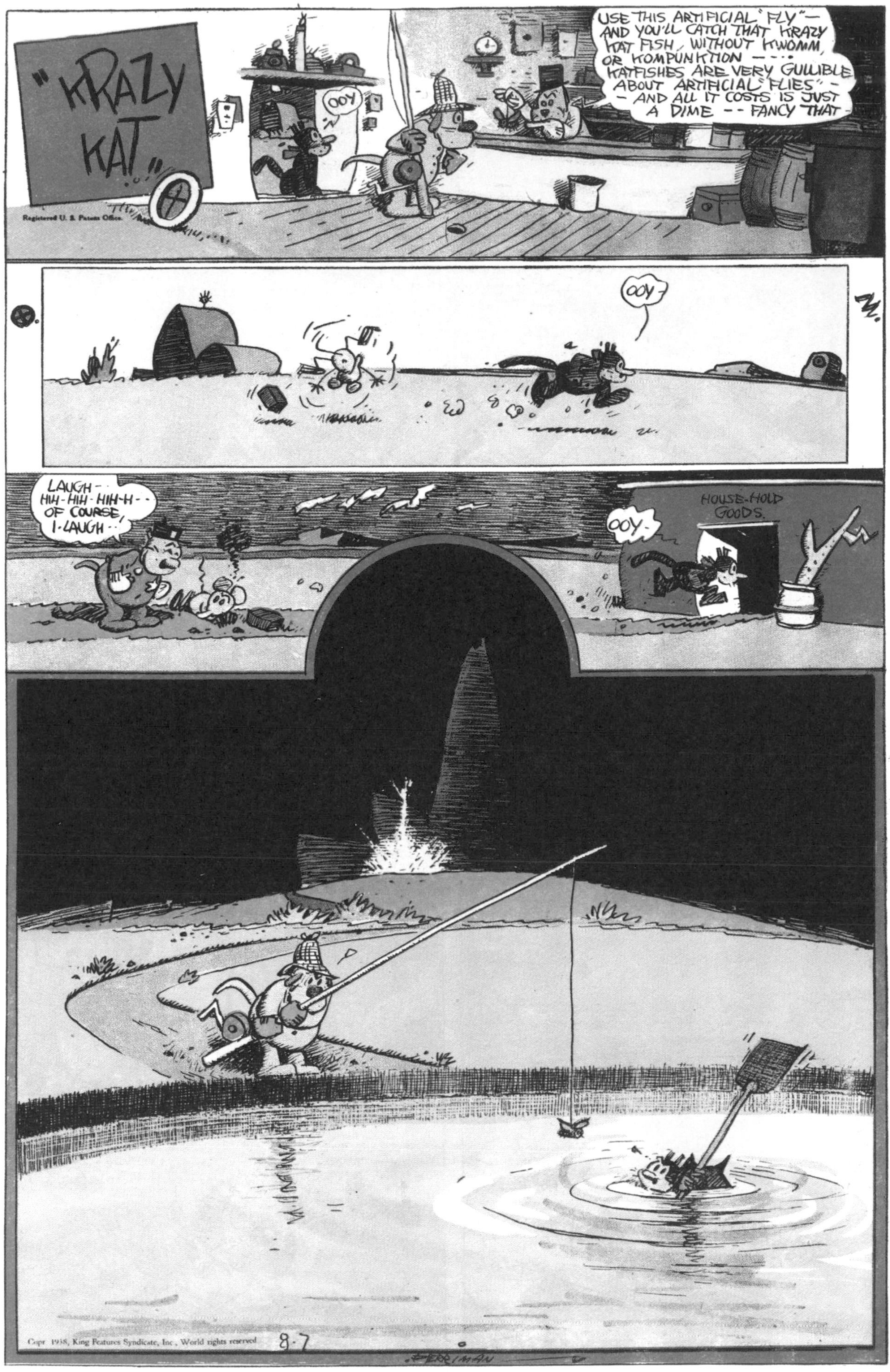
"KRAZY KAT."
Registered U. S. Patent Office.
OOY
USE THIS ARTIFICIAL "FLY" — AND YOU'LL CATCH THAT KRAZY KAT FISH, WITHOUT KWOMM, OR KOMPUNKTION — — — KATFISHES ARE VERY GULLIBLE ABOUT ARTIFICIAL "FLIES" — — AND ALL IT COSTS IS JUST A DIME — — FANCY THAT
OOY
LAUGH — HIH - HIH - HIH-H — — OF COURSE, I-LAUGH — —
HOUSE-HOLD GOODS.
OOY
Copr 1938, King Features Syndicate, Inc., World rights reserved
8-7
HERRIMAN

August 7th, 1938.

"KRAZY KAT"
Registered U. S. Patent Office.
YEEVA-YO YEEEE
?
IT'S A OLE GRIKH YIMPIL MINT OF WAR DOLLIN' A "KETTA PULP."
SO, O-O ?
FIRTZ YOU GIVE IT A YENK AN' PULL IT DOWN - LIKE THIS.
YOU DO, HEH ?
THEN YOU PLACE A KOBBIL ROCK ON IT RIGHT THERE --
A ROCK ? - HUH, WHY NOT A BRICK ?
THEN - Y LET GO."
"JAIL"
JAIL
WELCOME
8-14
Copr 1938, King Features Syndicate, Inc., World rights reserved
HERRIMAN

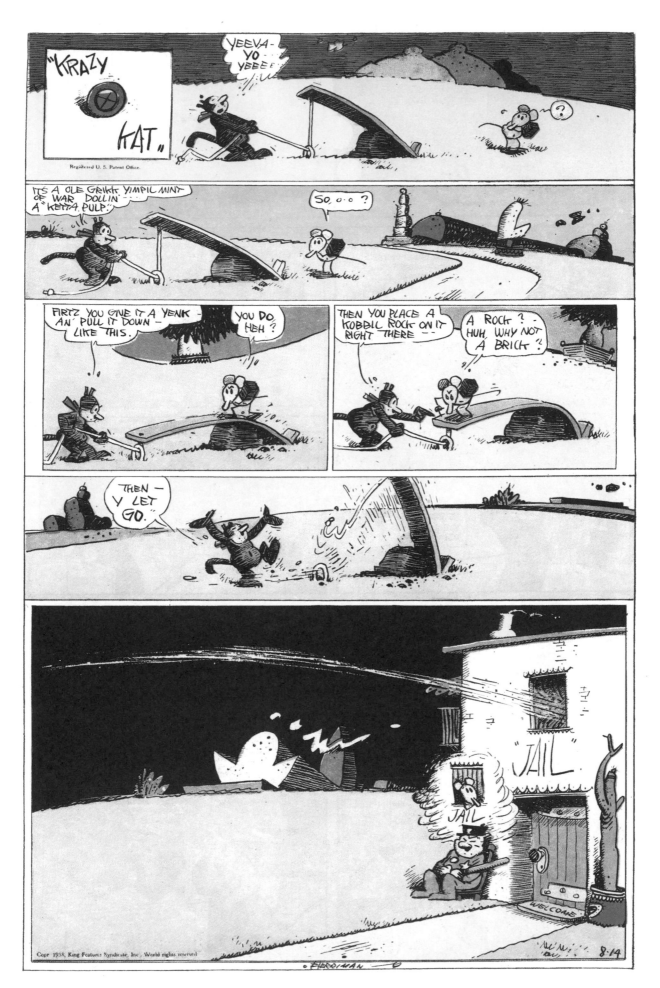

August 14th, 1938.

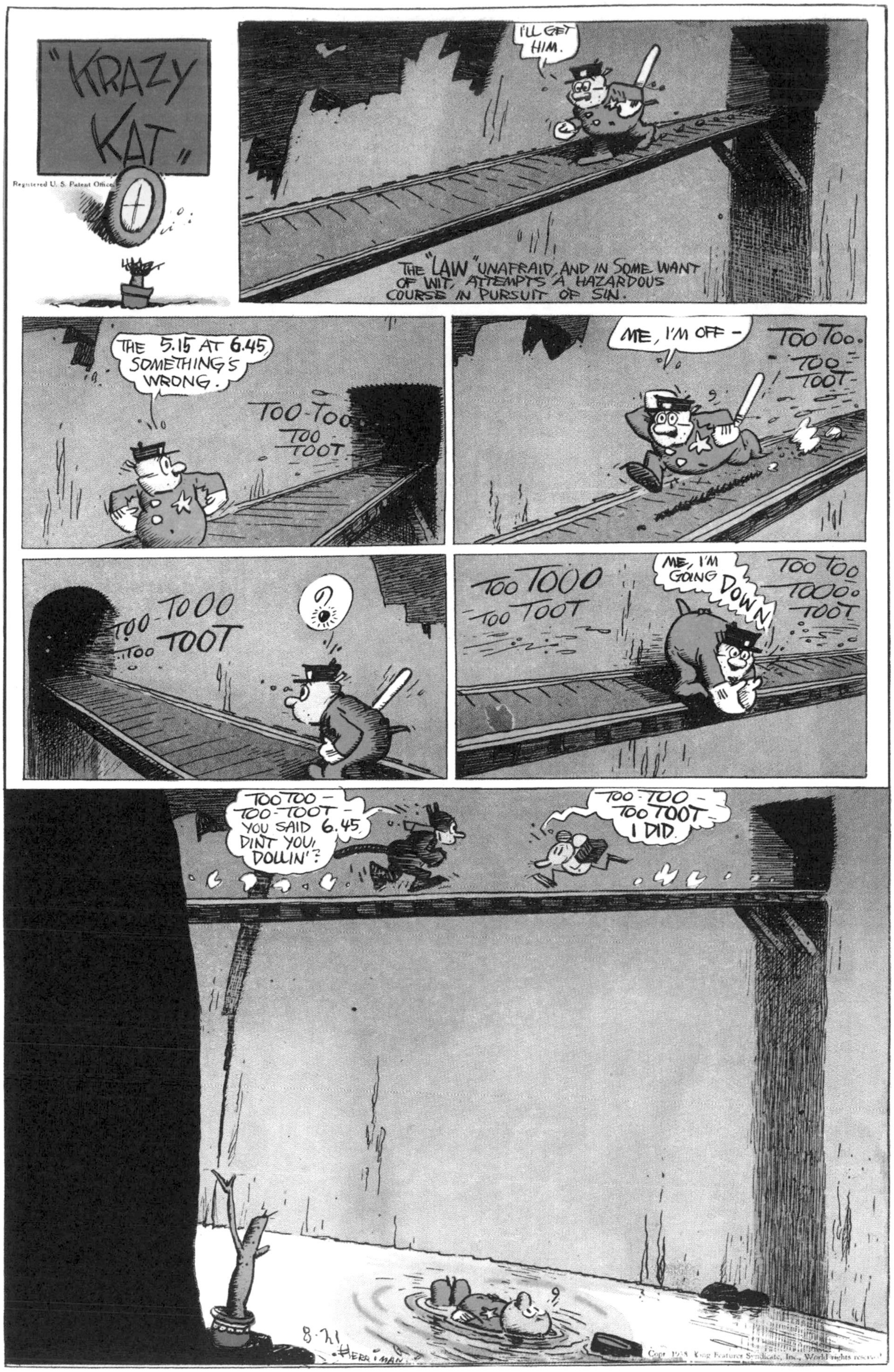
"KRAZY KAT"
Registered U. S. Patent Office
I'LL GET HIM.
THE "LAW" UNAFRAID, AND IN SOME WANT OF WIT, ATTEMPTS A HAZARDOUS COURSE IN PURSUIT OF SIN.
THE 5.15 AT 6.45 SOMETHING'S WRONG.
TOO-TOO TOO TOOT
ME, I'M OFF –
TOO TOO TOO TOOT
TOO-TOOO TOO TOOT
?
TOO TOOO TOO TOOT
ME, I'M GOING DOWN
TOO TOO TOOO TOOT
TOO TOO – TOO-TOOT YOU SAID 6.45 DINT YOU, DOLLIN'?
TOO-TOO – TOO TOOT – I DID.
8-21
HERRIMAN
King Features Syndicate, Inc., World rights

August 21st, 1938.

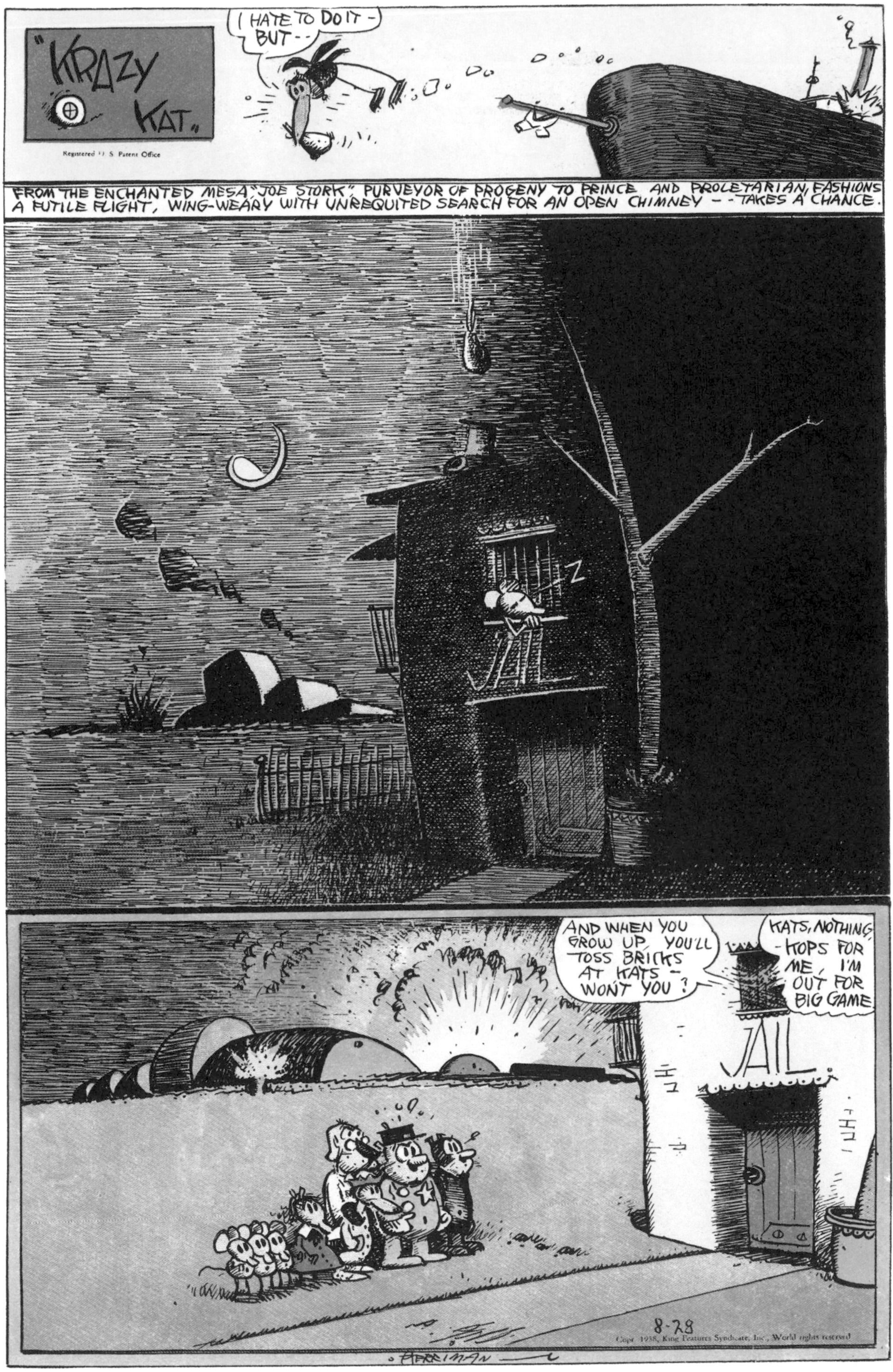
"KRAZY KAT."
Registered U. S. Patent Office
I HATE TO DO IT - BUT - -
FROM THE ENCHANTED MESA "JOE STORK," PURVEYOR OF PROGENY TO PRINCE AND PROLETARIAN, FASHIONS A FUTILE FLIGHT, WING-WEARY WITH UNREQUITED SEARCH FOR AN OPEN CHIMNEY - - TAKES A CHANCE.
Z
JAIL
AND WHEN YOU GROW UP, YOU'LL TOSS BRICKS AT KATS - WON'T YOU ?
KATS, NOTHING, - HOPS FOR ME, I'M OUT FOR BIG GAME
JAIL
8-28
Copr. 1938, King Features Syndicate, Inc., World rights reserved
HERRIMAN

August 28th, 1938.

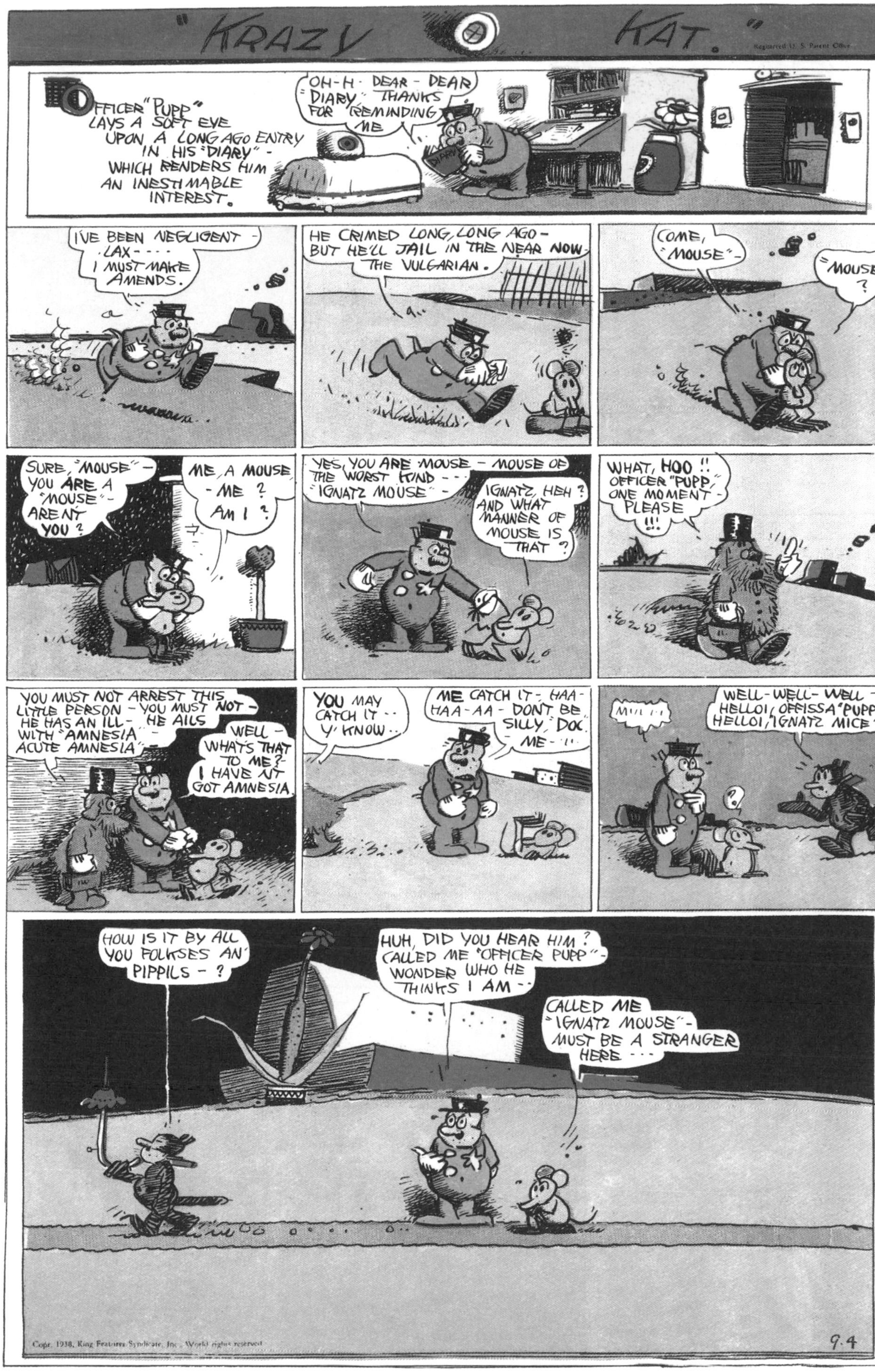
"KRAZY KAT."
Registered U. S. Patent Office
Officer "Pupp" lays a soft eye upon a long ago entry in his "diary" - which renders him an inestimable interest.
OH-H - DEAR - DEAR "DIARY," THANKS FOR REMINDING ME
I'VE BEEN NEGLIGENT - LAX - - - - I MUST MAKE AMENDS.
HE CRIMED LONG, LONG AGO - BUT HE'LL JAIL IN THE NEAR NOW - THE VULGARIAN.
COME, "MOUSE" -
"MOUSE" ?
SURE, "MOUSE" - YOU ARE A "MOUSE" - AREN'T YOU ?
ME, A MOUSE - ME ? AM I ?
YES, YOU ARE MOUSE - MOUSE OF THE WORST KIND - - - "IGNATZ MOUSE" -
IGNATZ, HEH ? AND WHAT MANNER OF MOUSE IS THAT ?
WHAT, HOO !! OFFICER "PUPP," ONE MOMENT - PLEASE !!!
YOU MUST NOT ARREST THIS LITTLE PERSON - YOU MUST NOT - HE HAS AN ILL - HE AILS WITH "AMNESIA" - ACUTE AMNESIA -
WELL - WHAT'S THAT TO ME? I HAVE N'T GOT AMNESIA
YOU MAY CATCH IT - - Y' KNOW - -
ME CATCH IT - HAA-HAA-AA - DON'T BE SILLY, "DOC." - ME - !!
WELL-WELL-WELL - HELLO!, OFFISSA "PUPP" - HELLO!, IGNATZ MICE" -
HOW IS IT BY ALL YOU FOLKSES AN' PIPPILS - ?
HUH, DID YOU HEAR HIM ? CALLED ME "OFFICER PUPP" - WONDER WHO HE THINKS I AM - -
CALLED ME "IGNATZ MOUSE" - MUST BE A STRANGER HERE - - -
Copr. 1938, King Features Syndicate, Inc., World rights reserved.
9.4

September 4th, 1938.

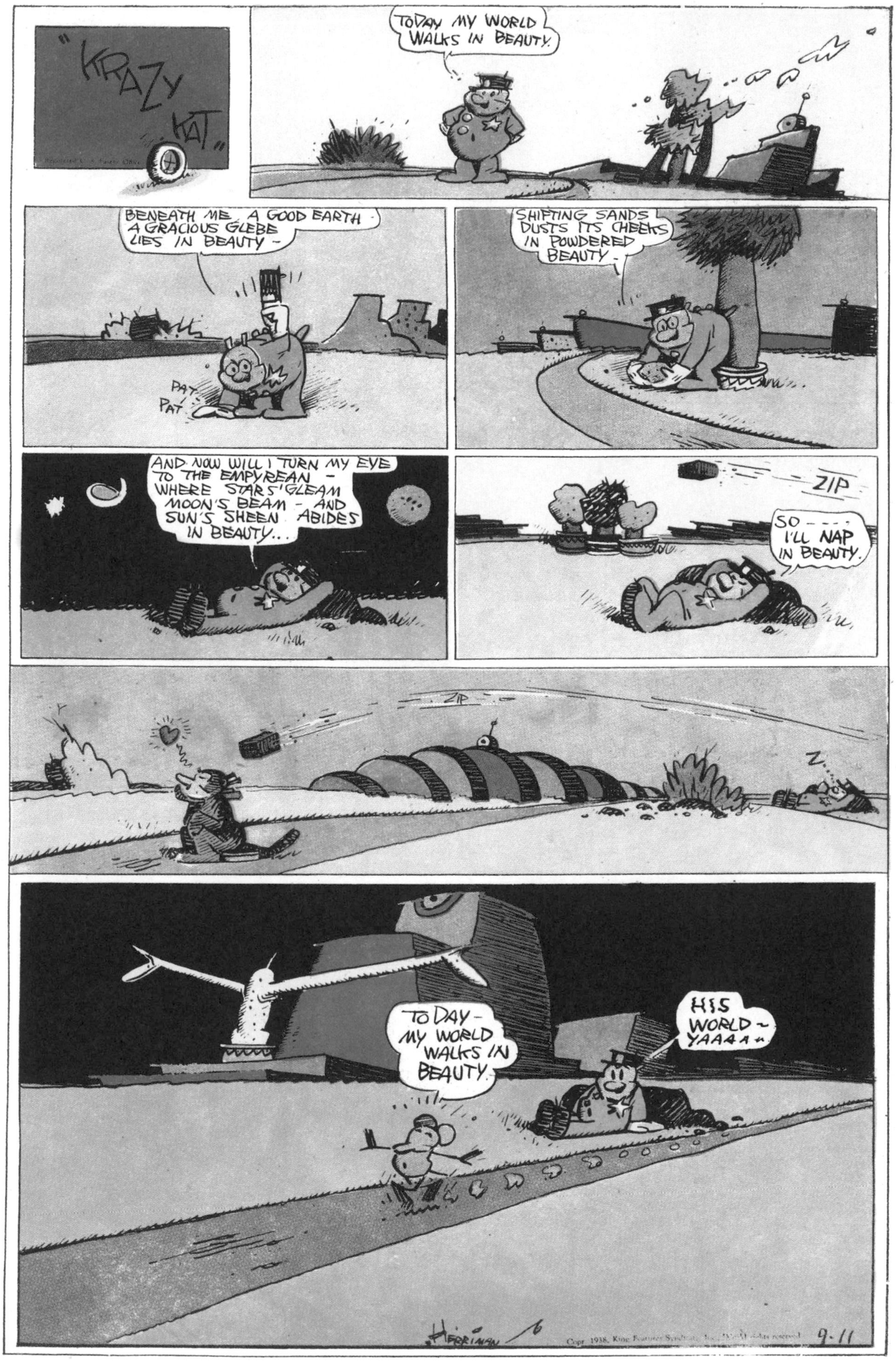
"KRAZY KAT"
TODAY MY WORLD WALKS IN BEAUTY.
BENEATH ME, A GOOD EARTH - A GRACIOUS GLEBE LIES IN BEAUTY -
PAT PAT
SHIFTING SANDS DUSTS ITS CHEEKS IN POWDERED BEAUTY -
AND NOW WILL I TURN MY EYE TO THE EMPYREAN - WHERE STARS' GLEAM, MOON'S BEAM - AND SUN'S SHEEN ABIDES IN BEAUTY...
ZIP
SO - - - I'LL NAP IN BEAUTY.
ZIP
Z
TODAY - MY WORLD WALKS IN BEAUTY.
HIS WORLD - YAAAAA
HERRIMAN
9.11

September 11th, 1938.

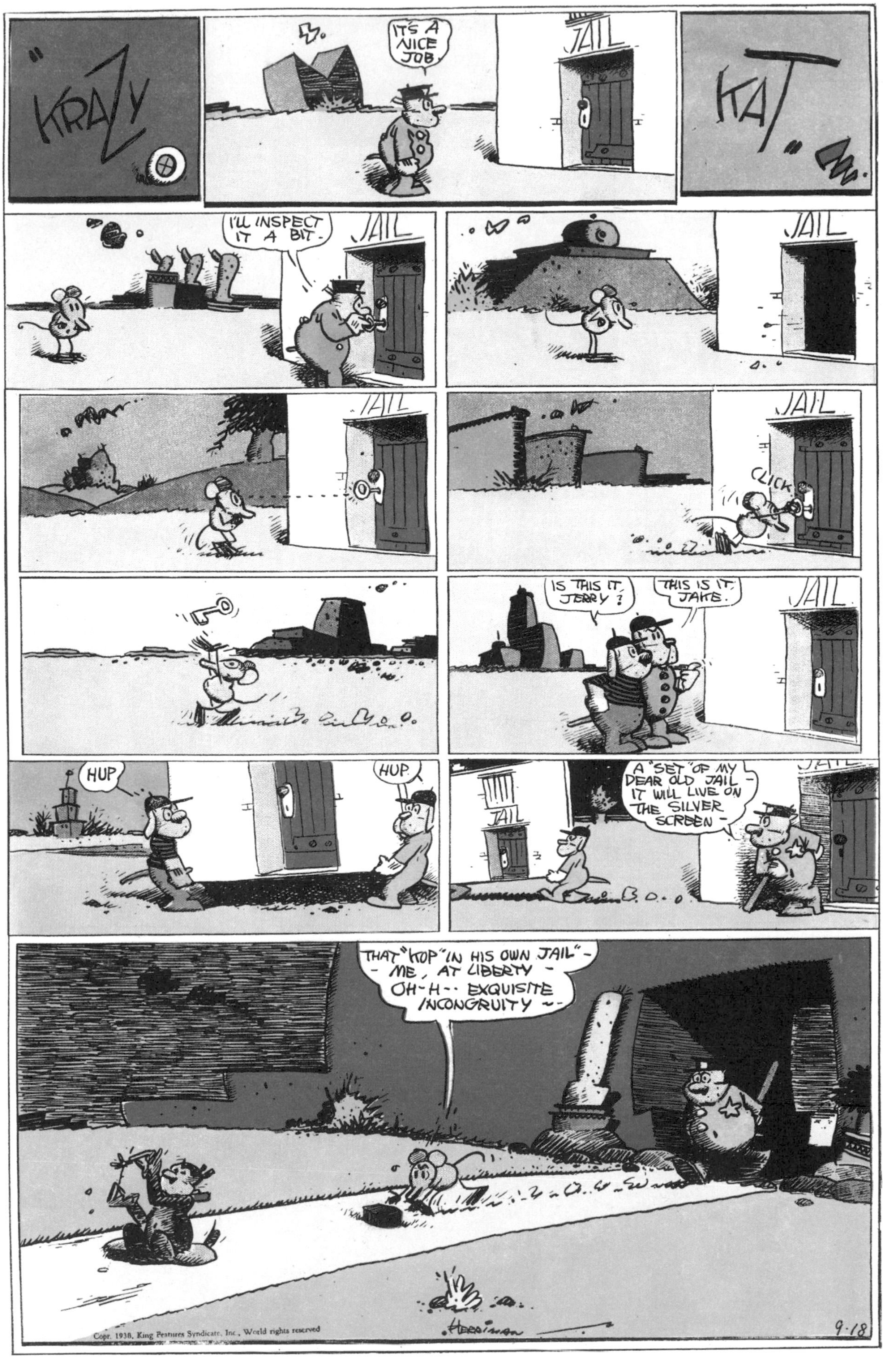
"KRAZY
IT'S A NICE JOB
JAIL
KAT"
I'LL INSPECT IT A BIT
JAIL
JAIL
JAIL
JAIL
CLICK
IS THIS IT, JERRY?
THIS IS IT, JAKE.
JAIL
HUP
HUP
JAIL
A "SET" OF MY DEAR OLD JAIL - IT WILL LIVE ON THE SILVER SCREEN -
THAT "KOP" IN HIS OWN JAIL" - - ME, AT LIBERTY - OH-H-- EXQUISITE INCONGRUITY ~~
Copr. 1938, King Features Syndicate, Inc., World rights reserved
HERRIMAN
9.18

September 18th, 1938.

"KRAZY KAT."
SOMETHIN' WRONG HERE SOMETHIN' TURVA TOPSA - IN CONGRESS - UJILLY THE JAIL SINN IS IN THE WERRA LEST PITCHA - - - "OFFISSA PUPP" MUST EXPLAIN -
JAIL
DID YOU KNOW THAT "IGNATZ MICE" WAS IN JAIL AT THE BIGINNIN' INSTEAD OF THE FINNITCH ? - DID YOU ?
HAVING PUT HIM THERE, MYSELF I AM QUITE AWARE OF IT.
THE RISSIN - I DEMEND THE RISSIN !!!
I ARRESTED HIM TODAY FOR THE BRICK HE MIGHT TOSS AT YOU TO MORROW -
AH- THEN IT'S FOR THE BRICK HE CAN'T TOSS TIDDAY AN' THE ONE HE HAS N'T TOSSED TIMORRA -
EXACTLY - MY DEAR "KRAZY" - WHAT ELSE DID YOU THINK ?
I HAD A IDA IT WAS FOR THE BRICK HE DID TOSS YESTIDDAY.
Copr. 1938, King Features Syndicate, Inc., World rights reserved. 9-25
HERRIMAN

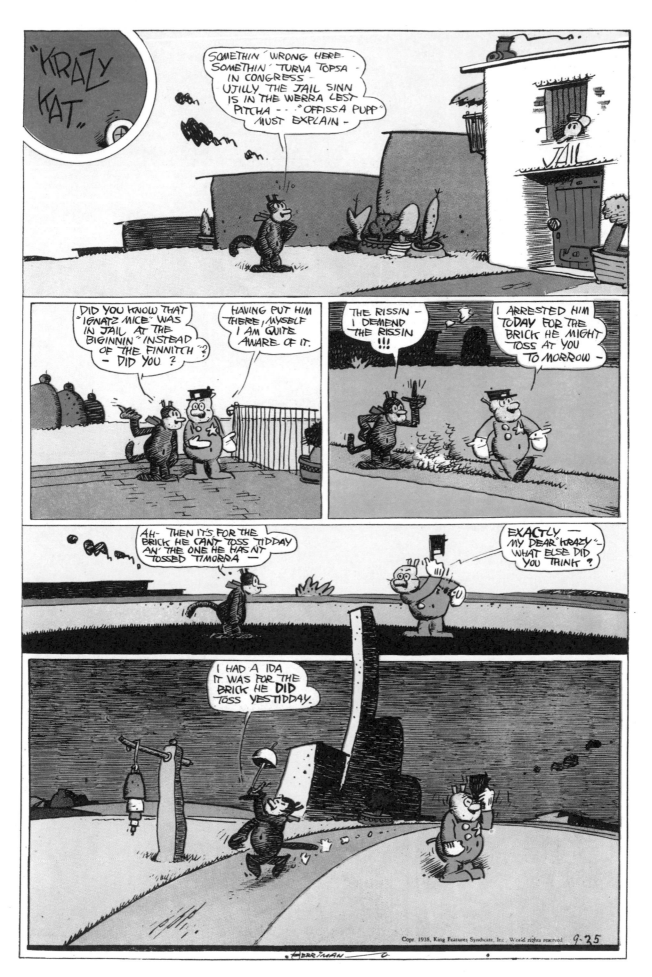

September 25th, 1938.

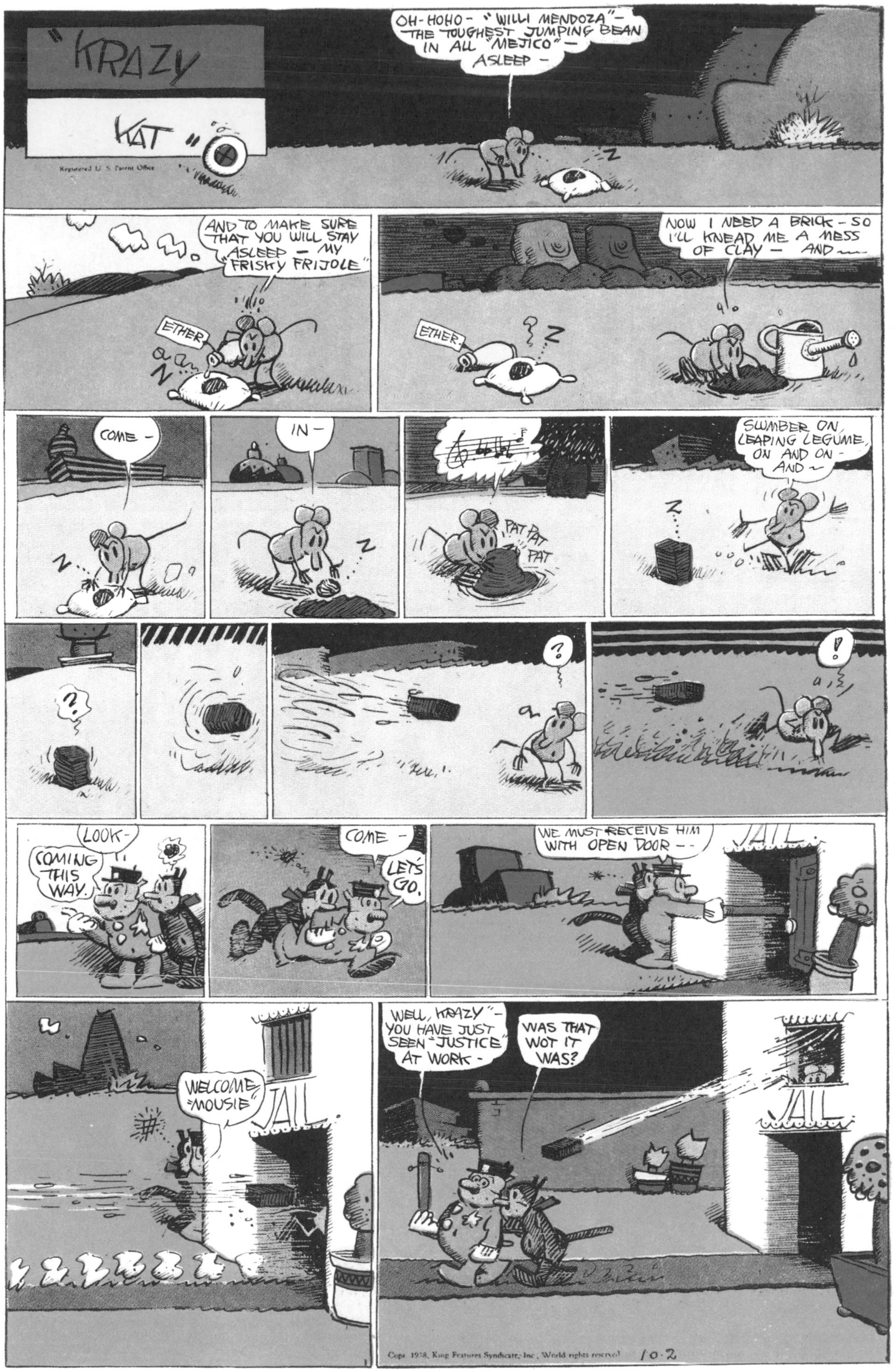
"KRAZY KAT"
Registered U. S. Patent Office
OH-HOHO- "WILLI MENDOZA"- THE TOUGHEST JUMPING BEAN IN ALL "MEJICO"- ASLEEP-
Z
AND TO MAKE SURE THAT YOU WILL STAY ASLEEP - MY FRISKY FRIJOLE"
ETHER
NOW I NEED A BRICK - SO I'LL KNEAD ME A MESS OF CLAY - AND
ETHER
Z
COME -
IN -
PAT PAT PAT
SLUMBER ON, LEAPING LEGUME, ON AND ON - AND
LOOK-
COMING THIS WAY.
COME -
LET'S GO.
WE MUST RECEIVE HIM WITH OPEN DOOR --
JAIL
WELCOME MOUSIE
JAIL
WELL, KRAZY"- YOU HAVE JUST SEEN "JUSTICE" AT WORK-
WAS THAT WOT IT WAS?
JAIL
Copr. 1938, King Features Syndicate, Inc., World rights reserved
10-2

October 2nd, 1938.

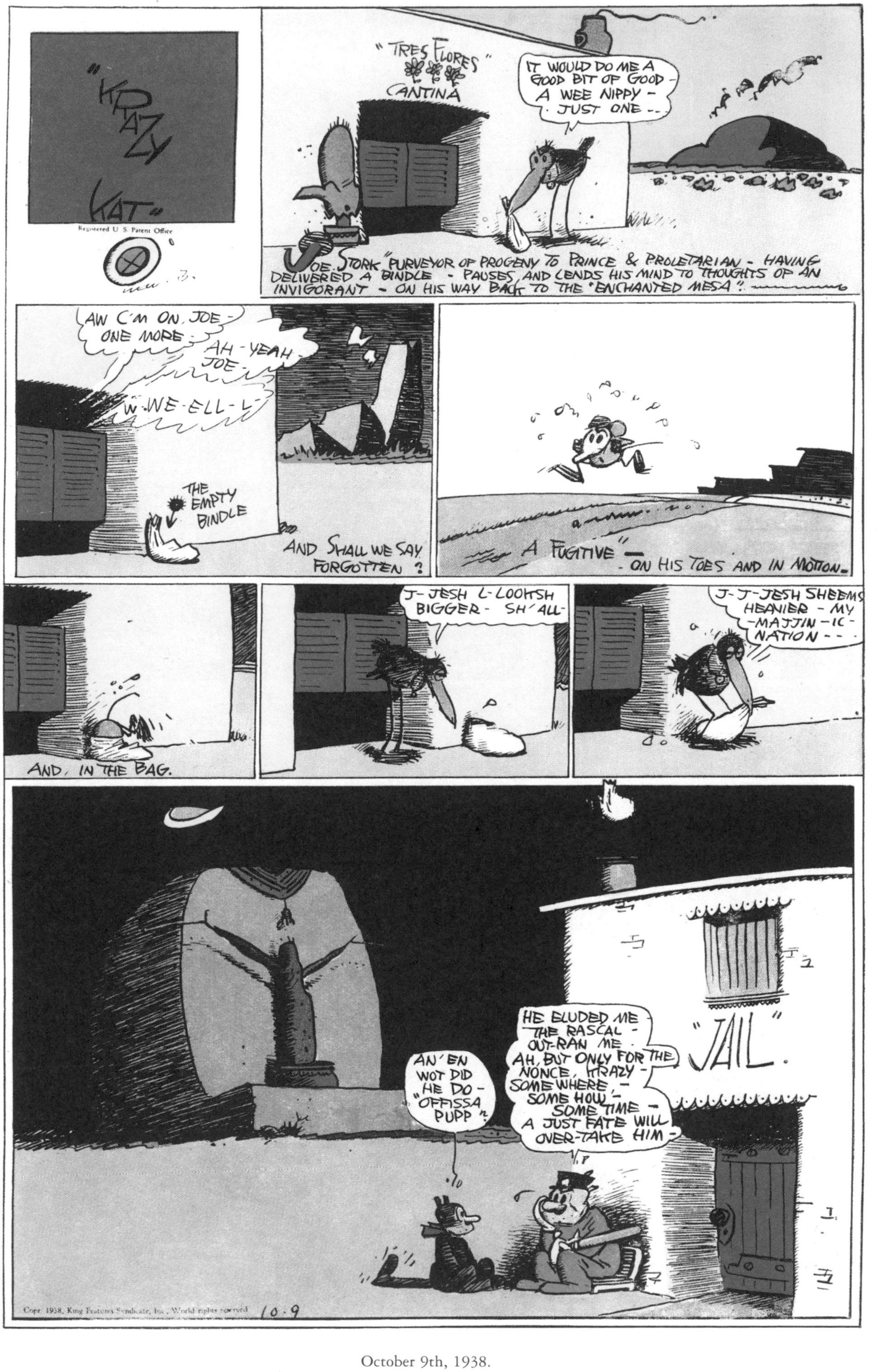
"KRAZY KAT"
Registered U.S. Patent Office
"TRES FLORES" CANTINA
IT WOULD DO ME A GOOD BIT OF GOOD - A WEE NIPPY - JUST ONE - -
JOE STORK "PURVEYOR OF PROGENY TO PRINCE & PROLETARIAN - HAVING DELIVERED A BINDLE - PAUSES, AND LENDS HIS MIND TO THOUGHTS OF AN INVIGORANT - ON HIS WAY BACK TO THE "ENCHANTED MESA".
AW C'M ON, JOE - ONE MORE
AH - YEAH JOE
W-WE-ELL-L
THE EMPTY BINDLE
AND SHALL WE SAY FORGOTTEN ?
"A FUGITIVE" - ON HIS TOES AND IN MOTION -
AND, IN THE BAG.
J-JESH L-LOOKSH BIGGER - SH'ALL-
J-J-JESH SHEEMS HEAVIER - MY -MAJJIN-IC-NATION - - -
"JAIL".
AN'EN WOT DID HE DO - "OFFISSA PUPP"?
HE ELUDED ME - THE RASCAL - OUT-RAN ME - AH, BUT ONLY FOR THE NONCE, KRAZY - SOME WHERE - SOME HOW - SOME TIME - A JUST FATE WILL OVER-TAKE HIM -
Copr 1938, King Features Syndicate, Inc., World rights reserved
10-9

October 9th, 1938.

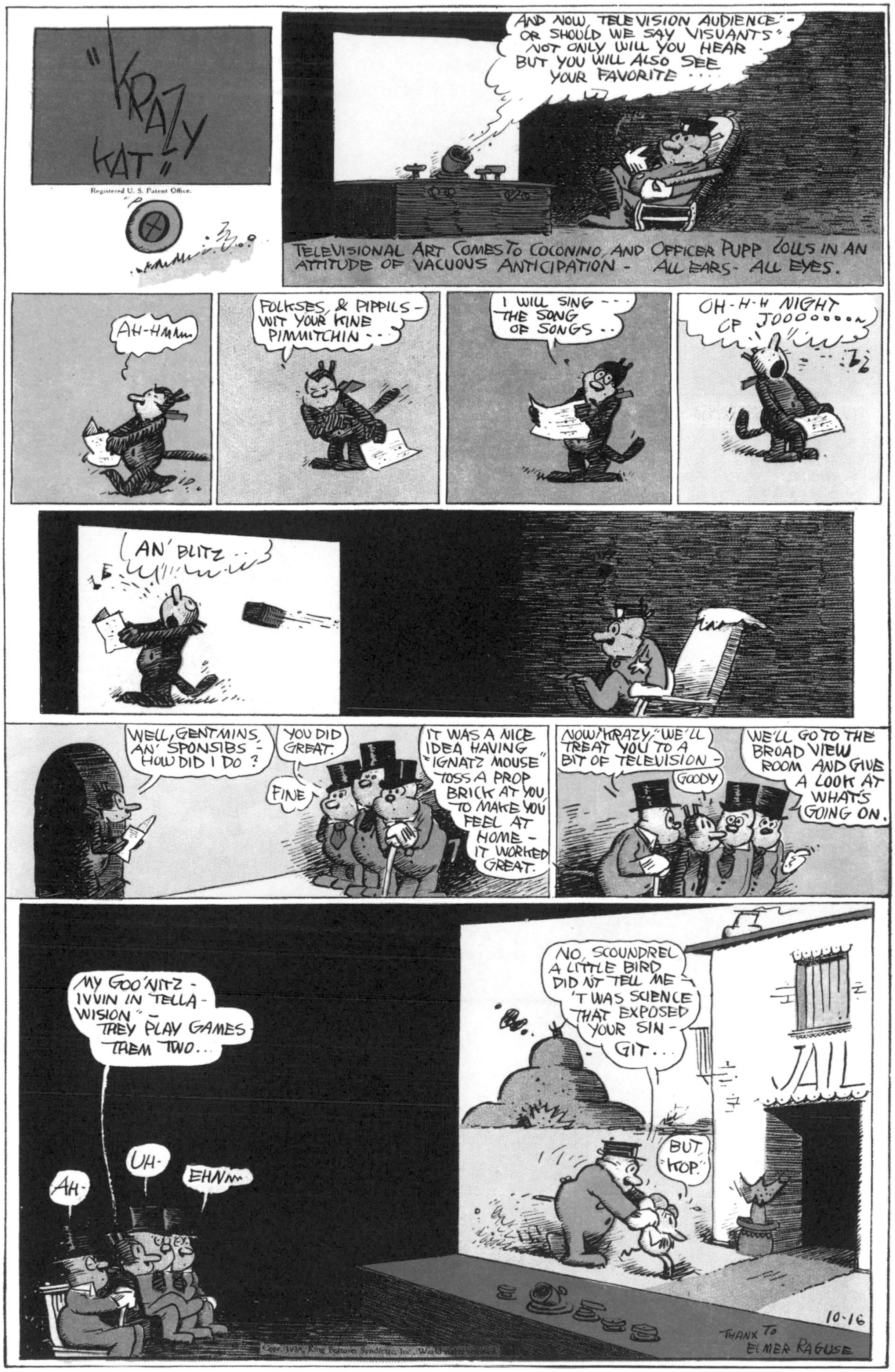
"KRAZY KAT"
Registered U. S. Patent Office.
AND NOW, TELEVISION AUDIENCE - OR SHOULD WE SAY VISUANTS - NOT ONLY WILL YOU HEAR BUT YOU WILL ALSO SEE YOUR FAVORITE ...
TELEVISIONAL ART COMES TO COCONINO, AND OFFICER PUPP LOLLS IN AN ATTITUDE OF VACUOUS ANTICIPATION - ALL EARS - ALL EYES.
AH-HMMM
FOLKSES, & PIPPILS - WIT YOUR KINE PIMMITCHIN - - -
I WILL SING - - - THE SONG OF SONGS - -
OH-H-H NIGHT OF JOOOOOOOO
AN' BLITZ - -
WELL, GENTMINS, AN' SPONSIBS - HOW DID I DO ?
YOU DID GREAT.
FINE
IT WAS A NICE IDEA HAVING "IGNATZ MOUSE" TOSS A PROP BRICK AT YOU, TO MAKE YOU FEEL AT HOME - IT WORKED GREAT.
NOW, "KRAZY," WE'LL TREAT YOU TO A BIT OF TELEVISION -
GOODY
WE'LL GO TO THE BROAD VIEW ROOM AND GIVE A LOOK AT WHAT'S GOING ON.
MY GOO'NITZ - IVVIN IN TELLA-WISION - THEY PLAY GAMES - THEM TWO...
AH-
UH-
EHNM
NO, SCOUNDREL A LITTLE BIRD DID N'T TELL ME - 'T WAS SCIENCE THAT EXPOSED YOUR SIN - GIT...
BUT KOP.
JAIL
10-16
THANX TO ELMER RAGUSE

October 16th, 1938.

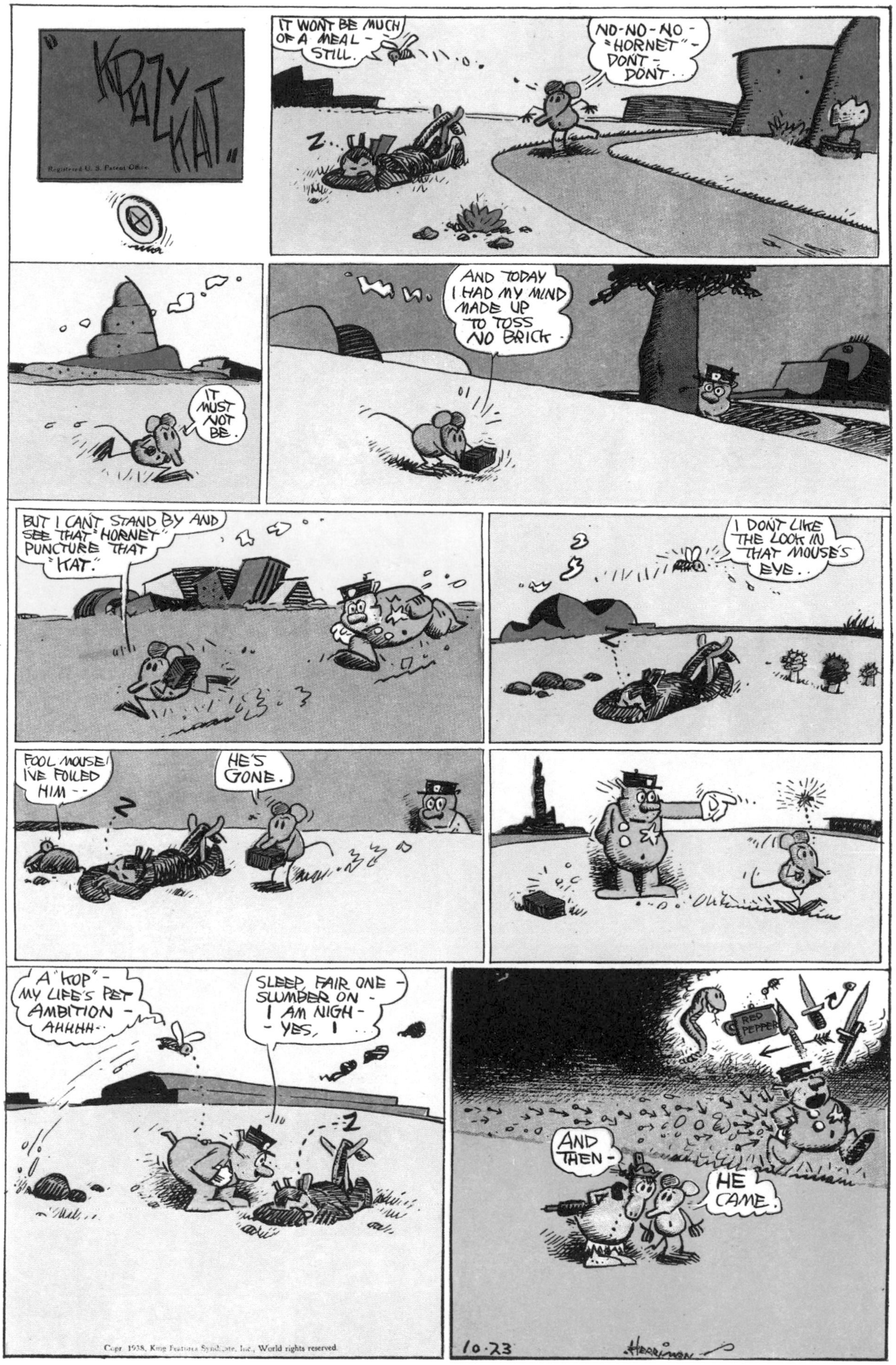

"KRAZY KAT"
Registered U. S. Patent Office
IT WONT BE MUCH OF A MEAL - STILL.
NO-NO-NO - "HORNET" - DONT - DONT.
IT MUST NOT BE.
AND TODAY I HAD MY MIND MADE UP TO TOSS NO BRICK -
BUT I CANT STAND BY AND SEE THAT "HORNET" PUNCTURE THAT "KAT."
I DONT LIKE THE LOOK IN THAT MOUSE'S EYE.
FOOL MOUSE! I'VE FOILED HIM - -
HE'S GONE.
"A "KOP" - MY LIFE'S PET AMBITION - AHHHH -
SLEEP, FAIR ONE - SLUMBER ON - I AM NIGH - - YES, I - -
RED PEPPER
AND THEN -
HE CAME.
Copr. 1938, King Features Syndicate, Inc., World rights reserved.
10-23
HERRIMAN

October 23rd, 1938.

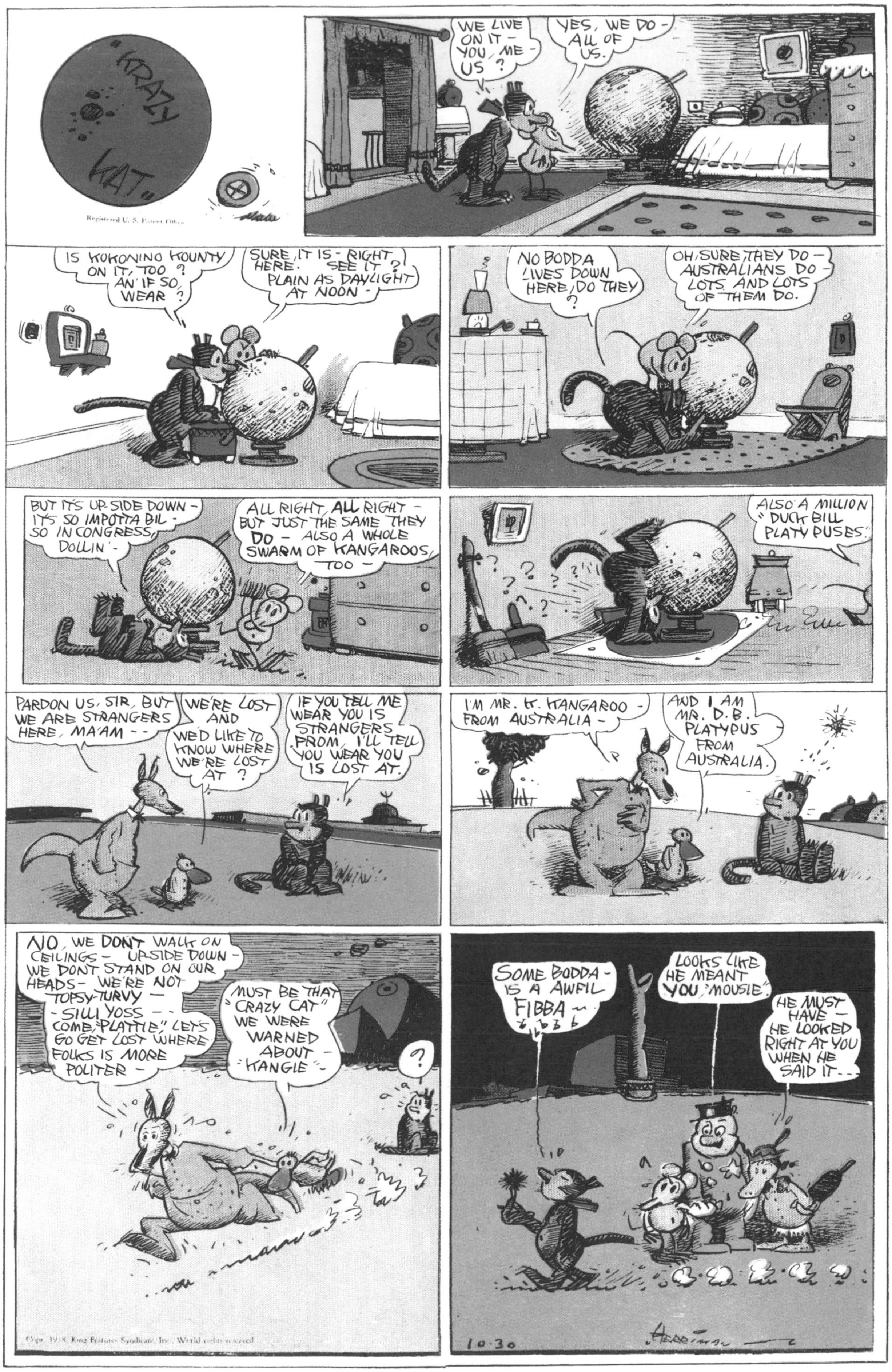
"KRAZY KAT"
Registered U. S. Patent Office
WE LIVE ON IT - YOU, ME - US ?
YES, WE DO - ALL OF US.
IS KOKONINO KOUNTY ON IT, TOO ? AN' IF SO, WEAR ?
SURE, IT IS - RIGHT HERE. SEE IT ? PLAIN AS DAYLIGHT AT NOON -
NO BODDA LIVES DOWN HERE, DO THEY ?
OH, SURE, THEY DO - AUSTRALIANS DO - LOTS AND LOTS OF THEM DO.
BUT IT'S UP-SIDE DOWN - IT'S SO IMPOTTA BIL - SO IN CONGRESS, DOLLIN' -
ALL RIGHT, ALL RIGHT - BUT JUST THE SAME THEY DO - ALSO A WHOLE SWARM OF KANGAROOS, TOO -
ALSO A MILLION "DUCK BILL PLATY PUSES."
PARDON US, SIR, BUT WE ARE STRANGERS HERE, MA'AM - -
WE'RE LOST AND WE'D LIKE TO KNOW WHERE WE'RE LOST AT ?
IF YOU TELL ME WEAR YOU IS STRANGERS FROM, I'LL TELL YOU WEAR YOU IS LOST AT.
I'M MR. K. KANGAROO - FROM AUSTRALIA -
AND I AM MR. D. B. PLATYPUS FROM AUSTRALIA.
NO, WE DON'T WALK ON CEILINGS - UPSIDE DOWN - WE DONT STAND ON OUR HEADS - WE'RE NOT TOPSY-TURVY - - SILLI YOSS - - COME, "PLATTIE," LET'S GO GET LOST WHERE FOLKS IS MORE POLITER -
MUST BE THAT "CRAZY CAT" WE WERE WARNED ABOUT - KANGIE -
?
SOME BODDA - IS A AWFIL FIBBA -
LOOKS LIKE HE MEANT YOU, "MOUSIE".
HE MUST HAVE - HE LOOKED RIGHT AT YOU WHEN HE SAID IT - -
Copr. 1938, King Features Syndicate, Inc., World rights reserved
10.30

October 30th, 1938.

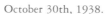

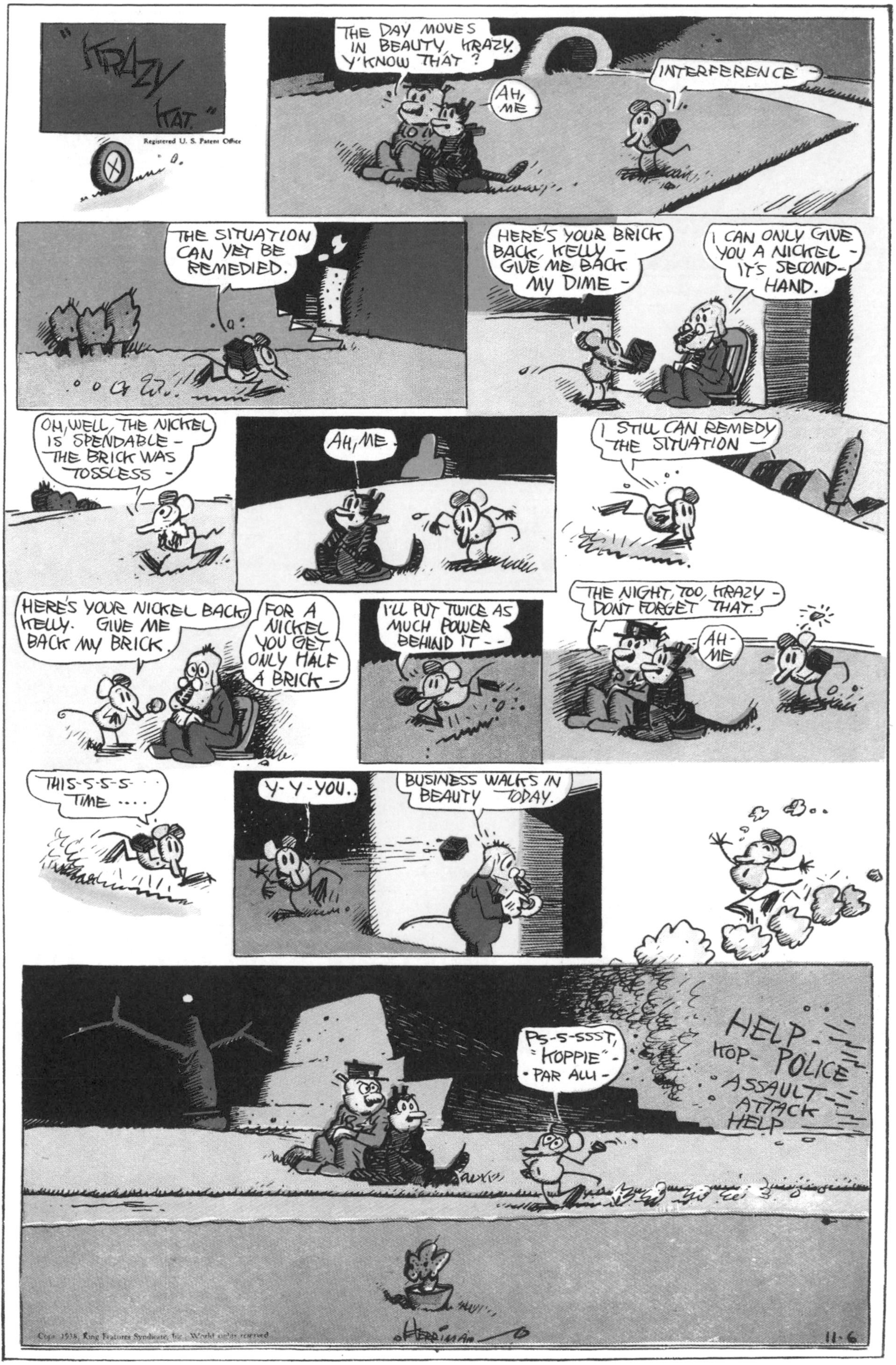
"KRAZY KAT."
Registered U. S. Patent Office
THE DAY MOVES IN BEAUTY, KRAZY, Y'KNOW THAT ?
AH, ME
INTERFERENCE -
THE SITUATION CAN YET BE REMEDIED.
HERE'S YOUR BRICK BACK, KELLY - GIVE ME BACK MY DIME -
I CAN ONLY GIVE YOU A NICKEL - IT'S SECOND-HAND.
OH, WELL, THE NICKEL IS SPENDABLE - THE BRICK WAS TOSSLESS -
AH, ME.
I STILL CAN REMEDY THE SITUATION -
HERE'S YOUR NICKEL BACK, KELLY. GIVE ME BACK MY BRICK.
FOR A NICKEL YOU GET ONLY HALF A BRICK -
I'LL PUT TWICE AS MUCH POWER BEHIND IT - -
THE NIGHT, TOO, KRAZY - DONT FORGET THAT.
AH- ME.
THIS-S-S-S- TIME ....
Y-Y-YOU..
BUSINESS WALKS IN BEAUTY TODAY.
PS-S-SSST, "KOPPIE" - PAR ALLI -
HELP - KOP- POLICE ASSAULT - ATTACK HELP
HERRIMAN
11-6

November 6th, 1938.

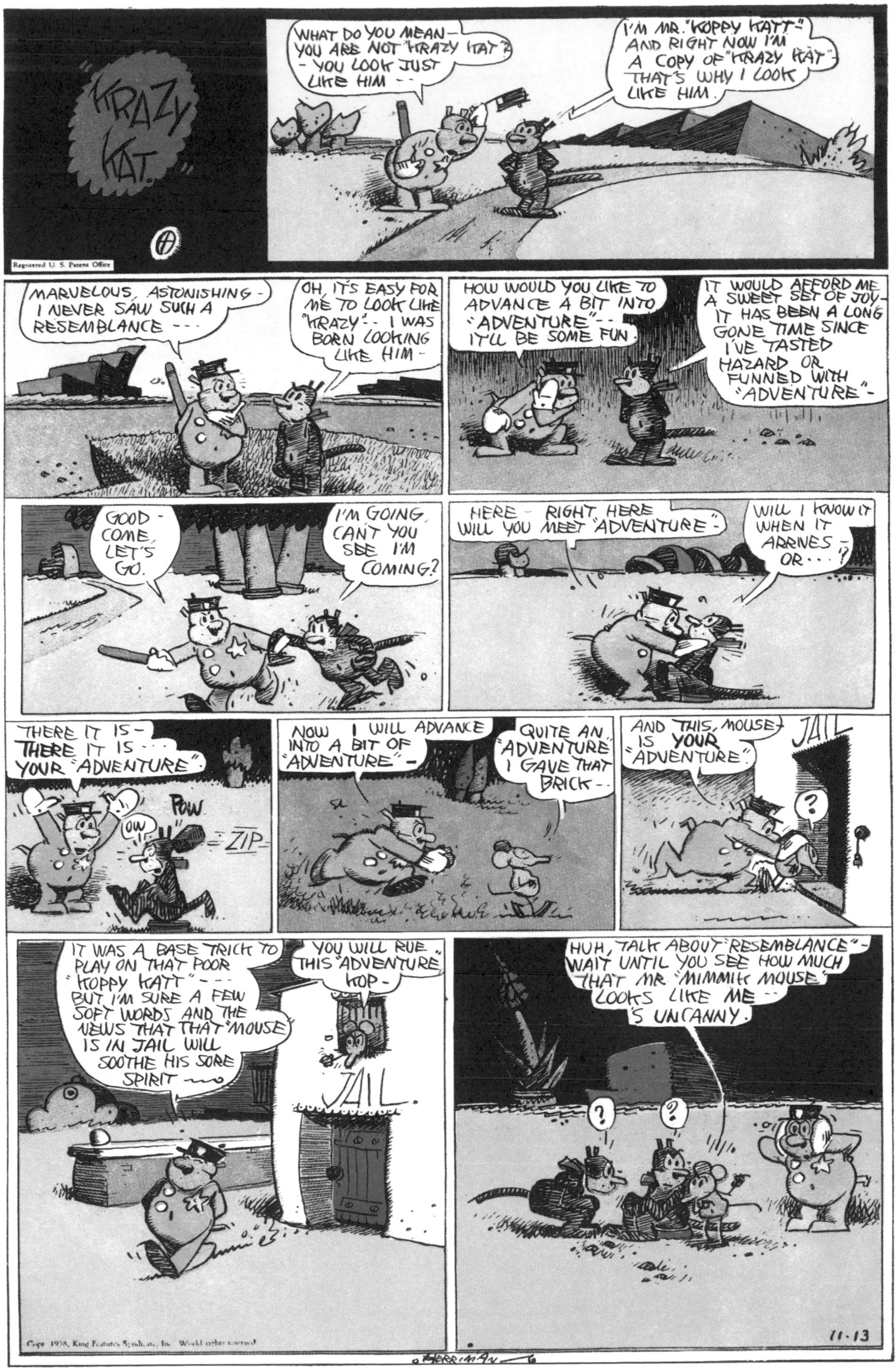
"KRAZY KAT."
Registered U. S. Patent Office
WHAT DO YOU MEAN— YOU ARE NOT "KRAZY KAT"? — YOU LOOK JUST LIKE HIM - -
I'M MR. "KOPPY KATT"— AND RIGHT NOW I'M A COPY OF "KRAZY KAT"— THAT'S WHY I LOOK LIKE HIM.
MARVELOUS, ASTONISHING— I NEVER SAW SUCH A RESEMBLANCE - - -
OH, IT'S EASY FOR ME TO LOOK LIKE "KRAZY" - I WAS BORN LOOKING LIKE HIM -
HOW WOULD YOU LIKE TO ADVANCE A BIT INTO "ADVENTURE" - - IT'LL BE SOME FUN.
IT WOULD AFFORD ME A SWEET SET OF JOY— IT HAS BEEN A LONG GONE TIME SINCE I'VE TASTED HAZARD OR FUNNED WITH "ADVENTURE"—
GOOD— COME, LET'S GO.
I'M GOING, CAN'T YOU SEE I'M COMING?
HERE — RIGHT HERE WILL YOU MEET "ADVENTURE"—
WILL I KNOW IT WHEN IT ARRIVES — OR - - - ?
THERE IT IS— THERE IT IS - - YOUR "ADVENTURE".
POW
OW
ZIP
NOW I WILL ADVANCE INTO A BIT OF "ADVENTURE" —
QUITE AN "ADVENTURE" I GAVE THAT BRICK - -
AND THIS, MOUSE— IS YOUR "ADVENTURE".
JAIL
?
IT WAS A BASE TRICK TO PLAY ON THAT POOR "KOPPY KATT" - - - BUT I'M SURE A FEW SOFT WORDS AND THE NEWS THAT THAT "MOUSE" IS IN JAIL WILL SOOTHE HIS SORE SPIRIT
YOU WILL RUE THIS "ADVENTURE," KOP —
JAIL
HUH, TALK ABOUT "RESEMBLANCE"— WAIT UNTIL YOU SEE HOW MUCH THAT MR. "MIMMIK MOUSE" LOOKS LIKE ME - - 'S UNCANNY.
?
?
11-13
HERRIMAN

November 13th, 1938.

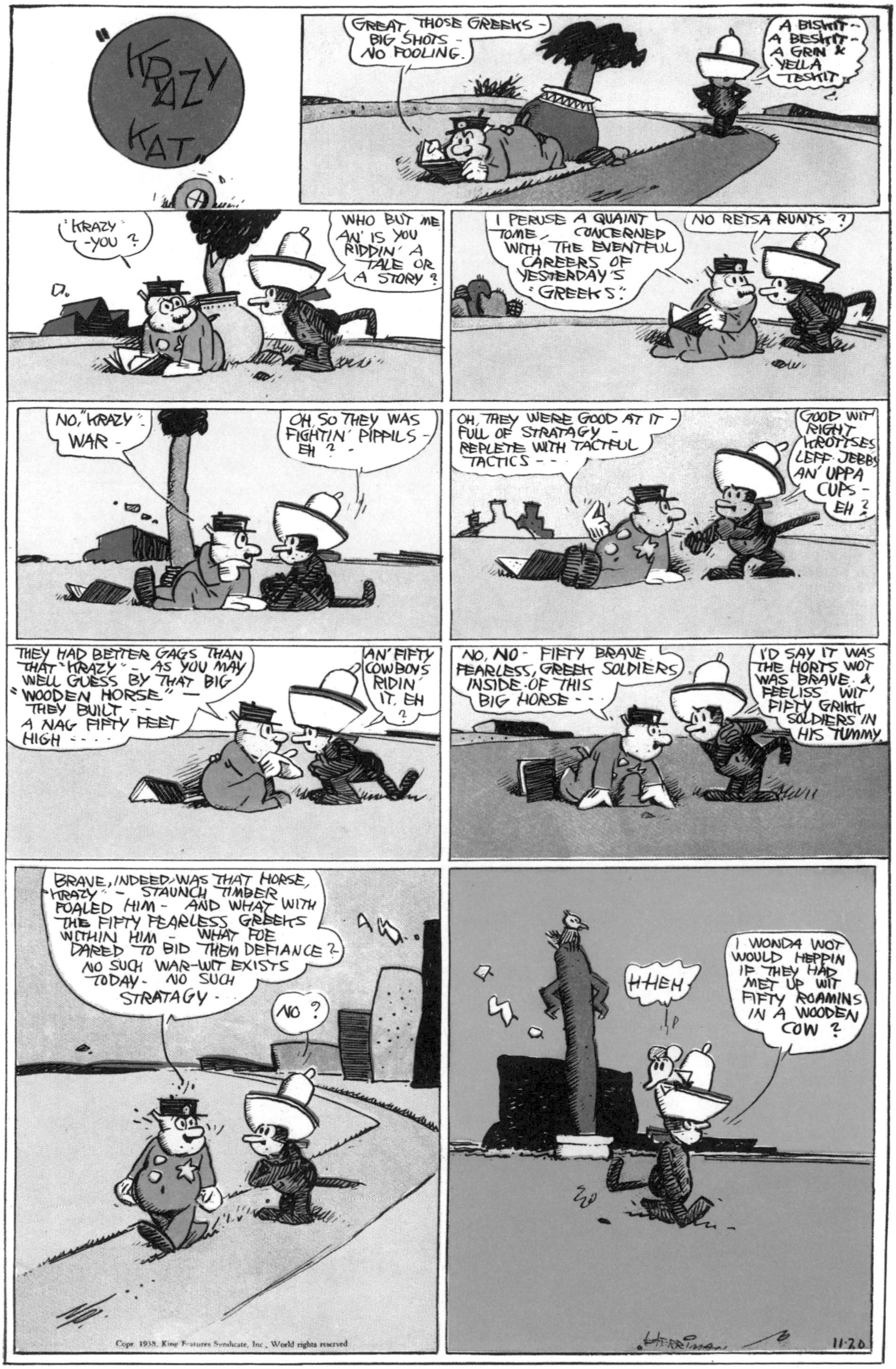
"KRAZY KAT"
GREAT, THOSE GREEKS - BIG SHOTS - NO FOOLING.
A BISKIT - A BESKIT - A GRIN & YELLA TESKIT
"KRAZY" -YOU ?
WHO BUT ME AN' IS YOU RIDDIN' A TALE OR A STORY ?
I PERUSE A QUAINT TOME, CONCERNED WITH THE EVENTFUL CAREERS OF YESTERDAY'S "GREEKS"
NO RETSA RUNTS ?
NO, "KRAZY" WAR -
OH, SO THEY WAS FIGHTIN' PIPPILS - EH ? -
OH, THEY WERE GOOD AT IT - FULL OF STRATAGY - REPLETE WITH TACTFUL TACTICS - -
GOOD WIT' RIGHT KROTTSES LEFF JEBBS AN' UPPA CUPS - EH ?
THEY HAD BETTER GAGS THAN THAT "KRAZY" - AS YOU MAY WELL GUESS BY THAT BIG "WOODEN HORSE" - THEY BUILT - - A NAG FIFTY FEET HIGH - - -
AN' FIFTY COWBOYS RIDIN' IT, EH ?
NO, NO - FIFTY BRAVE FEARLESS, GREEK SOLDIERS INSIDE OF THIS BIG HORSE - -
I'D SAY IT WAS THE HORTS WOT WAS BRAVE & FEELISS WIT' FIFTY GRIKK SOLDIERS IN HIS TUMMY
BRAVE, INDEED, WAS THAT HORSE, "KRAZY" - STAUNCH TIMBER FOALED HIM - AND WHAT WITH THE FIFTY FEARLESS GREEKS WITHIN HIM - WHAT FOE DARED TO BID THEM DEFIANCE? - NO SUCH WAR-WIT EXISTS TODAY - NO SUCH STRATAGY -
NO ?
HHEH
I WONDA WOT WOULD HEPPIN IF THEY HAD MET UP WIT FIFTY ROAMINS IN A WOODEN COW ?
Copr 1938, King Features Syndicate, Inc., World rights reserved
11·20

November 20th, 1938.

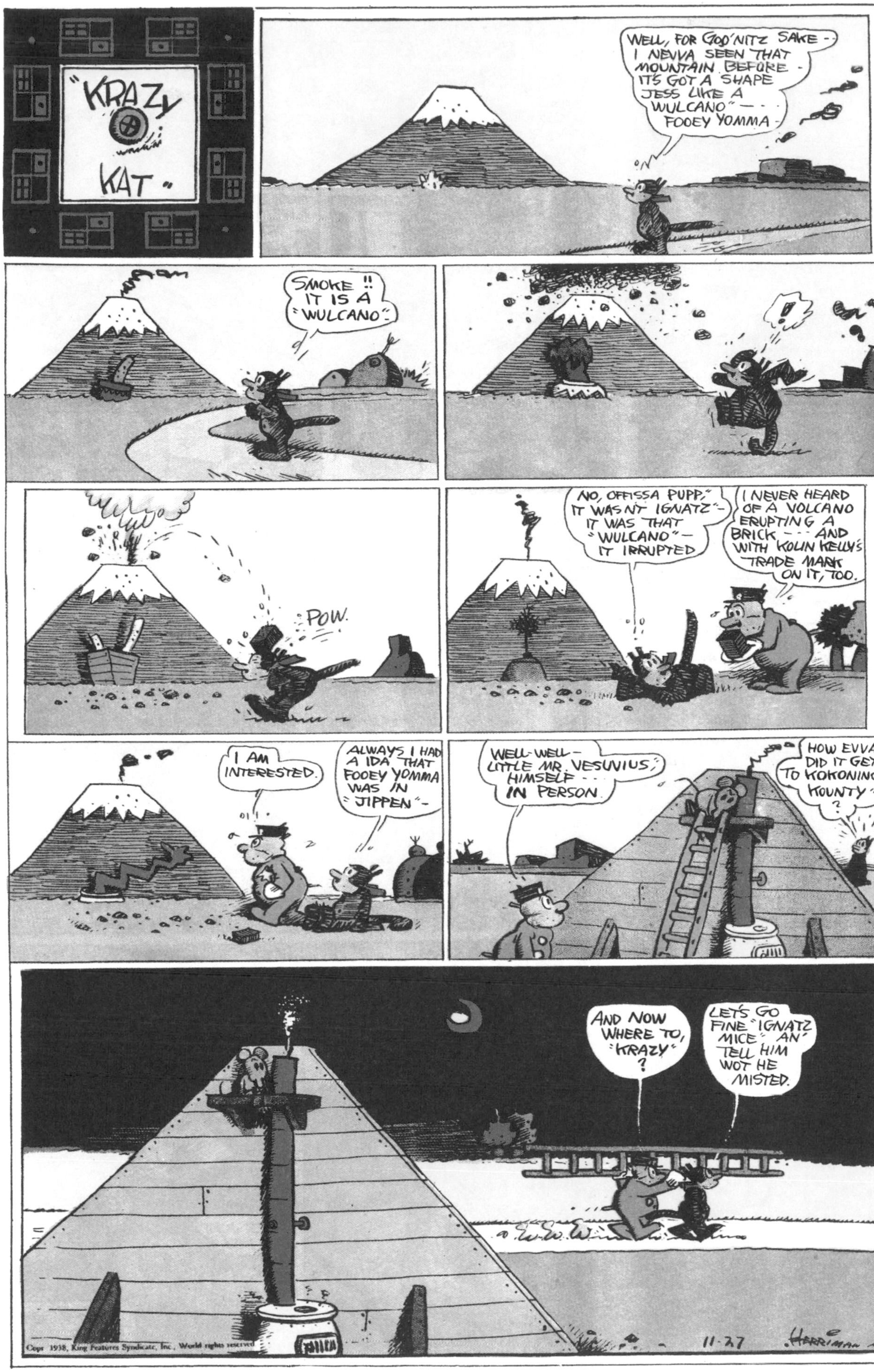
"KRAZY KAT"
WELL, FOR GOD'NITZ SAKE - I NEVVA SEEN THAT MOUNTAIN BEFORE - IT'S GOT A SHAPE JESS LIKE A "WULCANO" — FOOEY YOMMA -
SMOKE !! IT IS A "WULCANO"
POW.
NO, OFFISSA PUPP, IT WASN'T IGNATZ - IT WAS THAT "WULCANO" - IT IRRUPTED
I NEVER HEARD OF A VOLCANO ERUPTING A BRICK - - - AND WITH KOLIN KELLY'S TRADE MARK ON IT, TOO.
I AM INTERESTED.
ALWAYS I HAD A IDA THAT FOOEY YOMMA WAS IN "JIPPEN"
WELL-WELL - LITTLE MR. VESUVIUS, HIMSELF - - IN PERSON.
HOW EVVA DID IT GET TO KOKONINO KOUNTY ?
AND NOW WHERE TO, "KRAZY" ?
LET'S GO FINE "IGNATZ MICE" AN' TELL HIM WOT HE MISTED.
Copr 1938, King Features Syndicate, Inc., World rights reserved
11-27
HERRIMAN

November 27th, 1938.

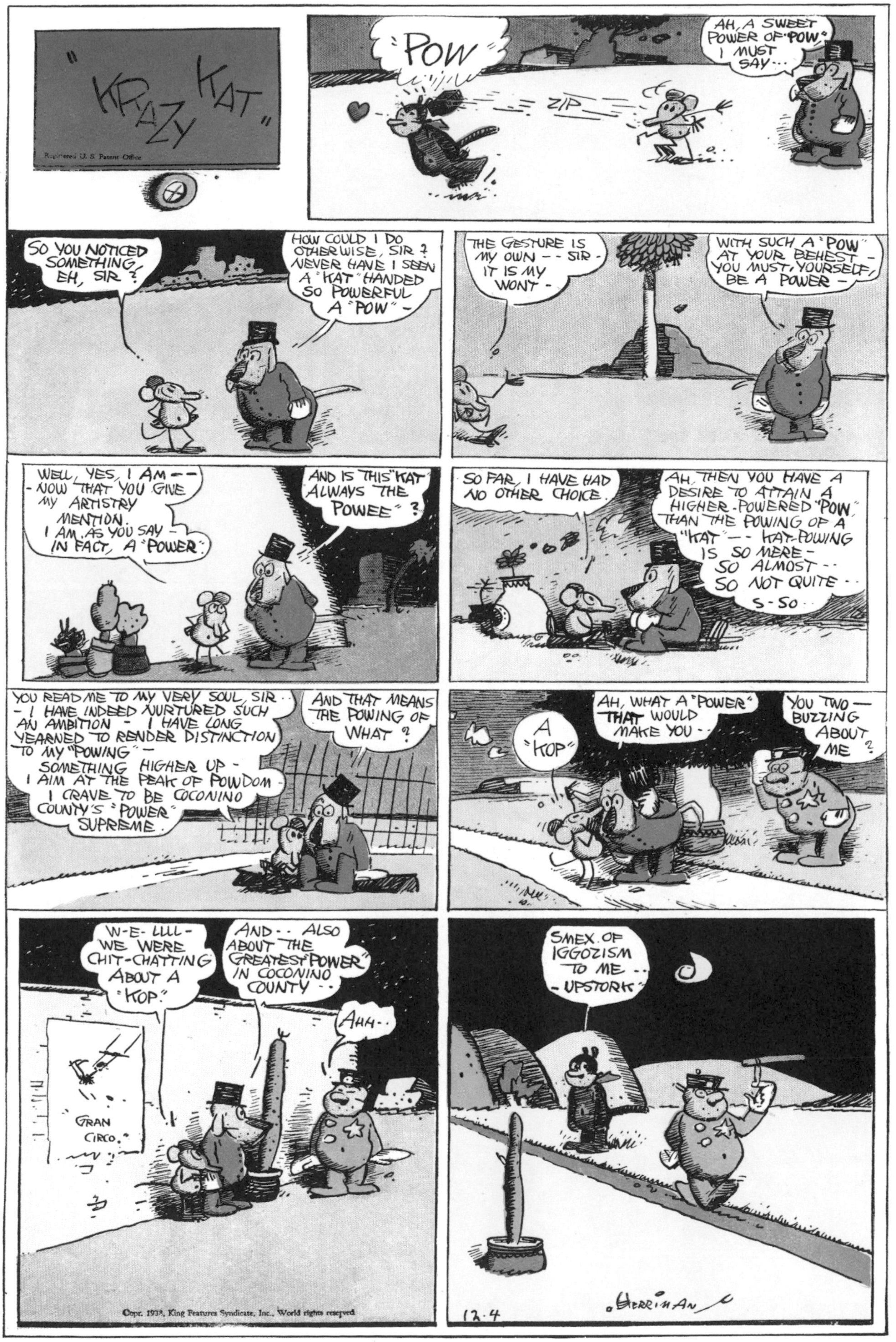
"KRAZY KAT"
Registered U. S. Patent Office
POW
ZIP
AH, A SWEET POWER OF "POW," I MUST SAY - -
SO YOU NOTICED SOMETHING, EH, SIR?
HOW COULD I DO OTHERWISE, SIR? NEVER HAVE I SEEN A "KAT" HANDED SO POWERFUL A "POW" -
THE GESTURE IS MY OWN - - SIR - IT IS MY WONT -
WITH SUCH A "POW" AT YOUR BEHEST - YOU MUST, YOURSELF, BE A POWER -
WELL, YES, I AM - - - NOW THAT YOU GIVE MY ARTISTRY MENTION. I AM, AS YOU SAY - IN FACT, A "POWER".
AND IS THIS "KAT" ALWAYS THE "POWEE"?
SO FAR, I HAVE HAD NO OTHER CHOICE.
AH, THEN YOU HAVE A DESIRE TO ATTAIN A HIGHER-POWERED "POW" THAN THE POWING OF A "KAT" - - KAT-POWING IS SO MERE - SO ALMOST - - SO NOT QUITE - - S-SO - -
YOU READ ME TO MY VERY SOUL, SIR - - - I HAVE INDEED NURTURED SUCH AN AMBITION - I HAVE LONG YEARNED TO RENDER DISTINCTION TO MY "POWING" - SOMETHING HIGHER UP - I AIM AT THE PEAK OF POWDOM - I CRAVE TO BE COCONINO COUNTY'S "POWER" SUPREME.
AND THAT MEANS THE POWING OF WHAT?
A "KOP"
AH, WHAT A "POWER" THAT WOULD MAKE YOU -
YOU TWO - BUZZING ABOUT ME?
W-E-LLLL - WE WERE CHIT-CHATTING ABOUT A "KOP."
AND - - ALSO ABOUT THE GREATEST "POWER" IN COCONINO COUNTY - -
AHH - -
GRAN CIRCO.
SMEX. OF IGGOZISM TO ME - - - UPSTORK -
Copr. 1938, King Features Syndicate, Inc., World rights reserved
12-4
HERRIMAN

December 4th, 1938.

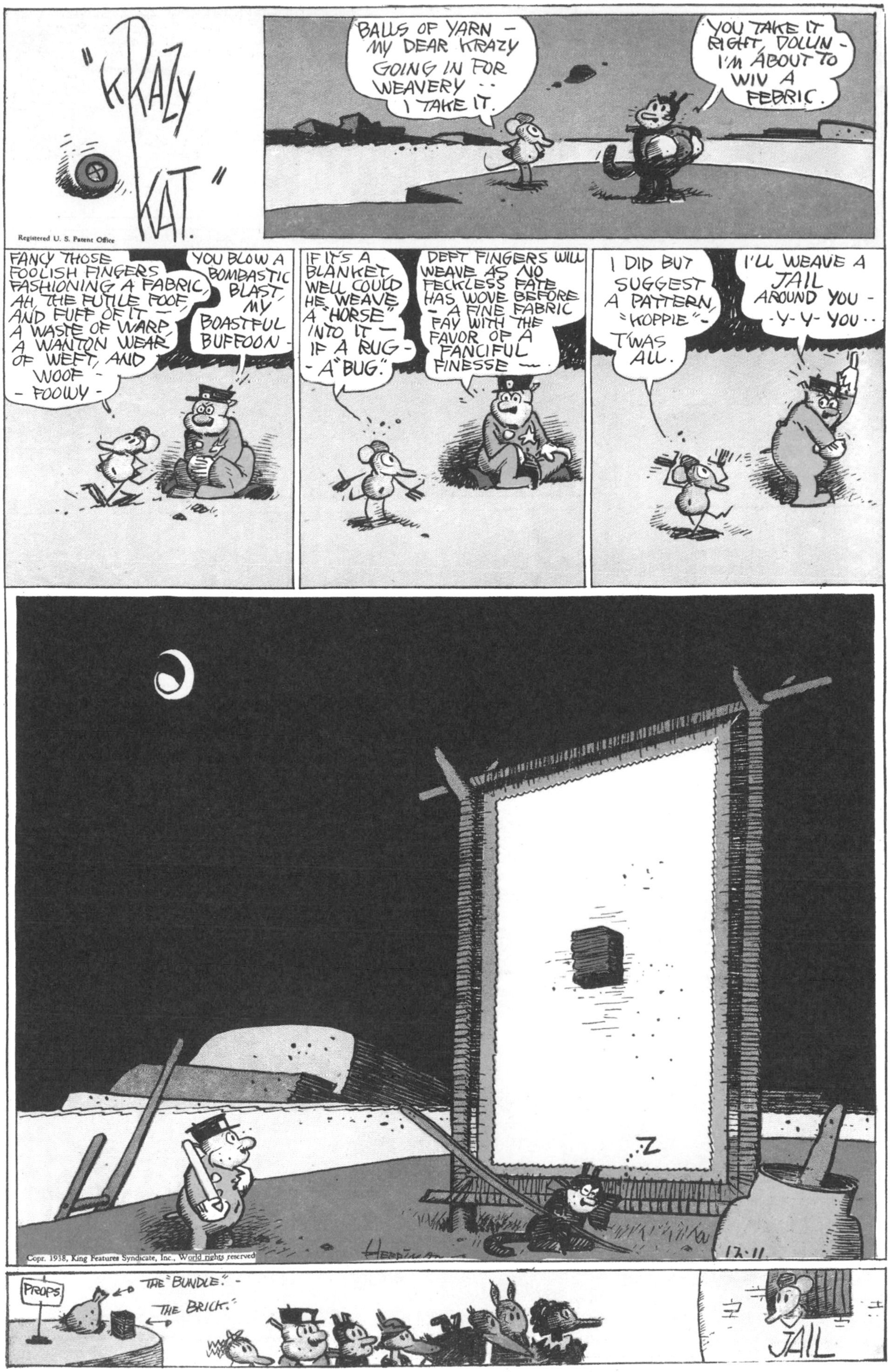
"KRAZY KAT."
Registered U. S. Patent Office
BALLS OF YARN — MY DEAR KRAZY GOING IN FOR WEAVERY .. I TAKE IT.
YOU TAKE IT RIGHT, DOLLIN — I'M ABOUT TO WIV A FEBRIC.
FANCY THOSE FOOLISH FINGERS FASHIONING A FABRIC, AH, THE FUTILE FOOF, AND FUFF OF IT — A WASTE OF WARP, A WANTON WEAR OF WEFT, AND WOOF — FOOWY —
YOU BLOW A BOMBASTIC BLAST, MY BOASTFUL BUFFOON —
IF IT'S A BLANKET, WELL COULD HE WEAVE A "HORSE" INTO IT — IF A RUG — A "BUG."
DEFT FINGERS WILL WEAVE AS NO FECKLESS FATE HAS WOVE BEFORE — A FINE FABRIC FAY WITH THE FAVOR OF A FANCIFUL FINESSE —
I DID BUT SUGGEST A PATTERN, "KOPPIE" — T'WAS ALL.
I'LL WEAVE A JAIL AROUND YOU — Y-Y-YOU ..
Z
Copr. 1938, King Features Syndicate, Inc., World rights reserved
HERRIMAN
12-11
PROPS
THE "BUNDLE." —
THE BRICK.
JAIL

December 11th, 1938.

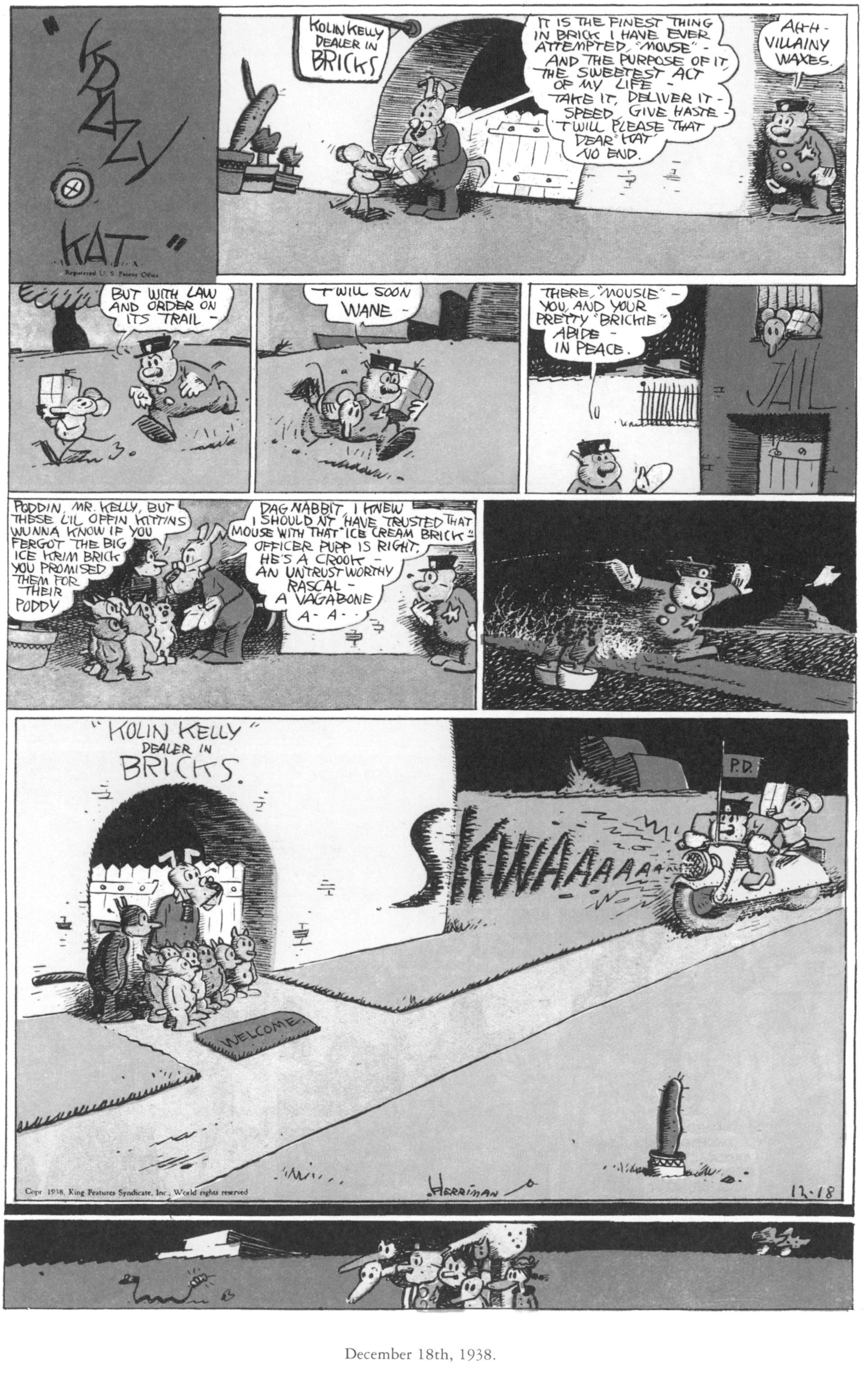
"Krazy Kat"
Registered U.S. Patent Office
Kolin Kelly Dealer in Bricks
It is the finest thing in brick I have ever attempted, "Mouse" - and the purpose of it, the sweetest act of my life - take it, deliver it - speed, give haste - 'twill please that dear "Kat" no end.
Ah-h - villainy waxes.
But with law and order on its trail -
'Twill soon wane -
There, "Mousie" - you, and your pretty "brickie" abide - in peace.
JAIL
Poddin, Mr. Kelly, but these li'l offin kittins wunna know if you fergot the big ice krim brick you promised them for their poddy
Dag nabbit, I knew I should n't have trusted that mouse with that "ice cream brick" - Officer Pupp is right, he's a crook - an untrustworthy rascal - a vagabone a - a -
"Kolin Kelly" dealer in Bricks.
P.D.
SKWAAAAA
WELCOME
Herriman
12-18
Copr 1938, King Features Syndicate, Inc., World rights reserved

December 18th, 1938.

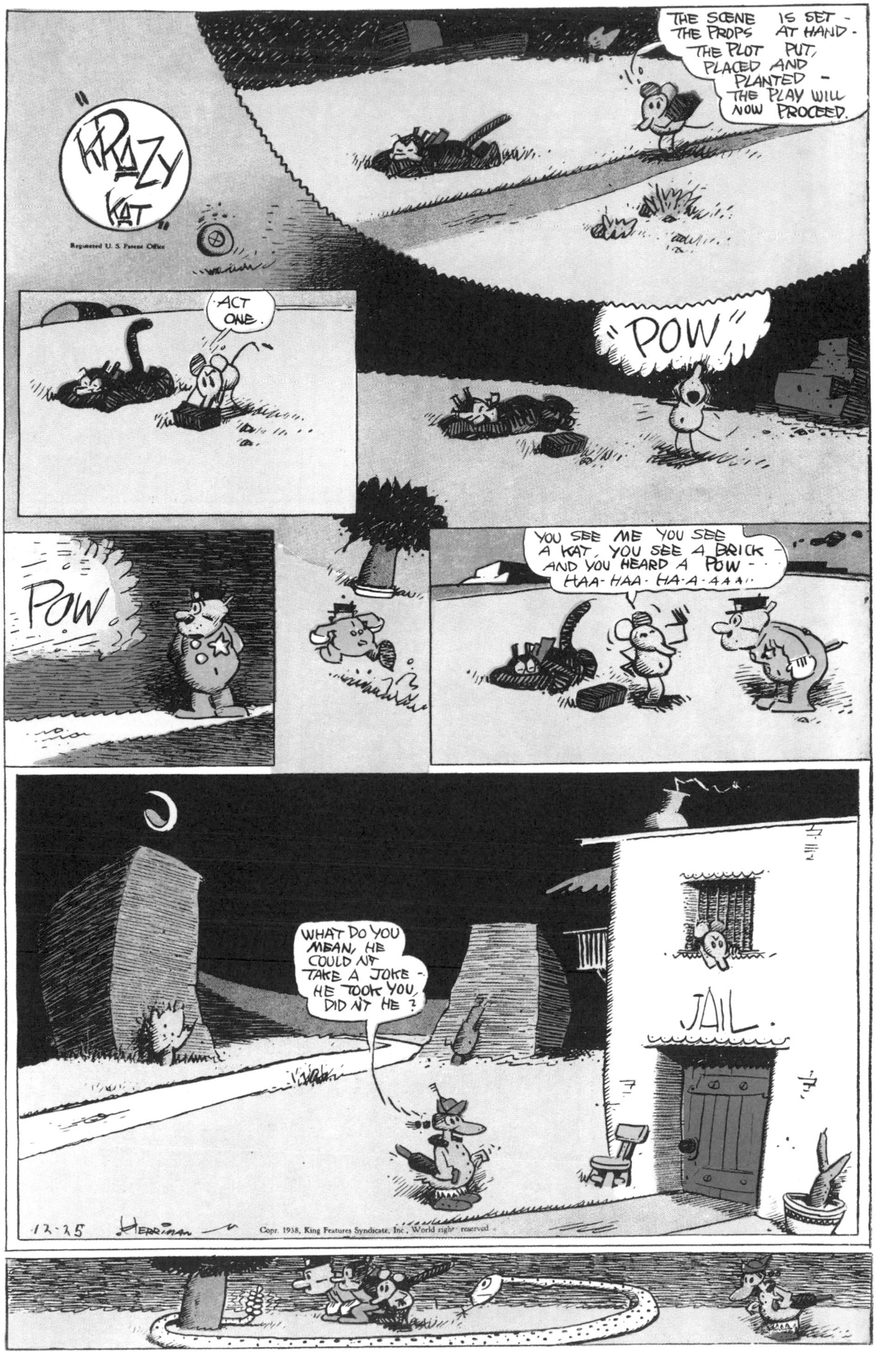

"Krazy Kat"
Registered U. S. Patent Office
THE SCENE IS SET - THE PROPS AT HAND - THE PLOT PUT, PLACED AND PLANTED - THE PLAY WILL NOW PROCEED.
ACT ONE.
"POW"
POW
YOU SEE ME YOU SEE A KAT, YOU SEE A BRICK AND YOU HEARD A POW - HAA-HAA-HA-A-AAA!
WHAT DO YOU MEAN, HE COULD N'T TAKE A JOKE - HE TOOK YOU, DID N'T HE?
JAIL.
12-25 Herriman
Copr. 1938, King Features Syndicate, Inc., World rights reserved

December 25th, 1938.

A presentation birthday drawing done for Herriman's close friend Beanie Walker, head writer for the "Our Gang" comedies at Hal Roach studios. Original drawing 9" x 8.25". Collection of, and many thanks to, Mr. John Fawcett of John Fawcett's Maine Antique Toy & Art Museum, http://home.gwi.net/~fawcetoy

The IGNATZ MOUSE DEBAFFLER PAGE.

4/18/37: Increased bafflement here. Where did Krazy get the pillow — or is it the heppy mittin he mentions in the preceding panel?

5/9/37: Don't esk me, but are those Mrs. Kwak Wak's nether habiliments aflutter on Joe Stork's flag-pole? (Don't try to esk Mr. Kwak Wak either; as far as I know he's never been seen in the strip.)

6/6/37 and 6/13/37: Ah, you think you caught us in a goof, running these two pages in the wrong order? O ye of little faith! In fact, 'twas either Garge or KFS who screwed up threescore and nine years ago when they dated these — as a close reading of the strips will show, the continuity demands that the strip printed on 6/13 precede the one printed on 6/6. We have merely restored the original intended order.

8/8/37: Aye, E. C. Segar passed this way.

6/19/38: This is the only KK kolor page to be a reprint; it first appeared on 6/8/35. We reprint it here because this version features significantly different coloring, as the floorboards, white in the 1935 iteration, have now aged to a nice orange.

10/30/38: The mighty KFS koloring team has forgotten to touch up K. Kangaroo's head in the final panel. Looks like a kritter in a kangaroo suit.

11/6/38: Offisa Pupp's kriminal delight at the going-on in panel six suggests that we may be konfronting a koppy kop here as well. — B.B.

The KAT LIBRARY, in progress.

All volumes edited by Bill Blackbeard (ably assisted by Derya Ataker on 1931-1932 and 1933-1934) and designed by Chris Ware.

Krazy + Ignatz 1925-1926.

"There Is a Happy Lend Fur-Fur Away." The first release in the series, with a gallery of supplements. $14.95.

Krazy + Ignatz 1927-1928

"Love Letters in Ancient Brick." Two more years plus such supplements as Herriman's "Embarrassing Moments." $14.95.

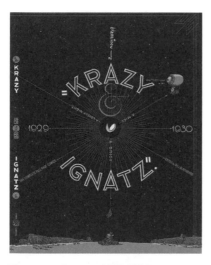

Krazy + Ignatz 1929-1930.

"A Mice, a Brick, a Lovely Night." Herriman returns to a more flexible layout, plus "The Krazy Kat Rag." $14.95.

Krazy + Ignatz 1931-1932.

"A Kat A'Lilt With Song." This one includes as a special bonus a 20-page portfolio of the 1931 daily strip. $14.95.

Krazy + Ignatz 1933-1934.

"Necromancy by the Blue Bean Bush." Includes the most obscure and hardest to find full-page strips. $14.95

Krazy + Ignatz 1935-1936.

"A Wild Warmth of Chromatic Gravy." The first in color, and Jeet Heer's definitive article on Herriman's ethnicity. $19.95.

All available at a fine comics shop near you, or, to order by mail, send a cheque or money order to

Fantagraphics Books
7563 Lake City Way NE
Seattle, Washington, 98115
1 800 657 1100

international calls, please dial 001 206 524 1967. or order on from website
www.fantagraphics.com
Please enclose $3.00 shipping and handling for the first book and $1.00 for every book thereafter.

Also, you may also wish to visit
www.specproductions.com/P006.html
to order the first two volumes of
By George! The Komplete Daily Komic Strips of George Herriman (focusing on *Baron Mooch, Gooseberry Sprig,* and *The Family Upstairs*) edited and published by Bill Blackbeard.

Krazy + Ignatz 1925-1934 hardcover.

This library hardcover binds the signatures of the first five books, but without the paperback covers. $75.00.